THE NATURE TRACKER'S HANDBOOK

THE NATURE TRACKER'S HANDBOOK

NICK BAKER

B L O O M S B U R Y
LONDON · NEW DELHI · NEW YORK · SYDNEY

a million
voices for
nature

The RSPB speaks out for birds and wildlife, tackling the problems that threaten our environment.
Nature is amazing – help us keep it that way.

If you would like to know more about The RSPB, visit the website at www.rspb.org.uk
or write to: The RSPB, The Lodge, Sandy, Bedfordshire, SG19 2DL; 01767 680551.

First published in 2013

Copyright © 2013 text by Nick Baker

Copyright © 2013 illustrations by Marc Dando

Copyright © 2013 in the photographs remains with the individual photographers – see credits on pages 283–285

Bloomsbury Publishing Plc, 50 Bedford Square, London WC1B 3DP

www.bloomsbury.com

Bloomsbury Publishing, London, New Delhi, New York and Sydney

A CIP catalogue record for this book is available from the British Library

Publisher: Nigel Redman
Project editor: Jasmine Parker
Design by Julie Dando, Fluke Art

UK ISBN (print) 978-1-4081-5150-1

Printed in China by C&C Offset Printing Co Ltd.

10 9 8 7 6 5 4 3 2 1

MIX
Paper from
responsible sources
FSC® C008047

Contents

Introduction

Why chase these scuffs in the dust?

Funnily enough, the answer to that question is not necessarily about finding the animal that made them. This may come as a bit of shock if you've just picked up this book expecting it will lead you to your favourite but elusive British mammal. Actually following a trail to its ultimate conclusion and meeting the maker of the marks rarely happens, even to the most experienced trackers.

For a start, you hardly ever get a complete trail, usually only a few footprints of the animal that passed and even then only when the environmental conditions allow. In learning to track you'll find yourself learning to read again, but from a book that has had its pages torn up and scattered to the winds and you have to piece them together again. So why bother?

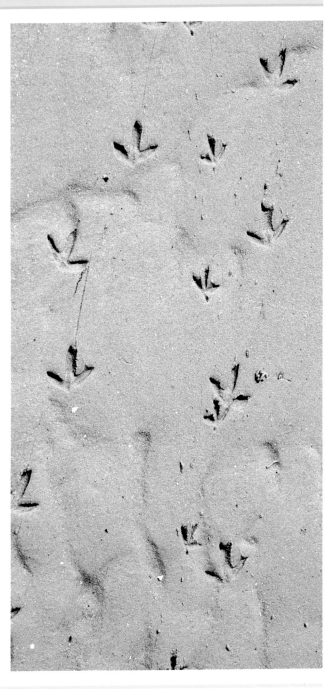

Sand is the perfect soft surface to see tracks such as these bird prints.

🐾 Pleasure of the chase

Just like learning to read, tracking wildlife is not so much about the end destination – the pleasure is in the moment and in the detective process. So you might not gain an actual physical closeness to your quarry, but by interpreting the signs it left behind you can get a very intimate 'look' at what it gets up to and develop a better understanding of what makes it tick.

They say that every animal leaves some kind of a trace, no matter how small, as it passes through its environment: perhaps an odour trail or a shed whisker. Take a square metre of, say, your garden hedge. Just imagine all the worms that have passed between the roots; the caterpillars that have fed on the leaves; the mice that have foraged for berries; the neighbour's cat whose curiosity has led him to sniff around and investigate the signs left by the mice; the Hedgehog that has holed up for hibernation among the roots; and the Badger that has rudely shoved his way through the tangle of branches on his nightly forays over the neighbourhood lawns. It's all there; the stories can be told if you know what to look out for.

Above: *Even the tiniest scratches and scrapes can tell a story. Here the concentration of claw marks on this section of log reveals where a Badger climbs over it regularly.*

Right: *Tracking skills can be applied to every living thing that moves; here trails in the fine wet sand plot the meanderings of a snail.*

Some signs are almost non-existent: a mere whisper of a trace, the detection of which may well be beyond the scope of this book, but sometimes a sign is very obvious: a tree stump covered in the feathers of a Blue Tit positively shouts 'Sparrowhawk' at the budding nature detective.

Ever since the first human climbed down from the trees, the art of tracking and being tuned in to the world around you has been a matter of life, death, going hungry or eating well.

Long before the advent of the supermarket, being able to find your dinner meant much more than identifying which aisle the frozen pizza could be found in. The original takeaway would run around and hide and do all it could to avoid being consumed, so our ancestors were kept on their toes. They would have had to interpret the signs and subtle clues left by their fellow species in order to avoid starving to death. Following the signs left by your quarry, or indirectly looking for the signs left by other predators which may well have lead to a fresh kill, were paramount to daily survival.

In some ways we've come a long way since then, and you may well argue that, other than for those who still hunt, these skills are redundant, the relics of a past beast. Yet hunting takes many forms: the naturalist armed with a camera may be trying to track down a subject in the quest for a perfect photograph. Using the available evidence can put the photographer in the best place for a shot – any fool can look, but only a good tracker looks in the right place. So for us professional (or aspiring) wildlife cameramen, naturalists and ecologists, being able to decipher the multitude of signs all around us is the difference between getting the information, the sighting, the photograph or the film we want and going home unsuccessful.

Tracker's funnel

A North American book I found recently describes the process of investigating animal signs and narrowing down the possibilities of which species may have left them as a 'tracker's funnel'. Awareness of whereabouts you are in the world and then which particular habitat you're in are essential first stages in making an accurate identification.

Although some animals are generalists and occur virtually everywhere, most have specific habitat requirements. Being aware what these are will help to fine-tune your tracking skills. For example, take the Red Squirrel. You will not find signs of it everywhere, as it mainly exists in the bioregion of Eurasia and in the ecoregion of northern Europe. Its preferred habitat narrows down the sites where you're likely to find it still further – it favours coniferous areas of northern forests that are not populated by the ecologically dominant and introduced Grey Squirrel. So unless you are standing under some pine trees in a northern European forest, you are not likely to find the tracks or other signs of this species. Initially, you may need to refer to field guides, but in time a lot of information will become programmed into your head and you will sift through it in seconds.

Part of the process of tracking is getting a sense of what you might expect to find living in any given habitat or bioregion. You won't get Red Squirrels leaving tracks in estuary mud, for example.

Get connected

'What made that track?' is one of the most natural questions in the world. I believe that an intimate connection with the natural world is what's missing in many of our lives. If we as a species can reconnect on many levels with the world around us and with the latent tracker inside ourselves, then I believe we have a chance, a future as a species. So to take the argument to its ultimate conclusion: although the art of tracking, for most of us, is no longer directly a matter of life and death, the process of connecting with nature is.

How to use this handbook

This book is a training manual for your senses, helping you to see again and showing you how to notice things as insignificant as a bent blade of grass or a trail in the dew. Knowing how to interpret these signs, combined with others, can help to build a picture of what has passed (sometimes when droppings are involved – quite literally).

Most books on this subject tend to feature just the physical evidence. What we are attempting to do, however, is to bring the animals back into the picture. So instead of simply stating that as an animal speeds up its trail changes drastically, I will attempt to show you the tracks in relation to the moving animal and show you how they are created.

The other day I was explaining the different ways in which small mammals eat hazelnuts, and someone in the audience asked how a dormouse makes such a neat job while a squirrel makes a right pig's ear of it. To answer the question, I had to visualise the mammal holding the nut and picture how it uses its teeth to get to the kernel. It's all quite simple and logical, and it is this approach that I apply all the way through this book.

Rather than arranging the subjects as a field guide with all the mammals herded between certain pages in one section and all the birds stuffed in another, I've tried to do something different and hopefully a little more user-friendly. The book is very simply divided and categorised by the type of sign that you might have before you.

The secret to good tracking is being able to visualise an animal, such as this running Hare, moving or feeding and how it created the sign that you are left to interpret.

Imagine you've found some droppings on your lawn: rather than expect you to know what animal may be responsible, which requires a degree of existing knowledge, I'm going to assume you are a total beginner. All you need to do is turn to the chapter with the unattractive title: The Pleasures of Poo. Likewise, the rest of the book is broken down into other general signs such as feeding activity, nests and holes – and in each chapter I give you some idea of which species may have left its mark.

Now let's cut to the chase, get down to the fun stuff and get tracking.

Stuff in the tracker's kitbag

The most brilliant thing about tracking is that you need very little, if any, specialist equipment – it's all about using your senses, particularly your eyesight. There are, however, a few handy bits and pieces that a keen nature detective would be wise to stuff in his or her pockets or rucksack.

Everything a tracker could possibly need can fit into the smallest of backpacks and most of it is relatively cheap and readily available.

🐾 Handy tracker tools

Notebook and pencil

These are undoubtedly the most useful bits of kit for me (pencils are always better in the field than pens as they don't freeze in the cold and the ink doesn't run if you get your paper wet). If you've got these simple bits of low technology with you, you can record every detail of a sign or make a sketch and not worry about forgetting any details. If your writing is good and your note-taking is accurate, you can use your notes for future reference and steadily build up a library of knowledge.

Tape measure or ruler

This is very important for measuring prints and track dimensions (so often key to identifying the animal that made them) and, of course, you can place it next to the track if you are taking a picture (more about cameras and photographing signs later).

You can make notes on phones and take digital pictures of almost everything, but nothing hones observation skills and makes details stick into your memory better than actually writing down, sketching and measuring what you've seen, and recording it in detail in a notebook (oh, and use a pencil – ink runs when it gets damp).

Some way of scaling tracks and signs in you notes and photographs is very useful and can make the difference in getting the identity right. A small ruler or tape measure is most useful.

Ziploc® bags

These are indispensable and come in a variety of sizes; every naturalist should carry a few about his or her person at all times as you just never know when you might need one. Specimen tubes are also invaluable. They're great for collecting all manner of specimens, such as feathers, droppings, pellets and bones. The other bonus is that they stop sometimes unsavoury items 'escaping' into the dark recesses of your pockets or bags (especially important if you're in the habit of keeping sandwiches and specimens in the same bag).

Ziploc® bags and specimen tubes are essential for bagging feeding signs, droppings, pellets, hair and feathers. Always remember to pop a label in as well, with date, location and any other useful information.

Labels

Just a quick jotting of date, place and description can save a lot of guessing later on.

Magnifying lens

This is a small and simple device that no naturalist should be without. Hang it around your neck or keep it in your pocket – you're sure to need to use it in the field. With a hand lens you can look into a backlit leaf mine and see the owner practically waving back at you, reveal the tiniest scratches made by a vole's fingernails on a nut, or see the barbules on a feather.

I favour the small jeweller's loops of x8 or x10 magnification as they fold in on themselves and are self-protecting. It's worth splashing out on a good one, with a screw pivot that can be tightened (they get looser with age). If you don't want to get too close to a decidedly 'niffy' carnivore's dropping or a decomposing shrew, you may prefer to carry a larger 'classic' magnifying glass and look the part of a nature detective.

A good magnifying lens will set you back a few quid, but a x10 hand lens is an essential bit of kit, allowing you to examine details such as hair colour or tooth marks. Stick it on a piece of string and keep it around your neck.

Forceps/tweezers

These come in handy for picking up delicate things and anything you wouldn't want to handle. You can raid a make-up bag or bathroom cabinet for a pair, or alternatively source them from a chemist.

Wooden kebab skewers and string

Lollipop sticks work just as well as kebab skewers and are useful for visualising and measuring trail patterns (more about that later).

Some of the things you'll want to investigate might be a little unsavoury and for these a pair of forceps is often preferable to fingers.

A camera provides an extremely handy and quick way of recording any scene for reference. Don't forget you may have one on your phone too.

String and sticks (or kebab skewers and twine) are handy for marking out a scene or plotting a set of tracks.

Camera

Taking digital pictures is a perfect way to build up your reference collection and record any sign in situ quickly and accurately. Gone are the days when you worried about what the chap developing your film would think of you when he saw pictures of a vole impaled on a barbed-wire fence (a shrike's larder in case you're wondering) or a slightly glistening Badger dropping (a work of art if stuffed with the wing cases of dung beetles). Even if you manage to take a plaster cast or trace, having photographs of footprints will prove invaluable. The most useful camera to have is one with a good macro facility as this enables the user to take photographs of some of the smallest and most delicate details (see pages 19–21 for more on photography).

There is a reason why crime scene investigators use flashlights – they illuminate details easily missed in all but the brightest of light conditions and they have the ability to focus your attention within the beam, so that you'll notice things you might have otherwise missed.

Torch

I always carry a small, lightweight LED torch, which is useful if you get caught out after dark. It's also handy for illuminating signs in dingy places, backlighting leaves and other objects, and creating side-lighting to show up the details and relief of footprints, especially when the ambient light is a little flat.

Above left: *A plaster-cast kit for recording footprints is a fun and useful tool for building a collection of prints for future reference.*

Above right: *One of the more recent additions to the tracker's kit bag is a very useful bit of technology called a trail camera.*

Below: *A tracking stick is little more than a stick and a few elastic bands, but it provides a very useful way to help beginners follow, measure and understand a set of tracks.*

Plaster-cast kit

More on this later, but basically this comprises a quantity of dry plaster powder, a pot to mix it in, another vessel to transport water and stuff to make a frame. See page 32 for more information.

Tracking stick

You don't need anything fancy, just a stick and a couple of elastic bands. This is a very handy bit of kit especially for those new to tracking. The magic is in how you use it… See page 41 for how to make one of your own.

Trail camera

The price of remote recording equipment is coming down, and it is now possible to buy a trail camera for a very small outlay. The purist animal trackers may not be that keen on them, but I love them and have played with several models over the years. They can help you confirm your hunches, place your tracking beds and generally throw light on what animals are out there. If you've got one that can record moving images, it will also tell you what they are getting up to. They are very much part of the modern animal tracker's kit.

Wet wipes

Last but not least, and I know this doesn't sound very 'rufty tufty' and true to the image of a wild animal tracker, but you'll find a small bottle of hand sanitiser or wet wipes indispensable – they'll give you the peace of mind that you're not transferring unmentionable bacteria to your cheese and onion crisps at lunchtime.

Codes of practice

When you're out and about it's worth remembering that more often than not you will be standing on ground that belongs to someone else. It is therefore important and respectful to other people, and the landscape, including the animals you're tracking, to obey some very basic rules of conduct – often referred to as the countryside code.

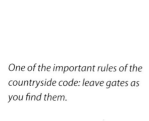

One of the important rules of the countryside code: leave gates as you find them.

Respect for the environment

I don't want to stamp loads of rules and restrictions on you before the book has even started, but I guess it's a sign of the times that I have to tip my hat in the general direction of common sense and spell out a few basics to you.

When out and about it's a good idea to stick to the countryside code; in a nutshell you can't go far wrong if you close gates and make sure you have the permission of the landowner if you are going to stray from footpaths.

Be aware that some animals are protected to a lesser or greater extent by law, and make sure you know of the ones that may be in your area and what you can and cannot do in relation to them, their habitats, nests, roosts and burrows. Bear in mind that it is illegal in some countries to be in possession of artefacts belonging to protected animals such as nests, eggshells, feathers, bones and other remains – check out the law protecting the animals that frequent your area. If in doubt, don't do it.

Your health

I have very clear memories as a kid of really upsetting my grandparents by poking around in a runny Badger dropping with a stick and announcing to the world that this one had been eating blackberries. Obviously this sort of behaviour can give you very useful insights into the fine details of an animal's life, but not only does it cross the line of what many people deem 'normal' behaviour, but also it does so for very good reasons.

There is a very good basic biological survival instinct in all of us that tells us not to put our fingers in this and stir it around (well, not without thoroughly scrubbing your hands afterwards anyway).

The droppings of some animals do carry nasty germs and diseases: toxocariasis from many mammals, particularly dogs and cats; psittacosis from various birds; salmonellosis and *E. coli* from almost anything and histoplasmosis from bats and rodents to name but a few. There are also diseases that you can pick up from the remains of dead animals, and a bird or a mammal carcass may either have been placed, laced with poison, to kill other animals, or it may have been a victim of accidental or illegal poisoning. Some poisons can be absorbed through the skin, so items should not be touched directly if there is any chance of poison involvement. So be aware, assume the worst and operate just like those good-looking *CSI* detectives you see on telly: wear gloves and a face mask if necessary, and wash your hands after touching droppings or animal remains.

If you need to explore faecal material, do it at arm's length with a stick; if you have to get closer, try to keep your face as far away as is practical and hold your breath. Some animal droppings do need a little sniff to identify the owner, for example to separate an Otter spraint (it smells relatively pleasantly, some say of summer meadows) from mink droppings (the word pleasant cannot in any way be used to describe their odour). Use your common sense and, for example, don't go doing the same to try to distinguish Fox from dog. There's a risk of contracting toxocariasis from the former, so it should never be attempted.

The high-tech tracker

After spending hours in the field trying to work out which animals are leaving signs of their presence, the dream of most trackers is to verify their hunches and to witness the animals in action. This is now possible thanks to some clever little digital devices.

I'm addicted to trail cameras – they close the gap between the tracker and the tracked, and the better you are at tracking, the better pictures you'll get. It's like leaving your eyes and ears out in the woods overnight.

Trail cameras

These neat all-in-one units, collectively called trail cameras, were originally developed for the hunting market in the US and have now found their way into the kitbag of the modern field naturalist. They vary a lot in price, quality and features, but all of them enable you to monitor a location remotely.

They consist of a small camera unit, with a tiny lens and the ability to record the information digitally on a memory card. Most have PIR (passive infra-red) sensors (the sort you find in security lights, which work on sensitivity to movement and temperature) and some kind of LED lighting, which is either red or infra-red and allows images to be captured on even the darkest night.

The units are compact and powered by batteries, although most have various other options of connectivity to monitors or mains power and can record reasonable stills or moving images; some can even do both as well as recording sound.

Some trackers don't approve of trail cameras and think that they make you lazy, but I think they have a valuable part to play in our understanding of the natural world. Anyone can follow an instruction manual and set up a camera, but if you apply the skills that you will naturally develop as a tracker you can position your device at a point where it will stand the best chance of capturing the action. Obviously there is an element of luck, but in my experience careful siting of the trail camera, using your tracker's insight, will simply get you a better picture. Another thing to remember when setting up your camera is security – you don't want someone to walk off with your camera and all your great action shots.

You can attach trail cameras to natural objects, or in the absence of the perfect tree trunk or rock, why not bring your own post? This camera is in a high-security 'bear-proof' box and is locked in place for extra security.

Trail cameras are basically a camera, a motion and heat sensor and a slot for an SD card – all neatly boxed together with batteries for power.

Ltl Acorn   ●   041°F   005°C   05.03.2012 23:07:01

I am now addicted to using my camera: I started off trying for the rats that live under my chicken shed, then I set it up outside a nearby Fox earth and then moved on to the local Badger sett. I now want to embark on other challenges. Can I capture the local Otter that I know uses the ledges under a road bridge? Can I identify the animal that left that poo on the lawn, and which bird has left very unusual probing signs on the spoil heaps of the Badger sett?

These cameras can give you great insight into what goes on when you are not around and they can also help you develop your ability as a tracker, not just by reading the signs to get the camera in the right position, but also by confirming or disproving your hunches. And what a bonus to actually see the animal that you feel you have got to know intimately via its tracks and signs. Both tracking and effectively using technology are about learning and developing a first-hand understanding and knowledge of animals' lives, and in this respect they complement each other very well.

If you find tracks, a trail cam is a useful tool to confirm who has been visiting your local wildlife area. Animals such as this Roe Deer are scared of humans and not easy to photograph in daylight, but here it is unaware of the hidden trail cam.

Tracks and trails

If an animal has feet and the conditions are right, it'll make tracks. String a few of these together and you've got a trail. There is, however, much more to the art of tracking than simply identifying and following a trail of dints made by the pads, hooves and claws of a passing animal. We can learn a great deal from a simple impression in soft terrain, and because of their visibility, footprints are an excellent starting point to get tracking.

The regular passage of Badgers' feet has flattened or worn away the vegetation to create this path. Such trails often connect the entrances of a sett with foraging grounds or other setts. Sometimes Badger-paths even travel under fences or cross over roads. Badgers repeatedly mark their paths with their scent night after night.

Where to find footprints

You'll only be able to find these noticeable signs of the passage of an animal if conditions underfoot are favourable, such as after a fresh fall of snow or at low tide on mudflats. Otherwise, you'll need to hunt out the softest substrates, such as the fringes of ponds, lakes and rivers, or even the edges of puddles on paths.

Snow

My favourite conditions for tracking occur after a fresh fall of snow – in snow, you should be able to see a number of different tracks quite quickly and get the chance to appreciate the varying gaits and trail patterns. Good trails will also introduce you to other signs, such as where an animal has urinated, defecated or even had a scratch.

Right: Trail patterns are clearest when a moderate snowfall is touched by frost. When snow is on the ground you'll see tracks everywhere.

Far right: A good tracker can look at a trail in the snow like this and recognise the 'maker' simply by the pattern and the rhythm of the trail.

The best kind of snow for tracking is fresh, fine-grained snow that has fallen on a hard level surface such as a path, road or ice. Here the prints will register clearly, especially if the snow is melting slightly. If the snow is too deep the size of the print can be misleading and if it is freezing, the surface crystallises and will blow about even in a light breeze. Even a dainty-footed animal can leave a large hole on the surface of snow, so it's best to get down as low as you can to the actual print which may well be on firmer ground.

Mud

Mud comes in many varieties, but smooth, firm, fine particulate mud is one of my favourites. Estuaries and muddy shores can be very rewarding for all sorts of tracks and trails. The margins of ponds and streams are also good places to look for footprints, though these will disappear in heavy rain. For this reason, it's often worth checking out muddy patches under bridges, as they seem to attract a variety of passing animals. You may also get good prints around the entrances of holes and burrows.

Fine but firm mud can be one of the most giving substrates, revealing many details, not just the pads and claws but even imprints of the hair between the pads, like this Wolf track does.

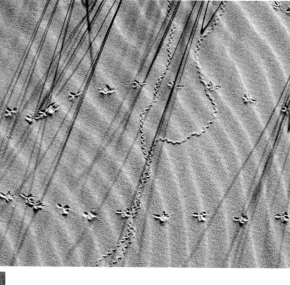

Above right: Sand is best if it is fine, damp or a little muddy – but tracks on sand rarely last and the window of opportunity rapidly disappears if the sand dries out or the wind picks up.

Sand

That iconic Robinson Crusoe image of a perfect lone trail of human footprints across the sand would only be possible if the sand was soft, moist and smooth, and more often than not in coastal situations it is. Beaches and sandflats below the high-tide mark have the potential to deliver great prints, particularly where animals forage along the shoreline, but the window of opportunity here is limited by the ebb and flow of the tides.

Identifying footprints

On encountering an impression in some soft ground, most people want to know whose foot made the print. The next questions that spring to mind are: what were they doing and in which direction were they heading?

Right: *An enthusiastic dog running fast made these tracks on the beach – you can almost feel the speed. See the disturbed sand and the way the dog's tracks are clustered in groups of four as it has bounced between touching down.*

Left and below: *Feet are very different, and learning how a foot touches down and how the various features relate to the impressions they make on the substrate, is all part of making you a tracker.*

Footprint types

We tend to think of the pad marks of mammals such as cats and dogs when we think of footprints – a nice flowery shape with clearly defined toes, maybe tipped with claws. This foot form fits many mammals from the big and the obvious to the tiny and often overlooked versions made by much smaller and more secretive animals, such as mice and shrews. Then, of course, there are the hoofed mammals consisting of the even-toed ungulates, such as members of the deer, sheep and pig families, and the odd-toed ungulates, such as horses. So there are three basic categories of footprints: those with pads, those with two hooves and those with a single hoof.

Mammals' feet

An understanding of the basic biology of animal feet and how they move is of immense use when you're out in the field trying to identify footprints and trails. When mammals evolved from their reptilian ancestors some 200 million years ago, they inherited the same archetypal foot plan of five digits, known as a pentadactyl (from 'penta' meaning five and 'dactyl', finger).

The big flat feet of a bear are classic of an animal that exhibits what we call the plantigrade footplan.

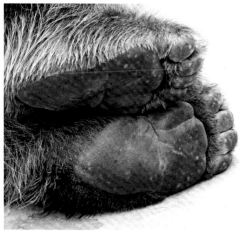

The biological convention is simply to number these digits from one to five starting with the shortest of the bunch, the inner toe, which is analogous to your thumb. Now press your hand down flat on a table top, and this demonstrates how those first primitive mammals would have walked: with their phalanges (finger bones), metacarpals (hand bones) and carpals (wrist bones) all pushing down together. In the rear limbs the bones are referred to as the phalanges (toe bones), metatarsals (foot bones) and tarsals (ankle bones). Many animals alive today still share this flat-footed primitive foot plan known as **plantigrade**.

This type of foot works well enough if you are a bear, shrew, mustelid (a group of carnivores that includes Badgers, weasels, Otters, martens and the like), Hedgehog and, of course, a human, but the problem is that it results in a relatively inefficient and clumsy way of moving. Every time a plantigrade animal puts its foot down there is a lot of resistance to forward motion created by such a large surface area coming into contact with the ground, and all those toe bones are heavy to swing around.

With the evolution of fast mammalian predators and the consequential need for the animals they were chasing to get faster in order to avoid being caught, something had to happen. The surface area of the foot was gradually reduced, enabling animals to 'step things up' by moving on tiptoe.

Cats walk on their tiptoes – they are what we refer to as digitigrade. Incidentally, the claws rarely show up in the tracks of members of the cat family.

These **digitigrade** animals stand only on their phalanges (fingers and toes). Bend your hand so only your fingers touch the table – this is pretty much the way a dog or a cat walks. Accompanying the touchdown of the toes was a moving forward of the body weight, the lengthening of the leg bones and a reduction in the number of toes. Digit number one still exists as the tiny 'dew' claw on the front foot in dogs and cats, but it doesn't make contact with the ground. So the footprint of a digitigrade animal usually only registers four toes.

Below: With reduced numbers of toes and standing on the very tip of them, these Reindeer feet exhibit the unguligrade footplan – ideal for running and moving at speed.

Bottom: You can't get fewer toes than one, which is exactly what a horse has – the most reduced and highly specialised of feet.

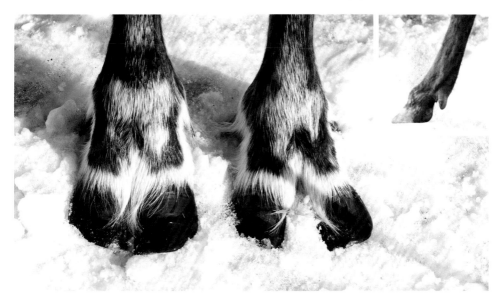

This design became refined even further in the hoofed animals, the ungulates, which are said to be **unguligrade**. The even-toed ungulates, such as deer, usually register only two slots or cleaves in their footprints, corresponding with toes three and four, which results in even less resistance from the ground and the potential to run much faster. If the ground is very soft, in some ungulate species, such as Wild Boar, toes two and five, known as dewclaws, also register in the footprint.

The ultimate specialisation for high-speed locomotion is the most reduced foot format of all – the single toe of a horse which moves on the tip of its single third digit, making its footprints one of the most instantly identifiable of all.

The chances of actually seeing the prints made by a bird of prey are slight – but here's a mean pair belonging to an eagle showing the classic toe arrangement of birds; three toes forward and one back.

The most basic and simple bird-foot layout is seen in the game birds such as pheasants, partridges and chickens.

Birds' feet

Fortunately for the tracker, birds don't show anywhere near the same diversity as mammals in their foot design, which makes recognising them relatively easy, but separating one bird from another can be quite a challenge.

The feet of birds are variations on the **digitigrade** type in that they walk only on their toes. A bird never has more than four toes – but instead of digit one (the thumb) being lost, it is actually digit five that has gone (except in some game birds, where it has become the spur and is positioned further up the shank of the leg) and the thumb has swung around to become the hind claw.

The total lack of a broad 'palm' or 'heel' pad and the elongated toes make bird footprints quite easy to separate from those of most mammals, and by noting the size, toe length, toe angle, toe arrangement, trail pattern (if there is one) and other details it is certainly possible to make an educated guess at what bird has hopped, bounced, waddled, shuffled or strolled past.

Since there are excellent books that specialise in classifying and separating the tracks of various birds and their families, all I do here is set you in the right direction, so that you start asking yourself the right identification questions.

The majority of bird footprints have three forward-pointing toes, with digit one (the hallux) pointing backwards. This is an arrangement known as **anisodactyl** (think of a chicken's foot) and is found in most perching birds from finches to pheasants. This can be split into other categories including **palmate** – ducks, geese, swans, gulls, terns and many other aquatic birds have a membrane that stretches between toes two, three and four; **totipalmate**, which translates as totally joined-up toes as, for example, in Gannets, Shags, Cormorants, etc; **semipalmate**, which means partially joined-up toes, found, rather obviously, in the Semipalmated Plover; and **lobate**, which describes the lobes of membrane that edge the toes in grebes, Coots and phalaropes.

Above: *Waterfowl often leave the details of the webbing in their tracks, but failing this the toe shapes, lengths and angle are all very telling.*

1: *The knock-kneed and fan-shaped feet of a Cormorant.*

2: *The lobed-footed Coot – conditions have to be really good for these flaps and flanges to show up in the track.*

3: *Woodpeckers (like owls and cuckoos) rarely leave tracks – their toes are arranged with two pointing forwards and two back.*

4: *Wading birds tend to have reduced backward-pointing toes with three relatively evenly spaced and sized ones facing forwards.*

The next most common toe arrangement among the perching birds is **zygodactyl**, which still has four toes, but this time with two pointing forwards and two backwards – the fourth toe in these birds has swung backwards to pair up with the first. It can be found in birds such as some owls, woodpeckers and cuckoos that use their feet for grasping.

Getting the measure of an animal

When you are learning tracking skills, try to make notes and measure the prints you come across. This will force you to get down close to the footprints, and you may well notice other details. It's also useful to draw or photograph a print with either an object of known size or a ruler in the picture.

Above: *A ruler is most useful to drop into a reference photograph. Here the size of the print clearly tells me that it was made by a Fallow Deer.*

Below: *Sometimes you might be caught out without your ruler, in which case use some other readily available item, such as some small change or a penknife, or even place your foot next to the print for scale.*

Foot figures

For mammals with pads, you need to measure the width and length of the footprint. To measure the length, use a ruler to measure from the very tip of the pad on the longest digit to the rear of the heel pad. You don't usually include the nails or claws, though a separate note of their length may be useful. Then measure the widest distance across. This all sounds so simple, until you try doing this with a tangle of spidery rat or shrew footprints, all superimposed over each other, in sticky mud!

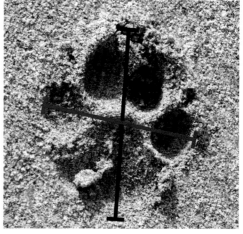

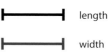

length

width

For animals with cloven hooves, take both length and width measurements, the length being the tip of the cleaves to the back of the heel. Also measure the separation of the cleaves at the tips and the length of the heel pads if the print has registered clearly.

For birds, you measure the overall length and width in much the same way, without including the claws. A separate measurement of the third (central) toe is handy, as are measurements of the claws and the angles between the toes. Measuring angles is, of course, very difficult in the field; it is better to do this from a photo, a tracing or a cast (see pages 32–33).

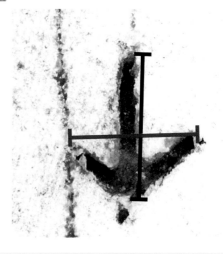

MAKING CASTS

Creating a cast is my favourite way of preserving a footprint – it enables you to build up your own reference collection so you can compare prints side by side and is especially handy if drawing isn't your forte. It's also a memento of the mark left by an animal that you may never actually set eyes on in the wild.

You'll need to have the following to hand:

- Suitable quantity of plaster of Paris or dental stone
- Plastic mixing bowl
- Spoon for mixing
- Container for carrying water – either full or empty depending on situation
- Some stiff cardboard strips, cut section of a plastic bottle or other frame
- Paper clips
- Knife
- Soap
- Rubber gloves

N.B. Take care when handling hot plaster of Paris to avoid burning yourself.

Position the frame

Surround your track with a ring of cardboard held together with paper clips, or a section cut from a plastic drink bottle or flowerpot – this is the frame that will hold your liquid plaster in place. Once it's in place press it firmly into the ground after removing any twigs or stones. To make doubly sure the frame won't leak, I lift it up and slice into the soil with a knife along the impression that it's made before replacing; it should then sit much better.

Get the plaster mix right

Pour water into your mixing bowl, add the plaster and stir slowly until it reaches the consistency of pancake batter (you can add a little more plaster or water to fine-tune the mixture). A flake of soap dissolved in water seems to make the casts less brittle. Dental stone, which you can get online, is a great substitute. It's a gypsum product like plaster of Paris, but is much tougher and gives a superior finish that is also easier to clean.

Pour the plaster into the frame, but not from a great height as this can damage the print and introduce air bubbles into the cast. Then gently tap the sides of the frame with your finger or a spoon to coax any stray air bubbles to work their way to the surface.

Lifting the cast

Leave for 10–15 minutes. The setting process produces heat (which is why you can't use this technique to make casts in snow), so if you wait for the plaster to cool down again you'll know when it has set. Then gently lift the cast – if it doesn't lift easily, I often dig underneath and lift it substrate and all.

The final touches

Leave the cast to harden to its maximum. Then use a brush to remove any traces of soil attached to the base of the print and moisten your brush to give it a final clean. You should now be holding a perfect rendition of the footprint you found except that it will be a negative impression. Finally wrap the whole cast in newspaper or bubble wrap to keep it intact in your bag.

Accentuate the positive

When your negative has thoroughly dried carefully paint the entire surface with a layer of Vaseline®, making sure you work it into all the cracks and crevices. Then place the frame around it and make a cast as before. Wait for it to dry thoroughly before gently prising the negative and positive casts apart using a knife; you should now have a copy of the original footprint. Occasionally a disaster occurs here because of an incomplete covering of Vaseline®, or if a track is particularly deep and a piece of the negative breaks off in the indentation on the positive. Frustrating though this is, time and experience will soon tell you which tracks will work and which will not.

Tracing tracks

It's as simple as – well tracing. Just draw over the track and you have all the details you need – you can even add notes and annotations.

This is a technique I've seen used in India to identify the tracks of individual Tigers. It's brilliantly simple, quick and clean, and helps you get to grips with what's in your area. It is, however, only as accurate as your tracing, so it's a good idea to get photographic back-up as well.

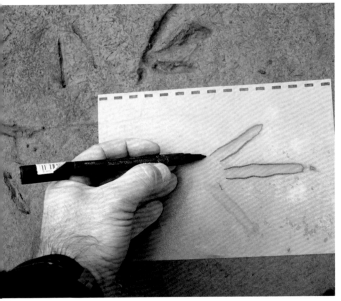

For a reusable 'tracing kit' all you need is a piece of Perspex (the sort you can get in any DIY store) and a fine wipeable pen or chinagraph pencil. For a more permanent version, you can used clear acetate sheets (often sold quite cheaply by stationery suppliers) and a fine permanent marker pen.

Simply drop the clear sheet over the top of the track and use the pen to trace the outline and any other features you wish to record; if your sheet is big enough you may be able to trace the whole set of tracks – two for birds and humans and four for most other animals. The trace can then be either photocopied or scanned and kept on a computer, then you can wipe the trace off the Perspex and use it again. If you've used acetate you can simply file it for future reference.

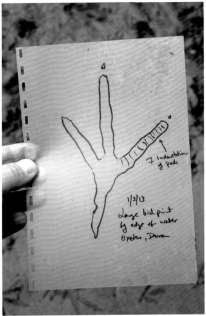

Tracking beds

If conditions are not suitable for creating footprints, you can intervene and create your own. I first realised the potential of this trick as a young naturalist when confronted with the many dints in the spoil heap outside the entrance of a Badger sett. I was looking to see if there were any cubs in residence, but it was difficult to make out anything – so I simply raked the surface of the loose sandy soil to make it flat and returned the next day, to be rewarded with a clearer

picture. There were cubs present after all, and what I learned put me in the right spot to get the most from my wildlife watching.

If, like me, you are on a continuous quest for perfect prints to add to your collection, experimenting with tracking beds can be a way of hunting out the impressions you need. Select the spot you want to make into a tracking bed, ideally a spot out of direct sunlight and with a soil made up of fine particles, remove all surface objects like stones, sticks and leaves, then break up the surface with a fork, hoe or rake and sprinkle liberally with water. Keep mixing the broken surface with water until you've created a fine muddy surface. It's even easier to modify muddy patches on paths by simply mixing and smoothing out the existing mud; the longer and bigger the tracking bed, the higher the chance that you will get a good set of prints and you may even get some good trail measurements. You can increase your likelihood of getting some good prints if you bait the area.

If you are recording the footprints of smaller, lighter animals, such as songbirds, reptiles and small mammals, mix your own mud pie and spread this out on a tray, which you can bait and position accordingly. For small mammals, I also make a cover to make them feel more secure and to keep off the rain.

If the conditions are not suitable for leaving tracks, then make some that are – the tracking bed is just that, a perfect smooth spot to place a foot and leave a clear footprint. Brush away any leaves, smooth the soil and don't forget to remove any stones.

DEAD USEFUL

Occasionally you will be presented with the gift of a dead animal. Horrible as it may sound, such a gift is very handy for getting precise measurements of the footprints of animals. Obviously take care when handling dead animals and obey the hygiene codes (see page 18). Sometimes you can actually use the foot of a dead animal to give you a perfect print for reference. Do, however, bear in mind that there is sometimes a variation between individuals and sexes.

This big elongated print, with claws clearly registered, says dog family – but is it a domesticated dog, Wolf or Fox?

No claws, a rounded toe and footpads shout 'cat!' to me.

Dog or cat?

The most commonly seen footprints belong to dogs and cats because we've surrounded ourselves with domesticated varieties of these animals. So here's how you tell them apart…

First check the tracks for claws: if they're present (and the track isn't on a steep incline), you've got a member of the dog family. Cats use their claws as tools for catching prey, so just like pocket knives, they need to be kept sharp and clean, and are kept in their sheaths until needed. Dogs, on the other hand, are designed to run down their prey and use their jaws for the kill. Claws to dogs are like running spikes for added grip, so you should see them in a reasonable track.

Now look at the shape of the interdigital pad: dogs lift up their feet and walk almost on tiptoe, so that the back of the pad does not register and the resultant print shows a back edge that smoothly curves in the middle. Cats have a scalloped back edge and a lumpy front edge.

The toe arrangement is the final giveaway: four toes register in both, but those of a dog have a pattern: the middle two are next to each other while the two off to the side are almost triangular. Cat tracks in comparison have four smooth, fairly even-sized toe prints.

Fox or dog?

So how do you separate the footprints of a dog and its ubiquitous cousin, the Fox?

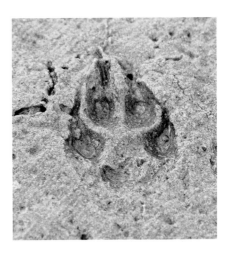

Both these canines, domesticated and wild, are intimately associated with our lives and, whether in the park, on a snow-covered driveway, on a woodland trail or on a sandy shore, there's a possibility of finding their footprints.

Telling them apart is actually really easy and one of the first tracking lessons I ever learned. Fox prints never really vary: the interdigital pad is small, only about the same size as each of the toes, and you can hold a straight edge (or draw an imaginary line) through the gap between the front two toes and the outer toes without touching a pad. The overall appearance of the print is one of neat proportions that fits smoothly into an oval, approximately 5 x 4.5cm.

Nice, neat and oval – you can get a line in between the furthest forward toes and those at the back. This is the print of a Fox, exhibiting the tidy design of nature and not the clumsy breeding of man-made dogs.

Domesticated dogs, on the other hand, have much more variable footprints, which can be more than 5cm in length or smaller (although be aware of the possibility of Fox cubs in the spring and early summer). Dog prints tend to have a much more splayed shape, rarely nice and oval, with a large, lumpy interdigital pad that is bigger than the toe pads. You also can't make the straight line fit between the front and outer toes.

In the fox print there is more space between the front and back pads than in a dog print.

cat

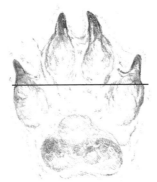

dog

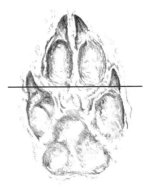

fox

Following the trail

Sometimes if footprints are not very clear, you can still tell exactly what species they belong to by their trail pattern. The pattern depends on several factors: how many feet the animal uses in contact with the ground, the mechanics of the animal, the terrain, and the type and speed of movement. Following a trail and trying to interpret an animal's behaviour is one of the more subtle skills of animal tracking.

Seeing individual prints is difficult, but the overall pattern and texture of this trail tells us that it is a regular path used by deer.

An animal walking, such as this Wild Boar, leaves a totally different trail than an animal moving faster. In the latter case the tracks tend to be closer together and straddle the middle of the trail.

Trail patterns: mammals

For mammals that use four legs, there are several patterns that, with a bit of practice, can easily be recognised. The main types of gait are walking; trotting or running; galloping; and bounding or hopping. Watching how animals move, in particular the sequence in which they move their feet and how long their feet are off the ground, will help you understand the various trail patterns.

When I'm interpreting a trail, the first thing I do is imagine the way the animal was moving, and it is this that comes with practice and experience. That instant recall of a moment is the pure essence of a good tracker; but it's also something that is really difficult to describe. I'm hoping the illustrations will help you become a veritable Miss Marple or Sherlock Holmes of a nature detective.

Walking

When an animal is moving very slowly, it may be browsing or grazing as it goes and is moving one foot at a time. The stride length is therefore short and if the animal is a species that over-registers (that is, the hind print superimposes over that left by the front foot) then that is what you'll see. Many mammals, such as insectivores, carry their bodies very low to the ground when walking, and in this relaxed state their tails and bellies tend to drag. This can often be seen and helps with identification.

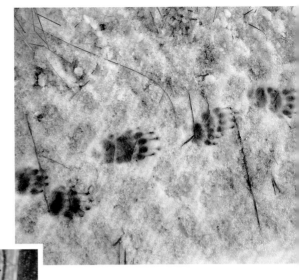

The heel mark of a Badger can sometimes be seen in snow. Also look for the larger claws visible on the forefeet prints.

Wild Boar are shy of humans and are most likely to be seen running, leaving clusters of footprints.

Trotting and running

At a faster pace several things happen: the stride gets longer and the spacing of the tracks is more spread out. Drag marks become less likely as the animal is now moving with purpose. More importantly, the feet are moving in a very clear and regimented sequence with the alternate opposite limbs being moved at the same time (so for this think right forefoot and left hindfoot, and then left forefoot and right hindfoot). There is a tendency for the rear tracks to slip over those left by the front feet. Those species that perfectly register have a tendency to become less perfect as they move from a trot to a run. Along with an increase in speed comes increased force placed by each foot, and the splaying of toes and slipping become much more common.

Rabbits (and hares) have a very distinctive pattern to their trail, whether they are walking or moving at speed as here – this animal is moving from the left to the right.

This Fallow Deer in mid gallop has none of its feet on the ground. The tracks made by a galloping deer will be spread out, expect to find groupings of all four hoofs at the points where it both landed and took off.

Galloping

Now the animal is moving at high speed and at some point in the gallop all four feet will be off the ground at once, so there will be big gaps in the trail as it literally flies along. When it does touch down, it leaves a group of four tracks, with any registration now totally lost.

Just as there are different modes of locomotion and trail patterns, there are different ways of measuring them. You need to be sure you are measuring stride lengths and trail widths based on the 'actual' prints and ignoring marks made by foot dragging, especially in deep mud, sand and snow.

For alternating gaits and 2–2 patterns, strides are the distance between the tip of the toe or the claw of one print and the next. With 3–4 and 4–4 gaits, the stride is measured from toe to heel, and in tracks that are grouped the group is measured from heel to toe.

When an animal gallops, generally the stride length gets bigger and the clusters of tracks tend to be spaced out as the animal flies along.

TRACKING STICK

Use this extremely simple and cheap device and you'll be surprised at how good a tracker you can become. It may be a straight branch grabbed when you find a fresh and beguiling trail, and marked with a knife, an indelible pen or movable, coloured rubber bands, or a special stick that you'll treasure and keep with you in your backpack.

Measuring mammal tracks

You need to record track length and then stride length – stride can be measured in a couple of different ways; it doesn't really matter which method you use as long as you're consistent. I tend to use the heel or the back of the track as this is where a lot of weight is placed and it therefore tends to make a better mark.

LF Left front
RF Right front
LH Left hind
RH Right hind

A = Track length

Place one end of your tracking stick in line with the heel of the first footprint, then slide one of your elastic bands to the position that aligns with the toes of the first print.

B = Stride length

This is the measurement from the heel of the first footprint to the spot where that same heel comes down again. Place one end of your tracking stick so that it is lined up with the heel of the first forefoot and slide one of the elastic bands to the position that corresponds to the heel of that same footfall in the following group of prints.

The advantage of the tracking stick is that it gets your nose down in the dirt so that you're more likely to see subtle signs, such as a trodden down bit of vegetation, which may come in handy if the next footprint is hard to find. You may need to consider whether the animal has changed gait and therefore whether its stride length has changed. In time you can leave the stick behind as your tracking skills and experience increase.

C = Trail width

This is the distance from the outside of one print to the outside of the opposite print.

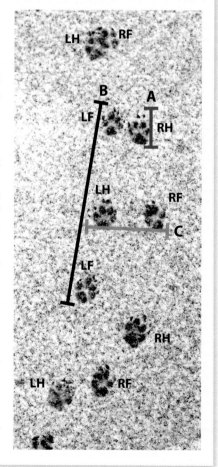

Above left and right: Pigeons stride along with their feet placed on either side of the track centre and will also often turn their toes in towards the centre.

Birds

Bird trails are a little easier to interpret than those of mammals, and with only two feet you have less to puzzle over. Ground birds, such as pheasants, partridges, waders and waterfowl, show a walking gait, while perching birds that spend more time in trees and bushes are generally not cut out for much walking or running around, so practise a hopping gait. Some birds, such as corvids (crows) and Starlings, are masters of both modes of locomotion.

A good example of a walking bird is a gull or pigeon. Both birds walk in as neat and tidy a fashion as walking goes for birds. Imagine the bird simply plodding along one foot after another, leaving straddled prints on either side of an imaginary line that runs between the two sets of prints. Different bird species straddle the line by different amounts and, for example, a pigeon has a much wider stance than a gull so its tracks are further apart. Waddling birds with webbed feet, such as ducks and geese, walk with their toes pointed inwards, and they make very distinctive tracks.

The webbing clearly identifies this as the track of a waterbird. The size and the impression of the turned in toes give it away as the trail of a goose.

One foot in front of the other. This Pheasant is about to place a foot almost directly in front of the one already on the ground.

This neat-stepping gait of a Pheasant leaves a very tidy trail, with the tracks of the left and right foot directly in a line and very close to the centre line of the tail.

Game birds walk in a very dainty manner for what appear to be such rotund and clumsy birds. Watch one next time you encounter it and you'll see how it places its feet neatly along a line, or rather overlapping it slightly, with each footfall. This is a good example of an unstraddled gait. Birds that hop create tracks of pairs of prints, the left and right foot registering side by side.

Just as in the mammals, if any of these birds start to run or speed up then the stride length increases and the tracks tend to become much more messy, with a tendency to show various drag marks where toes have scraped the substrate. With heavy birds, there will be more displacement of substrate and slipping.

To identify different species of bird, get as close as you can to the prints and look carefully for shapes, evidence of textures and claws, then carefully measure not only the track and the angles of the toes, but also the stride length and the trail width.

Mammals with pads

Having divided mammal footprints into the three main categories of those with pads, cloven-hoofed and hoofed, they can be divided into smaller groups based mainly on their shapes and also, handily, sizes.

Small mammals such as mice, voles and shrews are so light on their feet that conditions have to be extremely good for their prints to register.

The dainty feet of small mammals, with their long toes and their wide spreads, tend to create tracks that remind me of tiny little stars.

Rodents and shrews

These families of mammal are nearly all very lightweight and create dainty, scratchy, almost star-shaped tracks with toes well splayed to the front and out to the sides. The substrate needs to be quite fine for any decent prints to be left; in many cases simply being able to identify them as left by a rodent or an insectivore is often as far as a tracker can go. Although rodents have five toes on each foot, the front feet usually only show four unless really excellent prints are found. All these animals also have claws, which add to the elongated spindly look of the footprints, and shrews have a much longer thumb, which is situated lower and nearly always registers.

Rodents usually move with a hop (technically a gallop), which means that the rear feet normally land in front of the front feet, but there are other variations. Larger members of the family, such as Beaver and Crested Porcupine, move with the regular plod of a pacer, with alternating rear feet landing beside the track of the opposite front. Shrews move at more of a trot, their rear prints partially registering over the front tracks with a stride of 3–5cm depending on species.

The hopping gait of most small rodents indicates that the larger rear feet tend to land slightly ahead of the front feet.

Squirrels follow the classic rodent bounding and hopping gaits, but they are much larger than most smaller rodents and the tracks themselves tend to be more compact and less scratchy.

Beavers are not that small but they are a rodent. Being big and heavy they plod along with an alternating step, almost unlike any other European rodents, except marmots and Crested Porcupine.

Squirrels make slightly less scratchy star-shaped prints than most of the smaller rodents, but their rear feet especially can look almost like little human handprints, often with a clear outline of the foot and the three middle toes of about the same length.

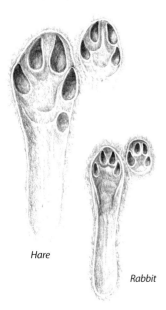

In the distinctive 'set of three' created by a Rabbit, the single pock mark in the track is created by the front feet, which are set very close together, while the two separate tracks are caused by the rear feet swinging past. This animal was heading away from the camera.

Rabbits and hares

The front feet make small, sharp-tipped, oval impressions, while the rear tracks can be similar but a little larger when travelling over firm ground at speed. With softer substrates and slower speeds, the rear tracks often give the impression of the full length of the rear foot. To differentiate between Rabbit and hare, try using a matchbox as a size guide: Rabbits make a track that is quite a lot narrower than the width of a matchbox (approx. 3.5cm), whereas a hare's footprint is the same size or bigger. The tracks will appear quite soft and indistinct at the edges because the undersides of the feet are clothed in pads of dense, forward-pointing hairs, but the long 'running spikes' of the claws will nearly always be visible. Because the first digit is positioned further back it rarely shows in a track, so most tracks show just three diffuse impressions of the toe and interdigital pads.

These animals move with a gallop even when travelling relatively slowly, so the rear longer feet register in front of the two front feet, which usually fall one in front of the other as the speed increases. The distance between the two groups gets greater as the speed increases. Remember also that the direction of travel is opposite to what it might seem. The pattern of the four prints makes an arrow shape, but the animal will have been moving in the opposite direction to the way the arrow seems to point.

Brown Hare: fore print 5 x 3cm, rear 6–15 x 3.5cm

Mountain Hare: fore print 5 x 5cm, rear 5–13 x 3.5cm (though tends to spread, making the track look wider)

Rabbit: fore print 2.5 x 1.5cm, rear 4 x 2.5cm

Hare

Rabbit

There is not a lot of difference between the tracks of hares and Rabbits – except size. Hares are quite a bit bigger and have a much greater stride.

Cats

Whether Tiger or tabby, the cat family's footprint fits nicely into a well-rounded oval, shorter than it is wide. The front paws are slightly larger than the rear ones and show four toe pads, but never claws, in general walking. The only time you will get the impression of claws from a cat is if they are slipping and need to find extra grip.

It is difficult to distinguish between Wildcats and domesticated cats by footprints alone – both have prints that measure about 3.5 x 3cm. A lynx's footprint looks the same as those of other cats but is much larger (7.5 x 8.5–9.5cm), with slightly larger outer toes (domesticated cats footprints have a balanced look to them as the toe prints are all the same size). A genet's prints show claw marks, so if you are in the range of this animal check for claw marks. (See pages 36–37 for a comparison between cat and dog prints.)

Trail patterns are what you might expect from a cool and collected predator – a diagonal stroll is typical, with the rear footprints overlapping the front ones, though slightly ahead; in soft substrate this overlap becomes almost perfect. At a walk there is a little straddle, but as the pace gets up to a trot the fore and hind prints become almost totally aligned; when the animal leaps you may get a variety of different arrangements of the prints, usually hind feet overtaking the front.

Stride length of a domesticated cat is about 30cm; at a trot this increases to 35–40cm (the trail of a Fox, especially if the prints are not that clear, can look quite similar, but the stride length, at 45cm, sets them apart).

Lynx stride length starts at 40cm for walking and can increase to 250cm if running.

The lynx is the largest of the cats in the region covered by this book, but you are much more likely to come across the tracks of domesticated cats or the similar Wildcat. The prints are all very similar; it is scale and stride-length that help identification.

The soft, rounded pads of a cat. Note the lack of claws. Unless gripping prey or slippery ground, they are always retracted and almost never show in a track.

Wild dogs

Fox The commonest wild dog print in Europe is that of the Fox and this really is the one to get familiar with and recognise. It is a small, typical dog print of about 5 x 4.5cm and you will usually see the impression of four toes with claws being evident in most tracks. Really good prints may display a hint of the fur that grows between the pads. (See pages 36–37 for a comparison between dog and Fox footprints.)

Fox

The normal mode of travel is a sprightly little trot, and the trail this leaves looks very linear. The tracks often directly register over each other and only just straddle the median line. They tend to have the look of an animal with a sense of purpose, unlike dogs' tracks, which are usually all over the place.

The stride of a trotting Fox is about 45cm, and when bounding in deep snow you get groups of four prints some 60–90cm apart.

Arctic Fox Very similar to the Fox, but the toes tend to splay more and are set wider apart. The feet register as being of slightly different sizes, although this can be difficult to detect. It has a walking stride of 40cm, increasing to 80cm when the animal is trotting and up to 70–80cm when it's bounding. The gaits are consistently smaller than those of the Fox.

The trail of a trotting Fox is very neat and purposeful: a line of oval prints that show a neat alternating pattern, with little straddle of the imaginary median line.

Arctic Fox

Raccoon Dog The tracks can be distinguished from a Fox's by different-sized front and rear footprints – the rear feet are smaller at 4.5 x 3.5cm. The walking gait has a stride of 25cm, and a faster bounding gait shows groups of four separated by 50cm.

Racoon Dog

Wolf Tracks of this largest member of the canine family always create great excitement and a flutter in the stomach of any tracker. The main difference between Wolf prints and the tracks of a large Alsatian dog is the overall shape – a Wolf's footprint is much neater and more slender, and the animal has that same sense of purpose as all the other wild canines.

The footprint, which has a large, three-lobed interdigital pad and blunt claws tipping the four toes, ranges from 10 x 7.5cm to 11 x 9.5cm. The front tracks are slightly larger than those of the rear feet.

Wolf

The most frequently found trail, when the animal is trotting or loping, has an even-spaced and neat pattern with a stride of about a metre. When the Wolf walks this reduces to 80–90cm, and when running or leaping strides of 150cm are not unheard of.

slow running   fast running

As the Fox speeds up or if it's bounding through snow the stride length increases and the print clusters become more spread out.

Mustelids

The weasel family is fairly diverse in size and habits, from the tiny weasels to the Wolverine. All mustelids are flat-footed and tread with their whole foot and not just the toes. I tend to split them into two categories.

The bigger mustelids such as the Badger and Wolverine have square, broad and boxy prints, while the smaller mustelids, the Stoat, weasels and martens, are much more dainty although the overall shape is still quite boxy. This group of active predators has a slender body plan, and this 'long wheelbase' leads to them moving in a very characteristic way. They shuffle along, leaving a trail that can range from partial registration, to the front and rear prints falling just behind each other, depending on the species. Most species, however, move by bounding or jumping – this results more often than not in four closely set prints with large strides between groups. Sometimes in soft or deep substrate, such as snow, one of the rear feet falls entirely in the footfall of a front foot, leaving a signature trail that appears to be made by a three-legged animal or, in the case of perfect registration, a nice line of paired tracks that look like stitches across the landscape. With low-slung bodies and relatively short legs, the mustelids often create a furrow as they bound along in very deep snow, and the prints still appear in the bottom of the furrow.

Badgers make probably one of the most easily recognisable footprints of any medium-sized mammal. Five toes are usually clearly identifiable in the footprints, as are the long claws. Track dimensions are 6 x 5cm for the hindfeet and 6 x 5.5cm for the forefeet, which includes the length of the claws. The large interdigital pad is broad with a rounded kidney shape to it, and the toes are arranged in a shallow arc in front of the interdigital pad.

Badgers plod and this produces a very distinct trail of partially superimposed tracks with a distinct straddle. The footprints are turned slightly inwards, and the stride length is only about 15cm. Trotting is much the same

Badger trail – the most commonly encountered tracks of the weasel family, the distinctive footprints show all toes pointing forward of the pad, and when walking there is an overlap of back foot over front.

Badger

with a larger stride, and it is only when galloping along in bounds that Badgers start to show the classic trail pattern of their mustelid cousins, with groups of four tracks separated by 40cm of ground.

A classic mustelid, this Pine Marten is creating the space between a cluster of four prints – the rear feet will now hop forward to land near where the front feet have just been.

Stoats, martens, Polecats and Least Weasels

have somewhat spidery tracks; the thumb is often missing unless a really good track is found, and the front track is universally larger and much more rounded than the rear prints. In the rare event that you come across their tracks (usually in snow), you will have to pay attention to the track sizes and stride lengths and even then, while you may be able to separate a marten from a Least Weasel, good luck with the rest.

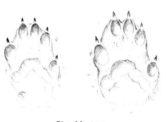

Pine Marten

Otter and Mink tracks are
more often found as they show up in the silt and mud around water; under bridges is quite a good spot for finding them. While Mink tracks are similar to those of the Polecat and its domesticated relative, the Ferret, Otter prints are quite distinctive as they are almost twice the size and, in good conditions, show webbing between the toes.

Otter

Otter tracks are often found in river and pond mud at haul-out sites, and here they are usually just ambling around. It takes an animal to get up a bit of speed before it starts to bound and create the classic mustelid track of sets of four tracks.

A selection of track dimensions and stride measurements of mammals found in Europe

Species	Track dimensions	Stride measurements/cm
Wolverine *(Gulo gulo)*	14–18 x 10–13cm	Walking 15–60, trot 35–50, galloping 90
Badger *(Meles meles)*	Front 6 x 5.5cm Rear 6 x 5cm	Walking 15–20, bounding 40
Otter *(Lutra lutra)*	Front 6.5 x 7cm Rear 6 x 9cm	Walking 35, galloping 50, bounding 80
Pine Marten *(Martes martes)*	Front 4 x 3.7cm Rear 4.5 x 3.5cm	Walking 50, bounding 60–90
Beech Marten *(Martes foina)*	Front 4 x 3.7cm Rear 4.5 x 3.5cm	Walking 30, bounding 40–60
Mink (American) *(Neovison vison)*	Front 3.5 x 3cm Rear 4 x 4.5cm	Walking 25, bounding 30–40
Polecat *(Mustela putorius)*	Front 3.5 x 3cm Rear 4 x 4.5cm	Walking 25, bounding 60
Stoat *(Mustela erminea)*	Front 2 x 1.5cm Rear 3.5 x 1.5cm	Galloping 20, bounding 30–50
Least Weasel *(Mustela nivalis)*	1.4 x 1cm	Galloping 25, bounding 25–30

A Fox chases a Mink through the snow, leaving two sets of tracks.

One-offs

There are a few mammals out there which make tracks and trails that don't quite fit into any of the afore-mentioned groups, because the animal is either highly specialised or is the sole representative of its kind in the region.

Hedgehogs One common insectivore that turns up quite regularly and leaves footprints not dissimilar to what you might expect from a giant shrew is the Hedgehog. Its tracks show many shrew-like qualities: five toes each terminated with a sharp little claw, and the thumb sometimes shows depending on the ground conditions. The sizes of both the front and rear prints are more or less the same, although the rear toes are less splayed and more forward pointing and so give the impression that the rear print is longer than the front.

Left: Because the Hedgehog lives close to humans, these mysterious tracks can show up quite regularly and unless you've got Hedgehog in mind they can catch you out.

The ambling walking gait has a wide straddle (over 6cm), with toes slightly turned in and a short stride length of 2–3cm. As a Hedgehog whips up into a run, the tracks tend to partially register; the faster it goes the more they overlap, until at full tilt the hindfeet may even be placed slightly in front of the forefeet.

Moles rarely leave tracks but when they do, they can leave you guessing. I've only ever seen their tracks after heavy flooding, when rivers have risen and displaced them from their usual haunts. Body drag is usually evident, but the track pattern and count can have you scratching your head. The highly modified front feet stick out almost like flippers, and because they are adapted to work as shovels they are quite inflexible at the shoulder and can only be pressed front edge down. This leaves a strange arch, peppered with tiny spike holes made by the five elongated and thickened claws. The rear feet leave five long, spindly toes that point forward. Moles often move their front feet several times for every one at the back, which sounds odd but once seen it makes sense.

Only once have I come across a Mole trail, in wet, smooth mud in a flooded field; the highly modified front feet leave a curious scraping mark.

Bats are highly specialised and obviously spend most of their time on the wing, leaving no tracks at all. However, occasionally at a roost, or in the mud by a puddle, you may find a track. Look for paired prints made by the rear feet, which are usually well turned out from the median line and are accompanied by a complex of regular scrapes and drags made by the wings and the single point of contact made by the thumb.

Seals leave unique trails as they drag their bodies along, reminiscent of the caterpillar tracks left by a tank or crane. Even if they weren't associated with sheltered, isolated estuaries and stretches of sandy and muddy coastline, their tracks would be a total giveaway. Their body plan is all about hydrodynamics, propulsion and steering in the water, which means that on land they are scuppered. They cannot lift their bodies off the ground so are reduced to dragging their great hulks about, mainly with the front limbs or flippers. The resultant track has a wide and smooth middle section, where the body dragged, with paired impressions made by the flippers on either side.

Bears The biggest tracks you'll ever encounter in northern Europe need no tracking genius to recognise. The two species of bear in Europe – the Polar Bear and Brown Bear – leave unmistakable impressions on the landscape and live in totally different habitats. A Polar Bear, the largest land-based predator in the world, has a footprint that is more than 30 x 20cm, while the European Brown Bear has a print of 23–30 x 17cm. The walking stride is up to 150cm and is a rolling, ambling gait with no registration and with the toes turning inward towards the median; at a run the bears lope along with some registration.

The biggest footprints in Europe – those belonging to the Brown Bear are unmistakable, no other animal has a footprint in the region of 30cm long.

Above both: *This distinctive trail consists of a shallow groove where the seal has dragged its body on the sand with flipper marks either side.*

Mammals with cloven hooves

Because the tracker is mostly looking at the impression made by the hard parts of the foot, it is often easier to interpret the tracks made by an animal with hooves.

Deer tend to use regular routes when they move to and from feeding grounds, creating worn paths like this one trampled by Fallow Deer.

Deer

Deer have a neat trail pattern that narrowly straddles the median line with tracks that run close but parallel to it.

Elk This is the largest member of the deer family that may be encountered in northern Europe and has huge footprints: the cleave length of a large male exceeds 15cm (and is up to 26cm if you include the dewclaw impressions). They are pretty distinctive but may be confused with those of domestic cattle, though cattle prints tend to have a much more rounded shape, while Elk prints have a very angular, almost rectangular look to them and sometimes leave dewclaw imprints unlike cattle. The toe pads also extend right out to the tips of the cleaves.

When the animal is moving fast or going up or down a gradient, the cleaves splay out, making the track break out of that classic 'rectangle'. Younger animals have more rounded cleaves.

The walking stride is about 90–100cm with a partial registration of the tracks, but as Elks speed up into a trot registration is mostly lost and the stride length increases to 150cm or more. When running, the stride is around 300cm and the tracks are grouped in separate clusters.

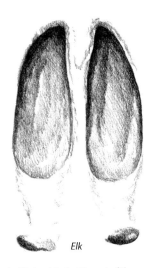

Elk

An Elk track is the biggest of the cloven-hoofed tracks you might come across within Europe. The fact that they often spread out and show the clear imprints of the dewclaw makes them look even bigger.

Reindeer Unless in the extreme north, where they exist as domestic populations, the tracks are about 14cm in length and always include the dewclaws. The feet of these animals are designed as snowshoes and are large and flat compared to those of other cloven-hoofed animals. The outer edges of the cleaves are convex and the inner edge concave, with the tips of the cleaves arched and rounded, so that the overall shape is large and round.

Reindeer

When walking, the tracks of the hindfeet almost perfectly register over those of the front, with a stride of 50–60cm. As an animal breaks into a trot, the stride reduces and the prints no longer register. At a gallop the tracks show as spread groups of four, some 200cm apart.

Red Deer Tracks are about 7.8 x 6cm. The cleaves are quite broad, with a curved outer wall and a fairly straight inner median surface. The outer walls are thick and well developed, as are the fleshy toe pads, which are very obvious in most tracks. The dewclaws rarely show in the print unless in deep

Red Deer

mud or snow, and the cleaves don't have a tendency to splay as much as those of other deer species.

The walking gait is very linear and only slightly straddles the median line of the trail. The stride is 80–150cm and the prints register imperfectly. When an animal breaks into a trot, the stride increases to 200–300cm, and the tracks become more splayed and stop registering.

As you might expect from a dainty-footed animal, the tracks of a walking deer are very neat, along a line, with little splay in the toes, they also overlap or register.

Sika Small to medium tracks 6cm in size, that look almost tulip-shaped because of the rounded outer wall and the sharp tip to the cleaves; the inner median surface is concave at the front. The thick outer walls cut into the ground, and this is often the only part of the track seen, making the slots look extremely thin and spaced out. The dewclaws may register in a slip or deep substrates and are very close together.

Sika

The trail pattern is much the same as those of other deer species, with a slight straddle and near perfect registration. The walking stride is 100cm, and in a trot the tracks show no registration and appear in pairs, heel to toe.

Fallow Deer Medium-sized tracks of about 6.6 x 4cm in a mature animal. The cleaves are quite distinctive in many individuals. They have a 'wobbly' profile, and the outer wall, unusually, has a concave element to it; the median surfaces between the cleaves are parallel along most of their length, even slightly convex. The tips of the cleaves are pointed but have a slightly hooked appearance. The dewclaws occasionally show, in steep inclines or deep substrate, and when they do they are very small and close together. The tracks splay a little when the animal is slipping, jumping and running. The toe pads are quite evident.

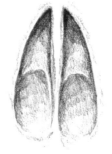

Fallow Deer

Tracks are close and narrowly straddle the median line; there is near perfect registration and a stride of 60cm when walking. Trotting has the effect of stringing out the tracks so that they run in pairs, heel to toe. At a gallop, the trail becomes stretched out, with groups of four prints separated by over a metre of ground.

Roe Deer This deer creates small tracks of about 5 x 4cm, with very narrow cleaves that look pointed towards the front. The cleaves are distinctly convex on the outside, and the way they taper off at the front gives the track an almost heart shape. The inner median walls are convex towards the back

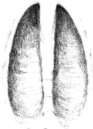

Roe Deer

The Fallow Deer has been introduced to most regions of Britain and has done very well at becoming naturalised. It is often the deer species to separate from the others – so pay attention to scale and stride lengths.

and concave near the front; toe pads are evident and dewclaws only register in soft substrate, when the cleaves are inclined to splay. The walking stride is 40cm, 60cm when trotting and 200cm when bounding.

Chinese Water Deer The tracks are small (3–4cm), neat and pointed; the inner median wall is parallel to slightly convex and there is a relatively large gap between the cleaves, making the overall track quite wide.

Chinese Water Deer

It has a typical deer trail pattern with a walking stride of 30–40cm. When trotting, the stride lengthens and registration is lost, and when running the trail is composed of groups of four separate tracks with around 100cm between them.

Muntjac The tracks are minute, with cleaves measuring less than 2.5–3cm, and usually asymmetrical, with the inner cleave smaller than the outer. The slots are narrow and have slightly convex outer walls; the inner median edges are slightly concave towards the front. Dewclaws register in slips, deep substrate and banks. The walking stride is 25–30cm, and as the animal breaks into a trot the cleaves start to splay. When running, strides extend to over 100cm.

Muntjac

Deer are creatures of habit and tend to take easy routes between feeding and rest areas. Here, the repeated passage of countless sharp hooves has eroded this bank – look close and you'll see the 'slots'.

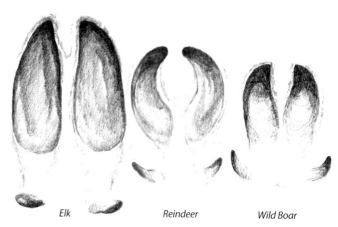

Elk *Reindeer* *Wild Boar*

In grassy, level habitat, the plants take a pounding and show the 'wear and tear' caused by many footfalls.

Wild Boar

In adult animals the large track reaches 12cm long (including the dewclaws) and over 13cm wide across the dewclaws. The prints at first glance resemble those of deer, but they always show imprints

of the dewclaws and this is where the track is always widest – a feature that easily sets the Wild Boar apart from other cloven-hoofed animals. The cleaves are very broad and rounded, with a convex outer wall and a concave median surface towards the front. Because the shape of the trotter is very low slung, it is quite common to see the impression of the sole of the foot between the cleaves and the dewclaws.

Wild Boar

When walking there is almost complete registration of the two sets of tracks, except for the two pairs of dewclaws which are visible. The tracks straddle the median line and turn out slightly. Stride length is about 40cm; when galloping, loose groups of four separate tracks are visible, with a stride of about 70–80cm.

Domestic stock

Humans have for a long time domesticated sheep, goats and cattle, and in many wild places the slots of these breeds will be found in close association with some of the wild cloven-hoofed animals. This can be confusing for the tracker just as domesticated dogs and cats have to be eliminated from the investigation before you can identify prints with pads.

Cattle

Red Deer

Fallow Deer

Sika

Roe Deer

Chinese Water Deer

Muntjac

Wild Boar are becoming more widespread in parts of their former range in the UK, and are still common on the Continent. They produce large footprints and are one of the few cloven-hoofed animals that routinely show the impressions of the dewclaws in good prints.

Cattle have the largest prints and, although they are quite variable in size, they are usually around 10cm long and about the same wide. The cleaves are rounded and the inner wall is distinctively straight along most of its length, with an abrupt concave section towards the front. The dewclaws only ever show if there is a steep slope or a slip. The trail is wide and straddled, with hardly any registration of the front and rear feet. The only similar tracks in Europe would be made by the wild relative of cattle, the Bison, which has a print with very rounded and teardrop-shaped cleaves.

Always be aware of the presence of domesticated stock. Cows are pretty obvious, but goats and sheep can get mixed up with deer very easily.

Sheep tracks are about 6 x 4.5cm and have very rounded cleaves at the front and back, which sets them apart from any of the small or medium-sized deer prints. They always remind me of a couple of slightly stretched out kidneys, facing each other with a very small gap between them and slightly concave inner medial walls. The trail pattern is narrow, slightly straddles the median line and is perfectly registered at a walk. At a trot the footprints separate out, distinctly turn out from the median line of the trail and the cleaves tend to splay. The walking stride is around 70cm and is longer at a trot.

sheep trail

Goats tracks are similar to those of sheep but have blunter cleaves, and they are much narrower at the front than towards the rear. The tips of the cleaves are often widely separated even when not splayed. I find the tracks of domesticated goats and Wild Goats difficult to separate; it usually comes down to context and reading other signs to tell them apart.

Goat

cow trail

Mammals with hooves

Horses and ponies don't really require much skill to identify from tracks, although you can still learn about gaits and have fun interpreting what the equines were doing, how they were moving and if were they wearing shoes.

There are no wild equestrians within the range of this book, although there are semi-wild populations.

The track of an equine is totally distinctive and the rounded arc of a pony, horse or donkey should be straightforward to recognise, even if the size is highly variable. A feral animal has a track that displays a rounded front and a deep notch at the rear. A shod animal, however, usually only shows the size and shape of the shoe.

These unshod donkey tracks show the natural contours of the underside of the foot; the same can be seen in unshod horse and pony tracks.

A foot that has a metal shoe clearly shows it.

Reptiles and amphibians

The name 'herptile', which is used to refer to amphibians and reptiles, has it roots in the Greek word *herpeton* meaning 'belly creepers'. Their legs, if they have them, stick out of the sides of their bodies and do not support their weight, which is a much less efficient way of moving as the toes and feet tend to drag more. The tracks may well show belly drag at points along the trail, and if like lizards and newts, they have tails, you'll see some kind of indication of this, too.

Occasionally in sandy places such as heaths, dunes and beaches you might get to see the light trail of a lizard. Look for the light and wispy drag-line of the tail that swings from side to side, with the stiff alternating steps which leave prints on either side.

Frogs and toads

The feet of frogs, toads and lizards are covered with various tubercles. These perform the same function as the pads on mammals and birds, but rarely do you get to see the fine details, just occasionally the drags of the long, widely spaced toes. The prints of a walking toad can look a little bird-like initially, but on closer inspection there is rarely a clear 'footprint' as such, but rather a series of striations in the substrate caused by the toes dragging. The outer lines and any pock marks are usually the hindfeet creating the thrust while those that run down the centre are made by the forefeet.

If you're in a dune system inhabited by Natterjack Toads, you may be lucky enough to find some prints, which are reminiscent of splats of ink in shape, with running marks made by the toes, often wider towards the ends of the digits.

If a frog or toad is hopping, then the dints created by the initial thrust of the hindlegs and the smaller dints made by the forelegs will be evident.

A fully grown Common Frog or Toad has a hind footprint length of about 2–2.8cm. In fact, the trail has very much the same sort of pattern, though much smaller in scale, as that of a hopping mouse or Rabbit.

Newts

The footprints of newts are not dissimilar to those of frogs and toads, but much smaller; a large track, say of a Great Crested Newt, is somewhere in the region of 0.8cm, and the majority are much smaller.

The thing that sets newts apart from frogs and toads is the fact that they possess a tail, and the narrow trail is a side-to-side, almost snake-like groove made by the tail, with pairs of tracks on the left and right sides that never superimpose on each other.

Rarely do you find frog trails, although occasionally you may find evidence of them around dune slacks or on very fine mud. Jumping frogs seem to be quite messy as substrate is displaced on leaping and landing, while the trails of walking toads look similar to lizard trails without the tail drag.

Lizards

The tails of lizards flex less than those of newts, and this is one of the characteristic differences between the two animal trails. A lizard's is generally quite neat, a clear, almost straight tail drag, with the footprint showing normally as a neat series of dimples that run parallel on either side. Only the very finest dust-like like conditions allow any clear imprints of the toe patterns. These usually show as repeating sets of grooves made by the toes (usually four out of the five toes leave impressions).

Newt tracks are rarely seen and are usually only visible on smooth mud.

Snakes and legless lizards

There are a few animals that leave trails but no tracks. Legless lizards such as Slow-worms tend to fall back on many of the same solutions as snakes. I have never knowingly come across their trails, but I've seen the animal use a gentle side-to-side serpentine locomotion, which I expect would be represented in their trails. Snakes have three main ways of moving across the ground, each of which leaves characteristic trail patterns, and many snakes switch between the different modes depending on the ground conditions they are experiencing.

Serpentine This is the classic undulation mode of locomotion used by many snakes where the animal throws its body into S-shaped curves that start at the head. The snake then uses its scales to effectively grip and thrust against fixed objects such as stones, rocks and branches. The result is a rather beautiful wavy trail, and on each sideways push of the body there will be evidence of a displaced ridge of material that will be pushed away from the general direction of travel, indicating which way the animal was moving.

Snakes and legless lizards move in a similar manner. Most typically they use the side-to-side motion, pushing backwards at the ends of the curves – leaving a small bank that gives the tracker some idea in which direction they were travelling.

Concertina This is one of the modes of movement that a snake uses in desperation to get up a sandy slope, and I've seen both Adders and Grass Snakes use it in the UK. The snake uses its body like a spring, forming a series of extreme lateral folds, then stretching forward with the head while pushing backwards with the loops of the body; it then bunches up around the middle of its body, pulling the hind portion up behind it before repeating the process. The resultant trail is a strange flattening of the ground, and a variety of smooth, curved, fine ridges of sand.

Rectilinear This is a caterpillar crawl and is a slow and steady way of making progress on level ground. The snake moves forward in a more or less straight line by sending waves of contracting groups of muscles along its body, then using these pulses to excert a grip on the ground with its belly scales. The trail left is more or less straight, but you may get a few undulations and other modes thrown in from time to time.

The trail of a Slow-worm is similar to a snake's, as on open ground it uses the classic side-to-side serpentine motion.

Ghost trails

There are many visible trails that do not necessarily show any tracks, but they are often subtle and generally do not last long, so as a tracker you need to be alert and keep your eyes peeled.

Sometimes subtle trails are apparent through vegetation. It might not be possible to identify easily which species made the trail without finding other clues first.

As an animal passes through fresh dewy grass, it wipes or displaces the dewdrops and creates a contrast with the rest of the grass.

Dulling

Some trails are aptly referred to as 'dulling' and are the product of a very specific time of day and weather conditions. When you get a bright morning with the sun sparkling on a heavy dew that has formed overnight, you can sometimes pick out a duller path through the grass. An animal moving through dewy grass knocks the droplets off and can create a clear indication of its passage through the grassy landscape. This phenomenon can also occur on frosty mornings. Interpreting exactly which animal has passed, however, can be another matter; you may only be able to

A test for the tracker is being able to spot a shining trail – caused by bent plants, usually grass, reflecting the sun's light in a different way than they do in the surrounding area.

Some animals will kick and move leaves as they pass. This can be quite difficult see in woodland, but here Roe Deer crossing a road leave a clearly visible trail of soil and leaf litter.

get an idea of the width of the animal. I tend to follow these trails until I get some further clues: the ground may get soft enough to trap a footprint, or the animal pushes through a hedge or leaves a dropping.

The exact opposite sometimes occurs at the height of the day, when the landscape can look quite flat and dull. An animal passing through a grassy landscape, however, can bend the grass so that it reflects the sunlight more, creating a ghost trail called a 'shining'. Also look out for 'leaf scuff' in woodland where an animal passing through not only depresses the leaves where each foot falls, but also gently scuffs and drags some leaves out of their naturally settled position as it moves each foot forward.

A well-trodden track

Sometimes a trail is used so frequently that it becomes greater than the sum of its parts and forms a well-worn track. In this photo is a trail left by Fallow Deer as they regularly move from a resting site to a feeding area.

Some animal trails are so well used that the animals' feet have effectively carved out a groove in the landscape. If you come across a well-worn track, follow it as far as you can and look for other signs as you go. You may find other features, such as what Badger biologists call an 'up and over' (but which also applies to many other animals with similar habits), where a hedge or bank has been surmounted by the animals so many times that it has become polished or eroded. Here you may find claw scratches or, if the animal has gone under some scrub or a fence, a hair or two may have got snagged. If you place your palm, preferably wet, on the ground, you may pick up more hairs that have been 'combed' out. If the path dives into some dense scrub or even under a fallen tree, the size of the resulting 'hole' will indicate the size of the animal – a Red Deer will not be moving under a branch that is only 50cm off the ground.

Sometimes it may be a little difficult to identify which animal uses a pathway, and it may be that many species all share a 'line of desire', which is the quickest route between two places. So once a track is established, it easily becomes a regular route for many species, including humans.

The fat feet of Badgers quickly erode a surface and form Badger highways.

Signs of feeding activity

Signs that animals have been feeding can be anything from a carcass, a broken feather or nibbled leaves to some old bones and split cones. You need to be able to recognise that an item has been nibbled, chewed or chomped. Then you can turn to the appropriate pages of this chapter to work out what kind of animal was involved.

Ponies have made a right mess of this broom bush, pushing into it and snapping off branches. Not all feeding signs are as obvious as this.

🐾 Trees and bushes

By far the most frequent feeding signs are those left by herbivorous animals, but sometimes their effects are on a landscape scale and can only be seen from a distance.

Next time you are out in an area where deer are found have a look for browse lines. They can help you identify the species and how many individuals live locally.

Browse lines

Where a large population of browsers exists, they will pretty much devour anything they can reach without too much of a stretch, producing a 'browse line'. For example, in dense woodland that has a large population of deer, they really will take every leaf, twig and bud up to a certain height above the forest floor. The tangle of vegetation that should make up the woodland understorey will be stripped out too, leaving just the near-naked poles of the thickest stems and trunks, which continue their leafy life just out of reach of the deer muzzles. Woods where there is a lot of ivy growth on the trunks often show this very clearly, as deer have a penchant for the

Here all the tender and tasty leaves and buds within easy reach have been stripped to the height of the animal feeding on them.

dark, glossy green leaves. The effect is sometimes easy to miss as deer activities occur below human eye level and are therefore not noticeable unless from a distance or when kneeling down.

Any herbivore can produce a browse line, the height being determined by the size of the animal. Rabbits and hares produce the lowest browse line at about 40–50cm, the diminutive Muntjac next at around 100cm, followed by Roe, Fallow and Sika that can reach up to 150cm, while Red Deer and cattle can manage about 200cm. Ponies have long and flexible necks and can browse even higher. Sometimes you can see more

Below: Rabbits are one of the most hard-working nibblers in the countryside and they can have landscape-sized impacts, surprising for such a relatively small animal.

Above: Ivy is a favourite food in the winter months. In this wood you never really see the deer but every single tree has been stripped of ivy leaves to exactly the same height.

than one browse line in the same habitat.

The incessant nibbling of Rabbits can also shape the landscape – think downs and coastal grasslands. They keep their 'lawns' closely cropped, particularly near their warrens, which gives them a clear view of a predator approaching. The continuous grazing stimulates new grass growth that is much more nutritious than old rank grass. Another large-scale effect of nibbling can be seen in some areas of woodland where there is a high population

of the non-native Muntjac, which, unfortunately, has taken to cropping huge swathes of Common Bluebells.

From a distance some woodlands look as though they are peppered with what appear to be recently deceased trees. On closer inspection, however, in spring and summer you will see that just the crowns of these trees have died and not the whole trees. The phloem and xylem vessels, in the cambium tissue, transport nutrients and water from the ground to the leaves, and this nutritious and sweet food source has not gone unnoticed by one group of adaptable rodents, the squirrels. The leaves have died because their lifelines, situated just behind the bark, have been severed. Grey Squirrels in particular are very fond of the cambium of thin-barked trees and most often attack maples such as Sycamore and Beech, but they also damage young oak trees before the bark gets too thick. They use their chisel-like teeth to strip the bark, then consume the sweet and juicy layers beneath. This unfortunate addiction of Grey Squirrels to certain tree saps has made them unpopular, particularly in the forestry industry, where squirrel damage costs millions of pounds a year in ruined timber.

Squirrels, mainly the introduced and naturalised Grey Squirrels, can have quite large impacts on forestry and tree health, stripping the bark to get to the nutritious sapwood beneath.

Bitten-off twigs

A twig that has been nibbled by **deer** is very different from a stem that has been snapped by a clumsy passing or indeed pruned neatly with secateurs. Deer only have front teeth (incisors) in the bottom jaw, and these work against a tough bony palate in the top jaw, so when a deer feeds it takes the twig into its mouth, then bites up, cutting neatly through the lower part of the stem but finishing off by gently tearing through the remaining portion. This leaves some frayed wood on an otherwise neatly executed job. The height of the nibbling should tell you which species of deer has been feeding, though there is quite a lot of overlap between the foraging heights of the different species. Deer forage best at head height, without having to stoop low or reach up.

Understanding that deer only have front teeth in the bottom jaw helps us to recognise their feeding signs.

Piles of hedge trimmings left by deer indicate where they have been reaching up and pulling down the long, spindly branches.

Below: Rabbits have the advantage of two sets of shearing teeth working together and they create neatly nibbled ends that look as though they've been cut by a pair of secateurs.

Rabbits and **hares** can be quite partial to leaves and buds, too, often standing up on their hindlegs to reach a desired twig or stem. Other than height, the most obvious way of recognising their work is again by closely investigating the cut surface. Rabbits, unlike deer, have incisors in both the upper and lower jaw, and these meet together like the blades of scissors. As you might expect, the biting teeth of these animals create a neat cut – no rough edges or frayed fibres here.

Right: You may not need to even look at the bitten ends of twigs to tell the cuts of Rabbits and hares apart. Rabbits work closer to the ground than hares.

FRAYING

This is a kind of environmental vandalism exhibited by antler-bearing male deer (Reindeer are an exception as the females also have antlers). Antlers are primarily for display and for use in the testosterone-fuelled battles for females that take place during the annual mating or rutting season. As they often get damaged and the status of individuals needs to be updated they are replaced each year.

After a pair of antlers is shed, a new set covered in a soft, velvet-like blanket begins to grow from the skull. When the antlers are fully formed, the velvet loosens and the buck or stag removes it by rubbing on any convenient tree, shrub or bush. The vegetation will be left totally trashed: not only will the bark be hanging off in rough-edged strips, but also plant tissue will often be gouged out by the action of the tines, and snapped-off twigs and bent branches will also be evident.

Fraying is most common in autumn, which is the rutting season for the majority of species. Roe Deer, however, 'fray' throughout most of the spring and summer months not only to clean their antlers but also, because they rut earlier, to disperse scent and mark their territories for other bucks to heed.

Sometimes the chosen branch for fraying gets nibbled as well. This sapling has been well and truly beaten up by a Roe Deer.

Muntjac also engage in fraying behaviour, but at a lower height from the ground and usually with their tusks. They can potentially breed all year, so evidence of fraying can be found at any time, most commonly on twiggy saplings.

Heights of fraying damage can help you to determine which species was involved – look out for other signs nearby if you're still unsure.

The culprit in action – this Roe Deer buck is transferring his personal scent from glands on his head and around his eyes to the shredded bark.

Levels of deer damage

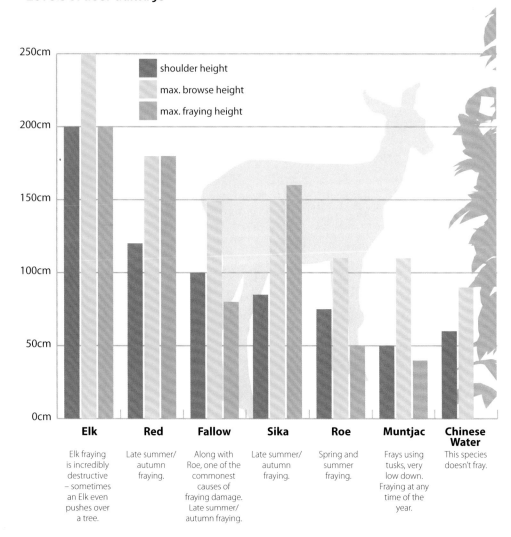

	shoulder height
	max. browse height
	max. fraying height

Elk
Elk fraying is incredibly destructive – sometimes an Elk even pushes over a tree.

Red
Late summer/ autumn fraying.

Fallow
Along with Roe, one of the commonest causes of fraying damage. Late summer/ autumn fraying.

Sika
Late summer/ autumn fraying.

Roe
Spring and summer fraying.

Muntjac
Frays using tusks, very low down. Fraying at any time of the year.

Chinese Water
This species doesn't fray.

This chart gives an idea of how high different species can reach. The teeth and the antlers are the many tools of destruction, and while you might expect the antlers to reach higher, usually the head of the animal is bowed a little when fraying. Some individuals stand on their hind legs to reach the really good stuff – we've not counted these troublemakers here.

The nutritious and sweet sap under the bark of this Alder has proved irresistible to sheep in this case.

Barking up the right tree

Bark may not seem very appetising, but for many animals it is a life saver when there is no real greenery available. At certain times of the year, the cambium is packed full of sugary sap and makes a nutritious snack for many animals. Stripping the bark for food is known as 'barking'.

The feeding signs of various animals

Species	Distance across all incisors	Notes and description
Small voles	1.5–2mm	Don't tend to damage woody material. Gnawed area has a smooth bevelled edge. They often discard fragments of outer bark below.
Water Voles	3.5–4mm	A neat job like other voles, but teeth marks are apparent on roots and waterside growth. Tend to tackle larger-diameter stems (20–30cm).
Squirrels	1.5–4mm	Often high off the ground; mainly bark on the main trunk, rarely the boughs. Hardly any tooth marks.
Rabbits and hares	6–9mm	Ragged/rough appearance of feeding area and eat into wood as well. The incisors have a groove down the middle, so bites often look as though they're made by four teeth.
Beavers and Crested Porcupines	8–25mm	Usually fairly obvious due to other signs in vicinity. Gouges in wood look roughly chiselled; chippings present.
Deer and sheep	10–30mm	Large and varied damage depending on species and breed. Height, etc. gives clues to identity.

Deer use their incisors, at the front of their lower jaws, to strip off bark with an upward slicing action; they then nip off the strip of bark at the top, leaving a messy frayed edge. The width of the teeth marks and the height that they occur will give you good identification clues. Deer tend to choose to strip bark in the winter when there is less green vegetation to be had than in warmer months. The bark is drier at this time of year and comes away in smaller strips.

Sheep and goats, which also strip bark, tend to nibble and strip shorter lengths of bark at a diagonal – the marks that are left are usually about 45 degrees to the trunk axis.

An awareness of animals' jaws helps us to understand feeding signs; deer use only their lower front teeth to tear the bark at the end of the bite, which tends to create a frayed edge at the top of patches of grazing.

Rabbits, hares, voles and squirrels also go in for a bit of bark bashing for much the same reasons, so any patches of stripped bark should be scrutinised closely for teeth marks and, of course, the height at which they have occurred.

Bark stripping carried out by **voles** is nearly always very neat and tidy. They tend to remove strips of the tough outer bark and discard these below feeding sites; they will then return to bite and scrape off the juicy cambium on the trunk. Tender, thin-barked twigs are often so thoroughly worked over that they look as though they've been carefully whittled clean with a sharp penknife – look for fragments of discarded bark below the damaged area. Tougher, drier bark, on the other hand, is less easy to work and the surface tends to be rougher and complete with tooth marks.

Field and Water Voles usually strip bark low down: branches, roots and the bases of trees are the most likely spots to see this sort of bark damage, especially if there is long grass or other vegetation allowing these timid rodents to work under cover.

You may see strange rings of stripped bark higher up a tree trunk after snow cover because the snow will have given a rodent a 'bunk up' and allowed it to feed from a higher vantage point than normal.

Voles are much neater than deer and their small incisors both top and bottom, create quite a smooth edge and a neat job of the whole process.

Bank Voles go in for a bit of high-level work in trees if the structure of the twigs and branches allows. You may find neat signs of chomping, often where a branch meets the main trunk. The gnawing patterns tend to be fairly distinctive: they tend to chew in one direction then in the other, probably to keep wear even on their continuously growing incisors.

Squirrel damage to tree bark often occurs high up, and any damage to areas of thick bark more than several metres above the ground is almost certainly going to be the work of squirrels. They can, however, feed at the same sort of level as deer and Rabbits, so before you jump to any conclusions it's always worth looking further up the trunk for damage of a similar age. The introduced Grey Squirrel is the culprit in most cases and is active in the summer months, often causing the premature withering of a tree crown if the bark is removed around the circumference of the tree trunk.

The appearance of the damage can depend on the type of bark and of course the season. This is squirrel damage: note the large flakes of stripped bark scattered around.

Rabbits and hares will also have a go at bark, and their bite can be identified by the neat work of their sharp incisors and the size of the marks, but more importantly because each incisor has a groove in the middle of it, so the resulting bite mark looks as though it's been made by four smaller teeth.

These branches from an apple tree have been stripped by Rabbits.

Assuming the tree hasn't been totally ring-barked, it will usually recover by forming calloused edges which in time will heal over. This can create all manner of interesting microhabitats for other life, including access to the tree for various species of fungus and wood-boring beetle. However, it can also hasten the demise of a tree and, in a commercial forestry context, can effectively ruin the value of the timber.

SCRATCHING POSTS

If you own a cat you will be familiar with its need to simultaneously stretch, and clean and sharpen its claws. Several wild animals engage in similar behaviour. Scratching posts are often living trees that have repeatedly had the front claws of an animal raked down them. The height of the scratches is well worth noting as it could help you identify the animal.

Badgers regularly use a scratching post, which will be situated near a sett entrance. They prefer Elder because it has a particularly spongy, soft bark perfect for removing caked soil from their claws and stuck between their pads. They may also be marking the tree, by smearing it with scent from glands between their toes. Badgers at full stretch will scratch posts up to a height of about a metre.

Cats, wild and domestic, also scratch trees to keep their claws sharp and serviceable, and perhaps to distribute scent from interdigital glands. Wildcats have been known to scratch the hard trunks of birch up to a height of 60–80cm, but you will be very lucky to find one. Lynx will do the same, but reach much higher up the tree.

Badgers at full stretch will scratch posts up to a height of about a metre.

Cats leave fine grooves in the bark so that the trunk looks almost downy, whereas the fraying caused by Badger claws has a coarser texture.

Bears also scratch tree trunks, leaving five large, blunt marks. The height (usually around eye level) and size of the resultant claw marks and the damage speak for themselves.

Above: *If you own a cat you will be familiar with its need to simultaneously stretch, and clean and sharpen its claws.*

Right: *Bears also use trees as an effective nail brush, but as you might expect their reach is much higher.*

Leaf damage

Whether a nibbled leaf is stripped back to nothing but the stem or perforated into some kind of vernal doily, you should be able to work out whose teeth did the munching.

The feeding damage of the Pea Weevil is a common sight. This insect takes multiple nibbles from the leaf edges of members of the pea family from beans to clovers.

Perforations

It'll come as no surprise that many species eat holes straight through the tissues of leaves. On the plus side you can normally eliminate mammals and birds from the equation as they bite, peck and tear at the fabric of the leaf, leaving plenty of tattered edges. The downside, however, is that the culprits are among the most numerous group of animals on Earth: the invertebrates.

A huge spectrum of damage can occur, from the occasional random hole in a leaf to the stripping away of the fabric of the leaf, leaving nothing but a skeleton of fine veins. The bigger beasts, such as robust slugs and snails, large beetles and caterpillars, will further reduce a leaf to nothing but a mournful midrib, a scenario familiar to those who have tried growing lettuce and cabbage plants in a slug-infested garden.

If you've got big (for an insect) chewing mandibles, then being able to eat through the middle of a leaf is rather like you or I trying to neatly bite through the middle of a pizza – close to impossible and rather messy. The tactic we politely embrace is chewing our way in from the edge.

Larvae of the Viburnum Beetle can rapidly reduce the leaves of Guelder Roses and other viburnum species to skeletons.

Small jaws can get a grip on imperfections in the middle of a leaf and start to chew holes – these are probably made by a beetle of some kind.

This analogy works if we apply it to a leaf: only little jaws in the middle of the leaf can find purchase on a vein, bump or minute corrugation on the leaf's surface; then once they are through there is no stopping them as they enlarge the hole. Invertebrates that fall into this category include many of the smaller foliage-eating beetles, such as leaf beetles (chrysomelids), some folivorous weevils, beetle larvae, thrips, some sawfly larvae such as the 'pear slug' (not a slug at all but a weird-looking grub of the Pear Sawfly), small caterpillars and earwigs.

Snails rasp at leaves and they can make holes in the leaf centre, and in time may reduce the leaf to nothing more than a skeleton – the presence of mucus trails is usually the giveaway in either case.

However, not all invertebrates have jaws that work in a side-to-side fashion; some, such as slugs and snails, have what amounts to a toothy rasp – hundreds of tough little teeth that work like a sheet of coarse sandpaper and scrape their way through the leaf surface. This versatile feeding tactic means that they can be responsible for random holes through to total consumption, depending on the size of the individuals doing the rasping as well as the toughness and palatability of the plant being eaten.

Slugs and snails famously leave a mucus trail that remains long after the animal has departed, and if they have been in one spot you are highly likely to discover the rope-like droppings of these molluscs attached to the leaf. Leaf skeletonisation by slugs and snails is generally a fairly coarse affair – they will leave the midrib and maybe a few of the smaller veins.

The Pear Sawfly often just scrapes away the living material on the surface, leaving characteristic transparent 'windows' in the leaf.

A colony of rapacious little caterpillars is what really turns a leaf to lace. They feed by scraping at the middle of a leaf and will at the same time leave very distinctive clues: they often spin a silken web either as a sheet to sit on or as shelter, and this will remain along with frass and moulted skins. If you follow the trail of feeding damage and silk you may even meet the caterpillars a little further on in their journey.

Above: *Silk is often laid down by many caterpillars at the feeding site, either as protection or as a way of coordinating their crowd.*

Left: *The silk trail around this nettle patch, combined with frass that has collected on leaves below, tells the tracker that the communal caterpillars of Small Tortoiseshell or Peacock butterfly are not far away.*

Rolls and folds

Cast your eyes over a nettle patch and you will probably see that several of the leaves are hanging in a peculiar way, and are either dropping from the main leaf stem or either side of the midrib. If you carefully grasp the nettle and investigate closer, you will notice that the leaf has been modified, only slightly, to provide a service to an animal within. A leaf that simply looks as though it's collapsed on itself is probably the work of one of a plethora of nettle-feeding caterpillars. Peacock, Small Tortoiseshell and, most frequently, Red Admiral create these living tents by simply chewing partway through the main stem, so it bends under its own weight, then a little nip here and there on either side removes some of the leaf's lateral support and it rolls in on itself. What the larva is left with is a perfect green tent that provides shelter, food and camouflage. Leaf tents that don't have any sign of nibbling

These rolled up rose leaflets have been galled by the Leaf-rolling Sawfly. The rolls feed and shelter the sawfly grubs.

Caterpillar of the Green Tortrix Moth; this one was found in a rolled up leaf.

at the bottom and have no dropped frass beneath them are worth treating with care as they may well be the final shelter containing the chrysalis. Many caterpillars and indeed spiders (although these won't eat the leaves) roll leaves by pulling the edges together and fastening them with silk to create bivouacs. A leaf roll in a nettle patch may well belong to the small, translucent green caterpillar of the Mother of Pearl Moth, while little green cigars in oak trees are formed by small and seemingly insignificant Green Oak Tortrix caterpillars. In a good year these animals can almost defoliate the oaks, but this doesn't happen too often as woodland birds such as Great Tits and Blue Tits time their nesting seasons to coincide with the life cycles of species such as this moth.

Missing chunks

Butterfly, moth and sawfly larvae, as well as crickets and grasshoppers, feed by lining up a leaf edge perpendicular to their mouth and then chewing, which leaves a smooth, semi-circular notch. The animals often move backwards and forwards during feeding, repeating the feeding arc each time they settle, until the resulting demolition has a distinctive scalloped edge. Sawflies are normally gregarious and will attack a leaf as a gang, working in from the leaf edges together until nothing but the midrib remains.

Most caterpillars of a good size work around the edges of a leaf, a style that suits their mouthparts, which work from side to side.

Grasshoppers, crickets and some of the large chafer beetles also create arcs, but with rougher edges.

Another noticeable form of leaf damage is caused by the industrious leaf-cutter bees. They often frequent our gardens and prey on the foliage of roses, using the leaf discs as building materials rather than food. If you notice very rounded, deep sections missing from the edges of a leaf and if the damage is fresh, sit and wait and you will see the bee come back for another slice. These solitary bees tend to forage near to their nesting sites and you may be able to track them and see a leaf being dragged and folded into a small hole in a plant stem or similar crevice in masonry. Inside, the leaf sections are used to line and form compartments or cells, into each of which the bee places a provision of pollen and a single egg before sealing it up.

Not to be confused with caterpillars of moths and butterflies, this team of Birch Sawfly larvae is working together to reduce this leaf to a single vein from the edge.

Leaf-cutter bees are responsible for the neat, semi-circular discs cut from the edges of leaves. The discs are carried away and used to construct the cells of their nests.

Marks and stains

The work of a group of insects collectively referred to as leaf miners often goes unnoticed, but it can be strangely beautiful and when

observed closely can reveal wonderful details and even the maker itself. Leaf mines are mostly caused by the larval stages of micro-moths, but other insect groups, including sawflies, flies and beetles, also etch their marks in the tissues of leaves.

The appearance of a leaf mine is highly variable and to an extent depends on the species doing the 'digging', the species of leaf being mined and the stage of development of both. Usually a mine looks

Life in a line – this swirly trail represents the entire larval part of the life cycle of a small moth caterpillar that mines its way between the top and bottom surfaces of a leaf.

like a discoloured blotch or an elaborate hieroglyph carved on the leaf, though it is, in fact, within the leaf.

The small larva or miner eats the nutritious cells in the leaf, avoiding the parts with high cellulose content or protective tannins. It tunnels its way through the green stuff sandwiched between the top and bottom leaf cuticles, as if it were burrowing between bed sheets, and completes its whole life cycle within a single leaf.

If you hold a leaf mine up to the light or place the leaf over the end of a bright torch and use a magnifying lens, you will be able to see the intricate details of the mine and its contents. The mine starts off narrow – where the egg hatched or the larva first penetrated the leaf tissues – but gets fatter as the insect feeds and grows. The frass or waste products are retained in the mine and can be seen as a random speckling, discrete piles or a dark stripe that runs along the mine like the central reservation of a motorway.

Start at the narrow end where the egg was laid and you can follow the course of the caterpillar's life through this Nasturtium leaf. Backlighting with a torch can reveal the details.

If you look at enough mines, you will eventually find one in which a larva is still alive and eating away at the internal workings of the leaf. In contrast, in a disused

LITTLE MINE, BIG DAMAGE

While most mines and miners are easily overlooked, they can occasionally be very destructive. The Horse Chestnut Leaf Miner, an introduced species, is currently sweeping across Europe. In the absence of any natural predator, this species is chewing its way through the leaves of Horse Chestnut trees in such huge numbers that it is creating a premature autumn for this popular park tree. Unless some other parasite or predator starts to exploit the larvae, we could lose large numbers of Horse Chestnuts over the next few years.

Horse Chestnut Leaf Miner larvae.

The effects of the Horse Chestnut Leaf Miner can be seen almost everywhere.

mine you should be able to see the empty pupa case and the hole through which the adult insect emerged.

The specific identification of mines is a detailed and rather specialised discipline that is beyond the scope of this book, but the shape and size of the mine, as well as the host species and the pattern of the frass deposited within it, can all be useful in identifying the species.

Lumps and bumps

There is a range of organisms that can create a huge variety of odd and often distinctive forms of damage to leaves, buds, stems and roots – these are collectively known as galls. A gall is a mutation of the host plant that is triggered by a foreign organism for its own benefit. The organism can be anything from a tiny wasp, fly, beetle, mite, larva or egg, to a bacterium or fungus.

Galls are created by various insects species; flies and wasps that modify the architecture of the plant to their own benefits. They occur in many species-specific designs.

Knopper galls are caused by the activities of a small wasp that deforms the acorn cup.

These nail galls on lime leaves are caused by the mite Eriophyes tiliae.

Galls

All galls are formed when a foreign organism starts to influence the living cells of a plant and the rate and way in which they grow and divide. The host plant's tissues are modified in often startling ways, creating the distinctive gall growths that are more easily identified than the animal inside.

Although galls rarely cause major long-lasting damage to the host the relationship is rather one-sided. The plant doesn't get anything from the deal, but the gall maker, by contrast, gets a cosy safe haven, protected from the attentions of predators.

There are more than 1,500 different kinds of gall in the UK alone, from spangle galls, which look like little flying saucers attached to the undersides of leaves, and the elaborate 'hairy' Robin's pincushions on roses, to the witches' brooms that create twiggy masses on the branches of birch. Again, identifying every individual gall you are likely to come across is beyond the remit of this book, but there are several specialist books on the market to aid the nature detective who wishes to know more and maybe have a go at identifying them.

The nut crackers

Nuts are rich in non-saturated fats and fatty acids and are laced with oodles of important vitamins and minerals, so it is not surprising that they are sought out by several rodents. Nut detective work is both fun and an essential skill for a wildlife tracker. An excellent time to look for nibbled nuts is in late summer before they ripen and go brown, and while they still stand out against dark woodland floors. Hazelnuts in particular, because of their smooth shells, will clearly show any signs of foraging activity.

The way a Hazel Dormouse works on it's namesake's nuts is so distinctive that surveys for the presence of this mammal can be carried out without even seeing the fluffy nutter itself.

The most common and visible procurer of the hazelnut is the squirrel – which has a very brutal way of getting to the kernel inside.

Common 'nutters'

In the UK we have six common 'nutters': Grey Squirrel, Red Squirrel, Wood Mouse, Yellow-necked Mouse, Bank Vole and Hazel Dormouse. Squirrel signs are the most obvious because of the animals' larger size (thus bigger requirement), diurnal activity and habit of feeding out in the open where they have a view of potential predators. Signs left by squirrels can be found in a woodland or hedgerow, or at a feeding station such as a fallen bough or tree stump.

CRACKING THE CASE: SQUIRRELS AND HAZELNUTS

Squirrels will tackle all manner of seeds and nuts, such as acorns, cherry stones, haws and hazelnuts, and they go about this in a distinctive way.

Hazelnuts are fairly smooth and slippery and getting a purchase on this surface is tricky. Before using its teeth, a squirrel will turn a nut several times, close to its face. It is smelling and weighing the nut, trying to ascertain whether an insect or fungus has got to the kernel before it; squirrels are pretty good at this. Look under a tree in which squirrels have been feeding and you will see the odd discarded whole hazelnut among the remains; these are squirrel rejects. Smash them open yourself and in most cases you will find nothing but a withered kernel within.

Squirrels have the uncanny ability to know if a nut is worth cracking, and any nuts left intact beneath a tree may well bear witness to investigations by the scratchy lines left by claws and teeth on the surface. Open them up and you will often find a shrivelled kernel.

A squirrel will find a weak point in a hazelnut shell, then force its lower incisiors into the casing.

A mouse will usually start at the broad end of an acorn, so the kernel can be pulled out.

Two halves of the same story come together to show the notch nibbled out of the end, then the way the teeth have sliced through the nut and created the big split to get to the goodies inside.

If the nut is a good one, the first thing a squirrel does is to hold the nut in its forepaws and nibble across one end. This creates a notch. The lower incisors are placed in this notch and the whole thing is, in most cases, cleaved neatly in half by the upward slice of the lower teeth. The two halves of the shell are then dropped while the kernel is consumed.

Squirrels cache their food: gather and hide it in different locations for future use.

If you find both halves of a nut, it is often possible to fit the two parts back together; this reveals quite clearly the initial notch. If you investigate the surface of the nut you will notice scratch marks made by the squirrel's sharp claws.

Rodent skulls

Look at the skull of a squirrel, mouse, Bank Vole or dormouse and the most distinctive things they all have in common are the four large front teeth, two in the top jaw and two in the bottom one. They are continuously growing, which is why any rodent has to keep gnawing and wearing them down. Each tooth has hard enamel on the front and softer dentine at the back, which means that the back of the tooth wears down faster than the front. This is what creates the angle of the blade, like a knife-blade that is ideal for inserting into cracks in nut shells.

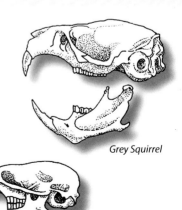

Grey Squirrel

Dormouse

Mice, dormice, voles and hazelnuts

These rodents are much smaller than squirrels and are physically unable to hold up the larger seeds and nuts, so they tend to ground one end in much the same way as a rugby ball is placed on the ground prior to a kick. Then they work away at the other end. The marks left on the nut should identify who did the nibbling.

Wood and Yellow-necked Mice hold the nut against the ground (most Yellow-necked Mice work into the side of the nut while the majority of Wood Mice work on the top end). They lean

it towards them and use their lower teeth to do the gnawing, working away at the side furthest from the body. The lower teeth work against the upper incisors, which grip the surface of the nut on the outside rim. This creates a distinctive edge to the hole (look closely with a magnifying lens to see the details). This lip is marked by the individual scrapes of the lower teeth and these always run at 90 degrees to the edge of the hole, giving it a corrugated texture, while the marks of the upper teeth can be seen around the outside of the rim. Similar feeding signs are also left on seeds.

Dormice do a similar thing, but once they have broken through the shell they work it differently. Their lower incisors still do the cutting while the upper ones grip, but instead of working across the hole's edges they work around it, creating a smoother effect that looks as though it has been turned by a carpenter.

Bank Voles use a totally different technique: holding the nut against the ground, they lean it away from their body and work the side of the nut that is closest. Once a hole is made they enlarge it by sticking their nose inside and gnawing with their upper and lower incisors. So they still create a corrugated edge but, unlike mice and dormice, leave very few scratches on the outside of the nut because they are working from the outside in.

From top, dormouse, Wood Mouse, dormouse, Bank Vole: *The three small mammal groups that tackle hazelnuts employ very distinctive techniques, all of which are reflected in the remains of the nuts.*

Feathered 'nutters'

A few bird species have worked out how to deal with the nut-cracking challenge. Watch a Great Tit in your garden and see how it holds down a sunflower seed with one or both feet, then hammers it repeatedly in the same place until it's broken through the husk. It uses exactly the same tactic to deal with a variety of nuts and seeds from acorns to hazelnuts. Nuts opened by these small birds have a characteristic small hole with uneven edges, and there will be a series of linear scratches radiating out from it, showing the numerous times the bird's beak has made contact with the shell. Fresh seeds and nuts are usually selected because as soon as the water content drops, they can become as hard as stones and impossible for even the most determined tit to crack. Magpies, Jackdaws, Jays and other crows are opportunists and will all sometimes hammer at nuts, leaving thick and triangular beak marks.

The Nuthatch's name says it all: this bird is the master of smashing open acorns, nuts and other seeds.

Nuthatch This bird has a pick-like beak that can tackle even mature and hard nuts. To solve the problem of the nut rolling around, the Nuthatch finds a tree with suitably fissured bark and jams the nut into a groove. It then goes at it hammer and tongs, delivering powerful blows to the trapped nut with its beak. This repeated hammering during the autumn and winter months is part of the soundscape of most European deciduous woodlands.

These Nuthatch anvils, as they are called, are rarely reused, but the birds will jam seeds and nuts into crevices and holes in the bark of trees as a means of storing them. Look for crescent-shaped beak marks on the nut itself and around the nut where the bird has missed.

Top: *Many tits, like this Great Tit, will carry a hard seed off to a spot where they can wedge the seed in place, before hammering away at it.*

Above: *The Nuthatch's use of bark fissures and holes that hold the food item in place before applying the hardwear, explains why you may find remains of nuts and seeds jammed into such crevices.*

Great Spotted Woodpecker This powerful bird uses an anvil or workstation and will often reuse a favourite tree if its bark is of the right texture to hold food steady. Its large, chisel-shaped beak has a knack of hitting a nut along the grain and often splitting it lengthwise, sometimes totally or at least making a longitudinal aperture through which to extract the kernel. Look out for the remains of hammered nuts, acorns and cones below a favourite anvil site.

Above: *The Great Spotted Woodpecker works in a similar way to the Nuthatch, selecting a suitable anvil in which to jam and hammer the toughest nut case into submission.*

Right: *On the Continent the work of the Spotted Nutcracker – another well-named bird – may well be evident. The birds apply the hammering technique to pine cones as well as to hazelnuts.*

Spotted Nutcracker If you are trekking in the mountains or far northern regions of Europe you may come across this specialised member of the crow family that has an exceptional knack with nuts. Although most individuals prefer pine cones, some seem to specialise in dealing with hazelnuts. The bird will grasp a nut or cone with one or both feet and hammer at it with its powerful and heavy bill. Favourite feeding sites – often stumps or fallen logs – are repeatedly used and are surround by a midden of smashed open shell fragments and tattered cones.

Cone crunchers

Pine seeds are packed with all manner of nutritional goodies. In many northern forests food can be thin on the ground, especially in the winter months. Therefore several animals have developed the knack of extracting these seeds from their cones in large enough quantities to make the effort worthwhile.

Cones represent a challenge, a lot of work for the little morsels that are the seeds – so only birds with the specialisms can energetically justify the effort. The Spotted Nutcracker is one such bird.

The ultimate specialist – the crossbill – has an asymmetrical twisted bill designed to twist and split cone scales.

Crossbills

If you find cones on a forest floor that have a ragged appearance, and each scale has a split running down the middle, they have probably been raided by a bird with one of the weirdest beaks in the world – the crossbill. Its beak is a specialised tool for extricating pine seeds with ease.

First, a bird snips off the cone from a tree and carries it to a more stable perch. If the bird is one of the 50 per cent that has a lower mandible twisting towards the right-hand side of its body, it holds the cone with its right foot, and with it angled upwards, inserts the tip of its beak beneath one of the scales at the top of the cone. As it pushes down, the lower mandible presses against the cone while the upper mandible pushes against the scale, and with a twist of the head it levers the scale away from the axis of the cone, creating enough space for the elongated tongue to scoop out the seed. The bird then systematically works its way around the cone, removing as many of the seeds as it can before dropping it to the forest floor. The cone is left with scales bent back and twisted, some of which are split along their length, an effect caused by the withdrawal of the upper mandible from the recess behind the scale.

The cones ravaged by crossbills have a very distinctive and ragged appearance.

Close-up of the most bizarre bill in the business.

There are several species of crossbill, and each is specialised to deal with the particular cones of different conifer species. The Parrot, Scottish and Common Crossbills, although all specialised to deal with Scots Pine, are able to exploit the cones most efficiently at different times of the year. The breeding season for these birds is during the winter months to coincide with when the pine seeds are ripening. The largest species, the Parrot Crossbill can breed earliest as it can access the seeds in the unripe cones, whereas the Common Crossbill breeds the latest and can only tackle cones that are already ripe, or smaller ones with thinner scales.

Squirrels are partial to pine seeds; they systematically strip the cone spindle of scales to get to the nosh.

The aftermath of a good squirrelling. The trick is to be able to recognise the difference between this and the work of other rodents, which will also feed on pine cones.

Squirrels

Wherever these mammals are present you will find the stripped spindles of various cones littering the floor of conifer woodlands. How a squirrel eats a cone depends on the size of the cone relative to the squirrel. It will usually start at the bottom of the cone, with the cone either lying on the ground or tilted with the base up; the lower cone scales are the first to bite the dust and are simply torn off to get to any seeds. Once the squirrel has got past the first few whorls of scales, it starts a systematic process of turning the cone while extracting the seeds. Small cones are simply turned in the front paws, while larger and longer cones are rested down on the ground. Watch for yourself how fast and efficiently a squirrel works a cone.

Great Spotted Woodpecker

Probably the least specialised of the cone crunchers are the woodpeckers – Great Spotteds have a penchant for pine seeds, especially in the winter when their usual insect prey is scarce. They use the same workshops that they use for busting nuts and apply much the same principles to pine cones. However, what they lack in technique for actually getting to the seed, they make up for in dexterity in getting the cone into a situation in which it can be worked. A bird will fly to its workshop, placing the cone securely between its belly and the tree trunk. It then tosses the old cone out over its shoulder, wedges the new one in place vertically and uses its chisel-like beak to chop into the cone. A discarded cone will not only look ragged and frayed, but nearly all the scales will be smashed and split.

Often a tree becomes a favourite 'anvil' for an individual bird, because the depth and size of the fissures are perfect for the job. Such a tree often bears witness to this fact with dozens of cones jammed in the crevices and surrounding the base of the tree.

When a suitable anvil is not present, a woodpecker jams a cone between its upright body and the tree trunk as it works on it.

When a Wood Mouse gets its teeth into a pine cone the damage is similar to that left by a squirrel, but generally a much neater job is made of it. Here a Wood Mouse has used the shelter of an old wasps' nest dug out by a Badger to eat spruce cone seeds.

Wood Mice

The most frequent cone nibblers among the small mammals (Bank Voles and Yellow-necked Mice) also partake of cones, but the signs they leave are difficult to distinguish. These rodents, however, have a really nervous disposition, and if they come across a complete cone, they will go to great efforts to drag their prize off to a secret location away from the gaze of owls, Foxes and Kestrels.

A cone processed by a Wood Mouse has a smooth central shaft, and there are no ragged or frayed ends. Interestingly, the mice often leave the tuft of scales at the apex of a cone intact just like squirrels do – there are few seeds at this end of the cone and it's simply not worth the bother to look.

Cones eaten by voles will often be found partially hidden in vegetation, with the scales bitten off more neatly than in a squirrel-eaten cone.

Fruit, roots and fungi

Packed with vitamins and sugars, fruit and tubers, as well as fungi, offer sustenance to many species. In doing so they leave a trail of tooth and beak marks, as well as a plentitude of stains and distinctive droppings that when put together can tell a clear story.

Birds such as this Starling will work on fruits in situ as well as on those that have fallen; either way the peck marks are usually very evident in the flesh of the fruit.

The ground below a bush in which birds such as Redwings have been feeding is often littered with fallen berries – most evident in snowy conditions.

Hips, haws and other soft fruit

Autumn is a time of plenty and many trees and hedgerow shrubs produce brightly coloured fruits and berries to entice animals to consume them. How can we tell what has been having a go at a fruit? **Apples** are a favourite among Blackbirds and other members of the thrush family, and they will readily peck away at a fruit until little remains but the hollowed out skin and the core. The texture of any flesh inside bears a characteristic roughness and there may be clear 'peck marks' on the outside of the skin. Many other birds, such as finches, tackle apples just for their pips, and they often target the small wild crab apples, which are easier to tackle than larger apples. Crossbills will also feast on small apples, leaving a distinctive ragged look, with fragments of the fruit discarded all around and some pieces of sliced flesh still remaining attached.

Small fruits, such as **haws** and **hips**, also contain seeds. Larger birds find it easiest to swallow them whole, and the seeds will pass out of the bird suitably scarified. Other seed-eating birds, such as various finches, are not so enamoured with the sweet flesh, so tear the fruits apart to get to the seeds. Mice also target the seeds, and often carry the whole fruit off to a secure private place to eat.

Voles, however, are rather fond of fruit flesh but not the seeds. They either consume fruit in situ, and I've seen Bank Voles scaling a complex trellis in order to feed on rose hips, or they carry their treasure to secure places. They leave behind small fragments of the fruit's outer skin and piles of discarded seeds. The difference between fruits dismembered by voles and birds is sometimes hard to tell, but as a rule birds are much messier and make smaller holes in the fruit, creating a hollowed out 'bowl' shape, while voles make a bigger hole to get to the seed and sometimes totally dismantle the fruit.

Wood Mice eat blackberries (amongst other things) and tend to eat only the pips, leaving the flesh of the fruit.

Cherries are attractive to many birds and usually the flesh is removed as few birds can tackle the stone itself. The only finch that can crack open a cherry stone to extract and eat the kernel is the

Cherries are enjoyed by many birds, but the evidence that they have been feeding is rarely seen as feeding signs. You are more likely to see the droppings left behind, which contain the stones that have passed right through the birds' digestive tracts intact.

Hawfinch, with its nutcracker bill. It grips the stone between four hard pads, two in the upper mandible and two in the lower, before cracking it open and extracting the kernel with its tongue. Research has revealed that Hawfinches exert a load of 60–95lb to break open a cherry stone. What remains below a cherry tree are the neatly split halves of the cherry stones. If the stones had been left by squirrels, you would be able to see a notch in them just like their discarded hazelnut shells.

Roots and tubers

Some wild animals are tempted to raid our crops over the winter months. Deer can cause damage to beet crops and will eat whatever is growing above ground, as well as uprooting the plant and consuming the nutritious beet. Any remaining beet will show the marks of the lower teeth only; more obvious will be other field signs such as slots and droppings.

Rabbits and hares also eat the leaves and parts of the tuber that protrude above the surface of the soil, but they won't dig up the tuber. Here the large marks of the gappy incisors are clear, especially around the edges. Often they work their way around the entire plant, leaving a characteristic shape not dissimilar to the cartoon image of an apple core.

Larger mammals such as Badgers and Wild Boar are also keen on tubers and bulbs. The aftermath of their efforts can be quite spectacular – they can leave anything from snuffle holes and scrapes to a total ploughing up of the surface turf (see the section on scrapes and soil disturbance on page 128).

Tubers are occasionally eaten by birds. These sugar beets have been partially eaten by Pink-footed Geese.

Rabbit damage can be confirmed by the presence of teeth marks.

The damage left by slugs and snails on the soft tissues of mushrooms is often evident as holes with a multiple scalloped interior surface.

Fungi

The soft pulp of a mushroom or toadstool can be a palatable treat for some species. Birds never actually eat mushrooms but will pick through the caps looking for the grubs of fungus gnats and other insect larvae; they leave a distinctive pock-marked texture where the beak has been used to peck into the flesh.

Slugs and snails love to crawl up onto the fruiting body and rasp away at patches; they leave a distinctive texture reminiscent of wind-eroded soft rock.

Mammals of various sizes quite happily sink their teeth into the soft caps of many mushrooms and leave a very neat imprint of their teeth – the size of the bite will help to narrow it down. A fungus nibbled by a squirrel has a chiselled look to it, the wide incisors making large gouges in the soft material. The signs of smaller rodents, by comparison, have a 'stripy' look to them as their teeth make shallower scratches as they feed.

Red Squirrels sometimes collect mushrooms and toadstools and carry them up into the trees intact, where they often wedge them into the forks of branches or impale them to be snacked on later.

The ragged edge of this toadstool tells us it's been nibbled by something with teeth; the size and shape of the marks will give us a clue as to who did it.

Nests

Nests – by which I mean any form of temporary or permanent structure created by animals in which to breed – are most obvious in winter once the veil of leaves has dropped. To work out who built a nest you need to take into account its size, where it's positioned, the materials used to make it and the type of nest.

Not all bird nests are as evident and obvious as those in this heronry.

A summary of nest types

Shallow scrape
Simple depression in shingle, sand or soil, e.g. Ringed Plover.

Shallow scrape (lined)
Lined with feathers and a few surrounding objects such as rearranged stones, e.g. Oystercatcher.

Feather-lined shallow cup on the ground
Down feathers line a simple hollow in the ground, e.g. ducks.

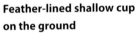

Floating platform of sticks and waterweeds
Mass of vegetation, with cup-like depression. Sometimes built on the bottom of a lake if shallow, sometimes tethered, e.g. grebes, Moorhen, Coot.

Heap of vegetation near water

Platform consisting of twigs or reeds gathered together at the water's edge, e.g. Mute Swan.

Domed nest on the ground

Defined cup with a domed, loosely woven roof; the cup is often attached to stems of reeds or bushes and is well camouflaged, e.g. Wood and Willow Warblers, Chiffchaff.

Simple platform in a tree

Thin criss-cross of twigs; the contents may be visible through the bottom of the nest, e.g. Woodpigeon, Collared Dove.

Large mass of twigs in tree, or on building or ledge

Bulky, untidy, heaped mass of coarse sticks, lined with grass, typical of crows and some birds of prey.

Large, ball-shaped mass of sticks
Spherical nest, with a domed roof over a platform, typical of a Magpie. If leafy and dense, possibly a squirrel drey.

Small, spherical/elliptical enclosed nest
Built of moss, lichen, leaves and hair with an entrance hole, e.g. Wren, Long-tailed Tit. Dormice and Harvest Mice make similar but looser structures.

Cup-shaped lined nest
Woven cup strengthened with mud and with a soft lining, e.g. thrushes, most small perching birds.

Nest made mainly of mud and either supported or stuck to a vertical surface under an overhang
Swallows and House Martins make these distinctive nests from mud and natural fibres.

If you find a nest and have difficulty identifying its owner, you can take several reference photos, but do so without disturbing the nest in the process. When you take the photos, try to include some background for scale. There are numerous websites now that have forums on which you can post such conundrums. Then all you do is sit back and wait for the responses to come flooding in.

DREY OR MAGPIE NEST?

Squirrel dreys, used both as shelters and nurseries, are rounded, domed structures and at a distance can be mistaken for the similarly shaped nests of Magpies (which are about double the size of a football). However, there are a few obvious differences. Magpie nests are usually fairly loose affairs, and when viewed from the side it is often possible to see daylight through them. Squirrel dreys, in contrast, are dense with every gap plugged and filled. In addition, Magpies build with bare sticks and twigs that are usually gathered after they've fallen. Squirrels, however, cut their own twigs, which will often have the leaves still attached, and the leaves become a visible part of the structure, making the drey a much more solid and enduring affair.

At a glance it is possible to confuse 'witches' brooms' with birds' nests. These odd-looking structures are caused by a fungal infection and are quite common on birch trees. The mutated growth sprouts twiggy stems, which can sometimes look like a messy nest.

Above: *The dense structure of this squirrel drey, as well the presence of leaves and its position in the fork of a tree branch, distinguishes it from a bird's nest.*

Magpies tend to make ball-shaped nests from twigs – composed of a nest cup that is quite dense with a thatched roof and sides which you can see light through. Often these nests are deep in a thorn bush or up high in twiggy growth.

Down-to-earth homes

It comes as a surprise to some people to learn that many birds nest on the ground. It's a logical strategy when there are no trees in open habitats such as grassland, marsh and moorland, but some birds still choose to make their nests on terra firma even in areas with plenty of tall vegetation.

The most basic nests are barely there at all – simple dents in the shingle of a beach or a loosely arranged group of pebbles are typical of many wading birds, such as Oystercatchers and Ringed Plovers.

Ducks in general will add a little extra comfort by lining the nest with feathers plucked from their breast. Eiderdown, for example, was once traditionally harvested for our own use by collecting these soft feathers from Eider nests.

The Eider duck in common with many ducks lines its nest with its own down – although in the absence of any other materials it tends to be constructed of this self grown material entirely.

The larger plovers and game birds, such as Pheasant and grouse, embellish their nests a little more using local materials like grass, leaves, twigs and feathers.

Waterside properties

Several birds associated with water or wetlands make the most of the fact that many nest predators aren't that keen on swimming, so they build their nests on the water or at least at the margins where it's unsteady underfoot.

Many ground-nesting birds, such as this hen Pheasant, make nests that are little more than a slight rearrangement of the material already present.

Grebe nests look like large, buoyant compost heaps and are nothing more than untidy piles of soggy waterweeds, which at some point in the season start to decompose and break down. These nests can be heaped up in the shallows, loosely tethered to emergent vegetation or indeed free-floating rafts. The size of a nest and its bulk will give some indication of the species involved: Great Crested tend to use bigger twigs and reeds, while the various smaller grebes use finer, more delicate and leafy material.

Tethered to water plants and made from them, the floating nest of a Great Crested Grebe is typical of its family.

The rails, including the Moorhen, Water Rail and Coot, tend to make fairly strong platforms, with a degree of 'weaving' to form a loose bowl-like depression, sometimes lined with finer weeds and leaves. The nests are usually started at water level and attached to emergent vegetation. Coot nests are bigger than those of Moorhens and have deeper, more defined nest cups.

Coots create a mound of rotting vegetation and this is one of the most common nests of its kind – size is a useful guide, but it can easily be confused with the nest of a Moorhen.

Right: Big nest for a big bird – the Mute Swan makes a huge pile of any vegetation that is available.

Swans create a fairly unmistakable huge circular nest about 1–2 metres in diameter on land or in shallow water. It has a proper cup and is lined with fine material but not down. Tell-tale swan droppings, combined with vegetation pressed down by clumsy feet and the odd moulted white feather, are giveaways if you feel you need further clues.

Minimalist penthouses

If you stare up into a tree and see what looks like an arboreal game of pick-a-sticks then you've probably just found a pigeon's nest! It really is just a few twigs criss-crossing each other supported by a few branches close to the trunk. Woodpigeons and Collared and Turtle Doves all go in for the same minimalistic approach to nest building.

The nests of the pigeon and dove family are often so minimalistic that they are little more than a mesh of twigs.

Open houses

The majority of bird species make a cup nest to hold a clutch of eggs or nestlings in a safe place, hopefully out of reach of predators. A typical nest is woven from coarse plant material, usually grasses, but some species use roots, heather fragments and plant stems and sticks. The resultant 'basket', depending on the species, can be a tightly woven affair or a much looser cup. To aid stability, the nest can be built around permanent features such as branches or roots, or it may even incorporate stems and living material into its infrastructure. Some species strengthen the nest still further by daubing on substances such as mud and saliva. Finally, many species insulate their nests with fur, feathers, fine grasses, wool, moss or hair to stop cooling draughts and help to retain body heat.

The cup nest is the norm and the materials, situation, size and construction technique can be telling. This is the work of a Blackcap – difficult to identify without seeing the eggs.

While you may expect to find this sort of nest in a hedge, bush or tree, many small birds of open habitat, such as pipits, chats, Yellowhammer, Twite,

Many birds build their nest cups directly on the ground and again it is habitat that is the big clue if the birds or their eggs are not present.

Skylark and Ring Ouzel, build this sort of a structure on the ground. However, it will usually be near a clump of taller rank grass, a bush or some other landscape feature that might provide some kind of cover.

The beautiful workmanship of the Song Thrush. Note the use of mud in the construction of the cup lining.

The biggest problem for the nature detective is that it is sometimes difficult to identify the different species from nests alone, as there is quite a lot of variation even within an individual species. What a nest looks like depends on what materials are available at the time of construction. However, with a bit of practice and some detective work aided by watching the birds at work, you'll soon start to feel more confident and make informed guesses, for that is often what they'll be initially. Size and habitat should be the main clues.

For example, the smallest nest in the UK, at only about 7–8cm in diameter, belongs to the smallest species: the Goldcrest. It prefers conifers and makes quite a distinctive nest, suspended beneath vegetation and constructed of fine lichen particles, moss and spiders' webs – the silk from these is used almost like thread to 'stitch' the construction together and also to bind it to the branches. At the other end of the spectrum, thrushes make quite bulky nests from plant material. They can be about 16cm in diameter, with a cup size of around 10cm. Blackbirds and Song Thrushes are relatively widespread and have similar-sized nests. You can tell their nests apart, however, by the way they are finished off. The Song Thrush leaves a bare mud floor to its nest cup, whereas Blackbirds line the nest with finer materials.

Compare the Song Thrush nest with another similar-sized thrush that of the Blackbird – similar in size and habitat, but the materials in this case are different and there is no mud lining to the cup.

Tree houses

Many nests are up off the ground and supported by being wedged in the forks of branches or placed on ledges. Let's start high and work our way down to hedge height.

Large, tatty masses of sticks in tall trees are usually the nests of members of the crow family. **Rooks** nest in colonies, and several dozen nests are often spread through the crowns of a group of large trees. Nests tend to have a conical shape, tapering to a point underneath the main, robust nesting platform.

Communal nests of Rooks can be seen from quite a distance, especially in the early part of the season when there is little leaf cover.

Herons also nest in colonies called 'heronries'. They start the nesting process in February and, unlike Rooks, vacate their

Below: The Grey Heron is another communal nester, it selects tall trees and those which are strong enough to take the weight of its massive nests.

heronries over the winter months. So if you find an empty colony it may well be a heronry, but the best way to find out for sure is to return in the early spring and see for yourself.

Carrion Crows/Hooded Crows also nest in trees. Their nests are a similar size to those of Rooks (about 60–80cm in diameter), but are not as deep. They look like large dishes of sticks, lined with finer material, which can include sheep's wool, plastic bags and string, but they are territorial birds so their nests are always found in isolation.

Big sticks, big bird. The chunky corvids can handle large building materials and are often responsible for single chunky, coarse nests.

Ravens make huge nests and often have traditional sites that are reused year after year. Although associated with crags and quarry faces, they are as opportunistic in choosing a nest site as they are when it comes to food and will nest in a surprisingly eclectic range of sites, from cathedrals and old barns to trees and crags. Nests in trees are easily identified by their huge size, which can reach 1.5–2m across.

Jays have a habit of hiding their nests in the solid V of a branch near the trunk, and also in dense, twiggy growth or ivy.

Messy piles

The nests of birds of prey are quite variable: a Peregrine's is no more than a scrape, while many other raptors, such as Hobby and Common Buzzard, simply take over the old nests of other birds, especially members of the crow family. You may think you are looking at a crow's nest, until three white Common Buzzard chick heads appear over the edge.

White Storks are famous for their massive ungainly piles of sticks, often located on tall trees, pylons and chimneys.

Generally speaking, if a nest is built from scratch it resembles a large pile of sticks and twigs, forming a platform with a depression in the centre. Ospreys famously produce monstrous heaps of sticks, which they add to year after year. This can eventually be their downfall, as the supporting tree can give way under the weight or increased wind resistance caused by the structure.

What the Osprey lacks in construction finesse, it makes up for with quantities. These massive nests are often near water.

ON THE EDGE

Nests positioned on exposed crags and rock faces can be more difficult to spot than you would think. Looking for piles of sticks and other material is one way, but more often than not from a distance they are not easy to see. Regular nests of Ravens and birds of prey can give away their locations with highly visible white streaks on the rock face from the continuous dribbling of white waste products from the nest ledges. In some situations these take on an almost lurid green coloration as the nutrients in the droppings are food for algae.

Classic crag nesters – the Peregrine and Raven often give away the presence of their nests by the stripe of mutes (droppings) that form a white streak directly below the nest ledge.

Wrens make a football-sized round nest, with the entrance hole somewhere near the bottom of the structure and well hidden.

Round houses

Some of the most beautiful and most cryptic nests are built like a hollow ball. Both the Wren and the Long-tailed Tit persuade a variety of materials to hold together to form a resilient, yet surprisingly flexible structure in which to rear their young.

A completely camouflaged, grapefruit-sized mass of leaves, grass and moss, built low down in thick vegetation, probably belongs to a **Wren**. The **Long-tailed Tit**, on the other hand, weaves a more elongated and delicate structure from mosses and lichens that is stitched together with hair and spiders' webs, giving the home great flexibility. The birds usually position the nest in dense thorny vegetation, though they will build a nest in the fork of a branch or even jam it into a cavity if pushed.

The **Dipper**, found in upland areas around swift-running streams, also builds a 'ball' nest, which may be sited on a bridge or in an old crumbly wall. You would rarely simply stumble across a nest. The Dipper's activities are largely confined to the water's edge.

Europe's smallest mammal, the **Harvest Mouse**, weaves a stunning structure from grasses and plant stems. Its tightly constructed nest is the size of a tennis ball and this distinguishes it from any bird's nest. The mice start their nest-building process near the ground by splitting the lower leaves of several grass plants and weaving the resulting ribbons together without detaching them from the plant. These living nests completely blend into their surroundings, so are very difficult to find. During the course of the season the nest will grow with the grass, so may end up much higher off the ground than when construction started. Breeding nests tend to have a single entrance, while winter shelters on the ground and summer resting nests tend to have a 'front door' and a 'back door'.

The master at weaving the raffia, dead and living grass stems, together is the Harvest Mouse – these nests are tiny, no bigger than a tennis ball.

For an animal also known as the 'seven sleeper' due to its habit of opting out and hibernating for up to seven months of the year, it is perhaps not surprising to learn that the **Hazel Dormouse** will also construct an excellent bedroom and breeding chamber. The dormice build their 15–20cm diameter spherical nest in a variety of locations: hollows in trees, bird boxes (a fact that has been embraced by dormouse workers in Europe, who survey for their presence by providing specially designed boxes, with the entrance hole facing the tree, and recording the number that get used) and also out in the open – I have found them woven into Bramble thickets and even wedged between the stems of Hazel trees.

Often built in crevices, tree holes and even bird boxes, the nests of Hazel Dormice can be made of any material to hand; a favourite is strips of honeysuckle bark and moss. I've seen them lined with feathers stripped from a nearby dead bird, too.

The nests are usually made of leaves and a dense weave of strips of vegetation, often honeysuckle bark, which splits really nicely into ribbons to create the main infrastructure; it also splits again and again into a fine bedding material, which is often used with fluffy plant seeds to create a cosy lining. The nest of a Hazel Dormouse could be confused with that of a Wren, though the latter tends to have a clear and reinforced entrance hole, whereas dormice nests rarely have an obvious entrance or exit.

Hazel Dormice make a similar nest for hibernation, but this is sited at or below ground level rather than above it, as are the nests made by voles. These, however, tend to be much more untidy, loose balls of plant fibres, which are often under logs, brash piles or even sheets of corrugated tin.

The **Edible Dormouse** is an introduced species in the UK, but is found widely throughout mainland Europe. It is a much bigger animal than the Hazel Dormouse and therefore builds much bigger nests. Although Edible Dormice often use cavities for their nests, which they may or may not line with plant material, they will also take over birds' nests and build nests in trees that look a little like squirrel dreys. The nest lining is usually made of green leaves.

Mice build nests, too, but their efforts look more like a bit of superficial redecorating. They will take up residence in cavities and burrows, and may line a chamber with leaves. You're more likely to see them when they turn up in nestboxes put out for other animals such as dormice, birds and bats.

The Edible Dormouse prefers tree holes, which it typically lines with green leaves.

NB: Both species of dormouse are protected by law in the UK and it is an offence to disturb them without a licence.

Often erected underneath objects or deep within tussocks, the nests of Field Voles are made from the finely shredded stems of grass and moss.

Adobe homes

Adobe derives from ancient Egypt and literally means 'mud brick'; some of the oldest buildings in existence are made from this very durable material. As well as being made from readily available materials, mud and clay constructions have excellent thermal properties, so that they stay cool when it's hot and snug when it's chilly.

It is therefore not surprising to find that many animals use mud to construct their nests. Probably the best-known species that build such nests are Swallows and House Martins. They would once have nested on cliffs, but now tend to just use man-made structures. The birds take beakfuls of wet mud and work it into place, one pellet at a time. They also periodically add fibre, such as plant stems, animal hair and feathers, to bind and strengthen the nest cup, which, once complete, is lined with feathers and other soft material. A new nest is composed of more than 1,000 mud pellets, but more often than not the birds carry out minor repairs to old nests which remain year in year out – there is a record of a nest being reused for more than 50 years.

The properties of mud have not been lost on humans and birds alike – it is readily available and easily moulded into the shape of choice. These Swallows have reinforced their open nest cup with straw, wool and feathers.

The nests of Swallows and House Martins are superficially similar, but are quite easy to tell apart. Swallows build a cup-shaped nest which is usually supported or sheltered in some way, while House Martins build on sheer surfaces and under overhangs outside. The nest cup isn't open and access is via an entrance hole.

House Martins nest against an overhang to create a ceiling.

Whose hole?

A hole, whether scraped into the dirt, bored through wood or pushed through sand, can be a front door, back door, bolt hole, emergency exit, ventilation shaft, dead end, or an excavation to access food or for a latrine. Whatever its use, a hole is a portal into an animal's private world, and the job of the tracker is to find out which species made it and why.

Who lives here? Sometimes the size of the hole is useful, but usually other clues will need to be sought for a positive identity.

Home is where the hole is

Life underground makes a lot of sense – it is, for the most part, a secure, safe and private place to live. Here, 20–30cm or so below the surface, whether in the middle of summer or in the frozen depths of winter, the environment is surprisingly stable. The insulative properties of the soil itself mean that air temperatures are moderated, so that it feels cool when it's hot and warm and cosy when it's freezing outside.

The first thing the nature detective should do is to thoroughly inspect a hole, being careful not to tread on any evidence and destroy what may be valuable clues. Heaps of excavated soil, if present, can be rich in all manner of clues, not least footprints. Make a note of any you find, but keep in mind that sometimes they may not be the footprints of the maker – a curious dog may have wandered by and stuck its nose in for a sniff, and in many instances more than one species may well live in the same burrow system.

Far right: The size and shape of this hole would fit a Rabbit; the presence of Rabbit down and droppings outside confirms this.

Foxes create their earths in a variety of locations as is befitting of such an opportunist. Often a foxy smell, droppings and food remains give the game away.

It is always best to start with a peek, using a torch or mirror to shed some light into the depths. It should be pretty easy to see if the hole is a dead end or a doorway into the darkness. If it is an animal's front door, you need to work out who the earth mover is.

It is surprisingly difficult to get a feel for the width of an animal, especially as field guides talk about shoulder heights and body lengths, but never an animal's girth. So while the bore of a hole is relative to the animal, getting a feel for which animal fits into each hole is a matter of building up experience.

Badgers have unmistakable homes, often with the presence of a semi-circular hole and a huge spoil heap.

In the UK the mammal holes you are most likely to encounter are those of a warren, sett and earth, the underground headquarters for Rabbit, Badger and Fox. These animals are all ubiquitous and their abodes are easy to spot, so you should be able to work these three out pretty easily.

A WORD OF CAUTION

If I find a hole, the first thing I do is peer into it, but do this with caution as you never know what may be lurking inside. I once found a large excavation that had appeared overnight in a local wood. I bent down enthusiastically to peer inside only to be sent flying backwards as the equally surprised Badger, feeling cornered in its summer-day rest, came bowling out, knocking me over and leaving me gasping on my back.

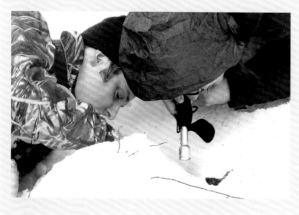

So now I nearly always carry with me a small torch or travel mirror, which can be very useful for investigating gloomy interiors. A very bright LED can easily be carried on a keychain and even some mobile phones have built-in torches. A mirror can be used to bounce natural light into unlit crevices and cracks or awkward spots – I often attach mine to a stick to look into tree holes and inaccessible birds' nests.

Badger

These fairly large and robust animals live in communities called clans, and each clan has a territory. Within that territory they can have several different kinds of burrow system, which vary in size from the biggest system, known as the main sett or clan HQ, with multiple entrances serving an underground network of burrows and chambers, through to various often smaller burrow systems that get used less frequently. These can be annexe setts, which are burrow systems close to the main sett and are often connected to it by well-trodden paths; subsidiary setts, which have a varying number of entrances but are not visibly linked by well-worn paths, as well as the occasional outlier, which may only have one or two entrances. The main sett can be quite substantial – one large sett excavated as part of a study consisted of more than 310m of tunnel and would have involved the excavation of over 25 tonnes of soil.

Badgers are good diggers and are well equipped for the job, but they still prefer easily dug, well-draining soil and the cover of woodland or scrub. They often dig into a bank, too, as this requires much less effort than simply going straight down. They are compulsive earth movers and even animals with huge setts, easily big enough to house the number of animals present, will continue to excavate. This makes an active Badger sett fairly conspicuous because each of the main entrances will usually have a large spoil heap of soil and bedding, creating a very distinctive 'doorstep'.

While the situations are different, all of these holes share the same characteristics: semi-circular entrance, large, fan-shaped spoil heap, often a groove in spoil along which material is excavated, soil worn smooth and well-worn paths joining the holes up – all of these qualities shout Badger.

Above: *Often (but not always) Badger setts have multiple entrances joined by a network of well-worn paths.*

Below: *Bedding is often discarded or brought out to air.*

There is a long list of clues that will help you in the identification of a hole made by a Badger. For a start there are usually several holes close by, though they can occur as individual holes or outliers. You may have to have a bit of a scout about to find other holes, as some are not that obvious or may be deep in undergrowth.

A Badger's entrance hole is almost semicircular, which neatly fits the profile of the animal. There will often be well-spaced claw marks in the soil, or rocks surrounding the entrance, particularly above the hole, and the flat bottom of the burrow entrance can have a polished look where the comings and goings of flat feet have compressed the soil.

When Badgers clear out a sett they drag soil or bedding backwards tucked between their body and front legs, and this creates a groove 30cm or more wide in the spoil heap. In fresh diggings you may get to pick out the pockmarks of tracks with the distinctive footprint at the bottom. Well-trodden paths linking the entrances, scratching posts, the presence of large lumps of soil and excavated rock (beyond the strength of a Rabbit or Fox), and very distinctive black hairs with white tips and roots are all clear signs that the holes you are looking at belong to Brock (Badgers). Many other animals, including Rabbits and Foxes, will also share a Badger sett, so the presence of their signs around the entrances will point to a communal property.

Below: *A large groove in the spoil heap is where the animals have dragged out material backwards as they've been digging.*

Below right: *Foot marks and characteristic footprints are rarely obvious in the soil; more likely is a concentration of activity evident by multiple prints.*

Rabbit

Warrens, like setts, occur in a various sizes and often have multiple entrances. Rabbits, like Badgers, may also live in groups where the soil type and shelter suit their requirements, so there will often be a network of well-used paths. However, both the holes themselves and the spoil heaps are much smaller, and the real giveaway will be the presence of Rabbit droppings deposited in prominent places all around the warren itself.

The Rabbit is a social animal, often living in large groups within a burrow system called a warren.

The presence of lots of small entrances and the distinctive round droppings identify this as a woodland Rabbit warren.

When in grassy areas the short-cropped lawn of grass near the holes makes Rabbit activity identifiable even from a distance.

Rabbits are as much incessant nibblers as Badgers are diggers. The result of this Rabbit habit is that any nearby plants will be grazed tightly to the ground, forming close-cropped lawns. Rabbits like to be close to a bolt-hole if danger threatens, so grazing close to home is their preferred option. This has the added benefit of keeping a clear area around their burrows so that the residents will easily spot a predator.

Occasionally you may discover a shallow, single-entrance burrow known as a stop. This is a breeding burrow used by a female Rabbit to give birth and nurse her kits during the first few weeks of their lives. One of the things that make these stops so difficult to find is that the doe will carefully 'close the door' by filling it with soil, plant debris and nest material.

Fox

Foxes are generally much more opportunistic than other woodland animals, and as they are clearly not cut out for digging as are Badgers and Rabbits, they prefer to purloin a hole already in existence, enlarging a naturally occurring cavity or Rabbit burrow or sharing a portion of a Badger sett. This makes a hole in which a Fox is resident seem a little less easy to identify. What Foxes do have, however, is a total disregard for the housework.

Right and below: Foxes hole up in many different kinds of places – the smell of Fox droppings and food remains can usually be detected near a Fox hole.

Foxes, unlike Badgers, bring their meals home. A direct consequence of this, especially when there are cubs in residence, is that the areas surrounding a Fox earth are often littered with the cast-offs from their meals: bones, feathers and fur. These in turn attract blowflies, and on a warm summer's day, the place will literally be humming in both senses of the word, as flies and a distinct foxy smell permeate the air.

Another small but relevant difference between the housekeeping of Foxes and Badgers is that Foxes don't use bedding in their dens, so if you have a hole in front of you with evidence of fresh bedding around the entrance the chances are it isn't being used by a Fox.

Small mammals

Small mammals such as mice, voles, Moles and rats make smaller holes, as would be expected from their smaller stature.

Shrews don't often dig holes, but instead form runs along the surface of the soil underneath vegetation and litter.

Voles, especially Field Voles, make neat holes approximately 2–2.5cm in diameter; there will often be evidence of well-used runs nearby and maybe other clues such as nibbled grass stems and droppings.

Wood Mice also make small holes, and depending a little on what they are burrowing into, there is often a little spoil heap left outside. Having said this, I had a pair of Wood Mice in my garden

Above left: *Small holes made by small mammals are problematic to identify – size doesn't help a huge amount.*

Above right: *These vole runs were under a piece of tin in an open space – so almost certainly belong to Field Voles.*

Below left: *A Common Vole will dig a nest underground to store food, raise offspring and to rest.*

Below right: *If there has been a covering of snow, the voles can remain active beneath its security. It's only when this cover melts that the full network of runs is visible.*

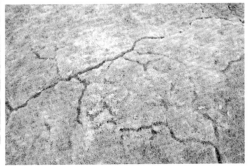

Wood Mice prefer hedgerows and woodlands with at least an element of a third dimension. They generally make their homes in the ground, but also settle in birds' nests and natural cavities.

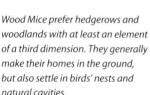

that excavated a huge spoil heap from a hole in a low-lying garden wall; I initially thought this was the work of rats, until I set up my trail camera and caught the pair hard at work.

Moles are one of the few small mammals whose signs almost anybody can identify. Their earthworks can be monumental for such a small animal, and they're one of the few mammals whose presence can be surveyed from a distance even from a moving car or train.

Directly below each conical Mole hill is a vertical tunnel that leads up from the horizontal tiers of burrows through which the Mole forces the loose soil excavated during the creation of his permanent tunnel system. The burrows are effectively traps for worms, which fall into them and are collected up by regularly patrolling Moles. The tunnel system is marked by the Mole hills and from a distance it is often possible to trace the rough outline of its extent by joining the dots. The size of the tunnel network is usually

Probably one of the most obvious and well-known mammal signs belongs to the Mole even though we rarely get to encounter this subterranean specialist.

Moles are most visible in pastures, where the short vegetation makes their activities most visible, but they are also abundant in woodland.

adjusted throughout the season, depending on temperature, moisture and food availability. During cold weather, heavy rains or very dry weather, soil invertebrates, especially earthworms, tend to go deeper or move and the Mole has to track with them, creating new or deeper tunnels – which is why we see more obvious Mole activity on the surface after such weather. Once a permanent system is established, assuming the weather is favourable for worms, Moles will slow down on Mole-hill production and eventually the spoil heaps will grow over or become dispersed by livestock.

Surface runs are sometimes visible and show where a Mole has run along just beneath the roots of vegetation. Occasionally, these will end when the Mole surfaces for a short while before diving back beneath the surface.

Look at a collection of Mole hills and you may be able to make out one or two, normally near the centre of the complex, that look considerably bigger than the rest; these signify the presence of the nest, which is usually situated deep within the subterranean maze. On shallow soils or those prone to flooding a larger hill is produced; a heap of more than 500kg of soil is termed a 'fortress', and it reflects the much bigger excavation project below ground. The fortress is a secure shelter above the level of the water table with the nest chamber often just below, at or even above the level of the surrounding ground.

While it is easy to locate Moles in areas of short grass, they are pretty widely spread and occur in other habitats, including woodland, where they are much less obvious. In pasture and rough grassland, where Moles travel just underneath the dense root mat, they push up a carpet of vegetation as they create temporary surface runs which show as distinctive ridges. These are usually used by the animals to survey pastures new or when they're in search of a mate. You may sometimes see an exit hole near the ridges where the Mole has popped out for a moment or two before descending into the loam again.

Mole activity such as this excavated surface run can sometimes be seen.

WHOSE HOLE – A QUICK GUIDE TO HOLE IDENTIFICATION

Shrews are often responsible for those random, loosely formed holes that just seem to pop up in soft soil, or more commonly in loose litter and moss.

Below: Water Voles' holes are quite distinctive. They can be confused with rat holes for size, but the presence of shredded and nibbled vegetation, often green droppings and burrowed runs is a giveaway.

Mice, voles and shrews

Small holes less than 3cm in diameter.

Rats and Water Voles

Holes 3cm up to about 7cm in diameter across. A rat hole tends to have a spoil heap that fans out from the entrance, while the holes of Water Voles are neater – both can be found by water courses.

Moles

Moles are almost always associated with 'Mole hills', the characteristic spoil heaps, or runs just under the surface. Occasionally they will exit the ground and leave a hole roughly oval in diameter and about 5cm across.

Rabbit

Rabbit holes are around 8–14cm in diameter across and can occur in many configurations, from singletons to vast warren systems with dozens of entrances, depending on the soil type and the size of the Rabbit population.

Badger

Badger holes are roughly semicircular and about 20–30cm across with large spoil heaps. Foxes, when they modify holes or dig their own, have smaller but rounder holes.

A Brown Rat burrow.

When a hole isn't a home

A disturbance of the soil, whether a scuff or a scrape, may have been left by someone's boot, or it may be the work of a wild animal. If you try to deduce the cause it'll help to hone your tracking skills, and you'll soon be able to recognise some of the more distinctive signs; others, however, are bound to remain a mystery…

Rabbits often scrape the surface of the soil, sometimes to get at roots and tubers, but more often than not this acts as a scent signpost, marked with glands between the toes and on the chin.

Badgers are the most tidy and hygienic of animals – tending to deposit their droppings more often than not in a small pit. These pits are often numerous at a latrine site, which is also usually connected to major pathways or even territory boundaries.

The size of a disturbance, of course, is always relevant; try to imagine how it was made. Was it created by pushing into the ground or was material excavated? Are there any signs of twisting? Maybe there are some other clues, fragments of food, footprints? Have a look around; sometimes there will be more obvious scrapes nearby.

Badgers

A frequently encountered scraped and scented signpost is left by Badgers in the form of a latrine. These mammals are highly territorial and mark their boundaries and paths with their latrines, which are so much more than a hygienic and neat way of answering the call of nature.

A Badger latrine is a shallow pit in which the animals deposit their scat

as well as secretions from anal glands which give others not just the information about who has been there, but also what sex they are, and whether they are in the mood for love and in breeding condition, and providing a clue as to when the message was left. So a latrine acts like a Facebook status update for other Badgers.

Sometimes Badgers leave distinctive little twists, known as snuffle holes. Here you can see where the snout has been forced through the grass and a worm has been slurped from its hole. You can see the worm's hole in the centre.

Above and below: Badgers disturb the surface of soil while feeding. It's not uncommon to see the turf torn up as an animal has systematically forged for worms or beetle larvae.

Feeding signs left by Badgers often involve quite a lot of scraping and shovelling, and can take on many forms befitting their eclectic diet. Worms, for the most part, are hoovered up like spaghetti, but just occasionally a worm or a beetle may be tangled up in roots. The Badger then has to work a little harder, pushing his tough but flexible snout deep and forcing his way into the ground. This activity, often accompanied by a twist of the head, produces distinctive 'twisted' holes in pastures called 'snuffle holes' (as the Badger huffs and puffs a lot when making them). In a woodland, the sign is less distinctive and any disturbance looks a little as though a small child has kicked his or her way through the leaves.

Badgers also investigate any other edible objects, from plant tubers such as Pignut, to subterranean bee and wasp nests – the excavation of these using the claws on their front feet can be pretty spectacular.

Rabbits and hares

Rabbits are also territorial beasts, and during the breeding season from early spring they get really feisty and the dominant males turn up their territorial activity. This involves the distribution of scent, particularly urine and droppings, which are often deposited in conspicuous places, including shallow scrapes. Rabbits also make scrapes when feeding, to access particularly tasty roots or tubers. The scrapes are usually quite shallow and have a smooth, neat look to them, with the signature pellets nearby.

Not all holes are to be lived in. Some animals such as Rabbits will dig for food or even for social purposes

Hares make many similar scrapes, especially while feeding, and instead of a burrow they construct a form; sometimes this is no more than a little hare-shaped dent in the ground or surface vegetation, or a shallow scrape made in the soil.

Squirrels

In winter, squirrel diggings are a common sight and can occur anywhere from lawns to woodland. A squirrel questing for an old food cache that it hid back in the autumn will make a fairly deliberate excavation. This is not very deep, but material pushed backwards by the animal's forepaws will usually be evident. Sometimes, if it was relaxed while it was foraging or if its food was spoiled, evidence of the stash will be present.

Squirrels will return to dig up acorns and nuts they have previously buried; this is most obvious when they've chosen the really short grass of your lawn.

Few animals possess the bulldozer-like qualities of the Wild Boar.

Here Wild Boar have worked their way along a path, lifting the turf with their snouts as they rooted for tubers, roots and invertebrates.

The key to this foraging is the very sensitive and flexible snout.

Wild Boar

Large animals such as Wild Boar and deer also make scrapes in the soil. A Wild Boar is the mammal equivalent of a bulldozer, and it will practically deturf an area in pursuit of roots, tubers and other edibles such as worms and insect larvae. With their heads down, boar systematically work over an area, pushing their snouts through the soil or leaf litter and leaving wide furrows. While they usually forage in patches of suitable ground, looking for wind-fallen fruit, and acorns and beechmast in the autumn and winter, they are also capable of ploughing large areas that prove particularly productive for food.

These dents in the landscape are scent baths for stags. During the rut, urine and soil is mixed then rolled and scraped about, which is the stags' way of making themselves smell good for the females.

Deer

Deer are smelly animals and tend to have numerous scent glands, the oily products of which are smeared and scraped over their habitats and bodies. During the rutting season Sika and Red Deer create churned-up 'wallows' in damp ground in which they urinate and smear their scent.

Fallow, Roe, Red, Sika and, to a lesser extent, Muntjac Deer scrape up the ground by pawing at it with their feet. The animals have scent glands between their toes, and the act of breaking up the soil surface undoubtedly distributes their smell. They may also urinate in the scrape, then rub their heads and antlers (further messing up the ground) in the loose soil to anoint their bodies. When feeding, deer create surface scrapes to access such tasty morsels as roots, tubers and fungi.

Here's a buck in the process of anointing himself with a heady mixture of dirt, his own urine and glandular perfume; the ladies will love him.

Bird holes

Beaks are handy tools for poking and prodding, and some birds even use them to chisel and pick out a home. These workings, whether large productions such as nest holes in trees and banks, or smaller, more subtle dents and depressions in soil, estuarine mud or cowpats, tell us loads about what has been going on: who's been working it and what they've been working it for.

A perforated bank, the perfect tenement for the colonial-nesting Sand Martins.

Holes in steep banks

Steep, eroded river banks are worth checking out for the nest burrows of one of Europe's most dazzling birds, the Kingfisher.

There is a handful of birds that excavate their nesting chambers in soil. Sand Martins need soft, easily excavated cliffs that are near vertical, a specialised requirement only found in areas of landslip, quarries and river banks. As the birds nest colonially their nest-sites are usually obvious at the height of the breeding season.

Single holes in river banks, usually high above the water line, are made by Kingfishers. They dig tunnels, some nearly a metre deep, using their bills as picks, then use their feet to pull out the loosened soil. They usually select near-vertical banks where the digging is easy. The ones I've found are most frequently under an overhang of some kind above slow-moving water. Watching from a distance will confirm whether your hole has Kingfishers resident; I've also found that the presence of flies buzzing around the hole usually means it's occupied.

Marks in the mud

Head to an estuary on a cold winter's day at low tide and the exposed mudflats will be heaving with all manner of different species of wading bird – from Sanderling to Curlew they are all out there, shoving their bills and beaks into the sediment. If you really watch the birds' feeding behaviour, you will soon start unravelling the marks left behind in the mud.

Different bills and a diverse number of strategies are employed to outwit the worms and other animals with a sedimentary life. Bills can leave lots of different holes in the surface of mud, and what remains very much depends on the nature of the mud.

The regular 'stitching' marks left by many small species of wader, especially Knot and Dunlin, are very distinctive. One of their feeding strategies is to randomly probe as they go, looking to touch and somehow sense a prey item below the mud like a very repetitive lucky dip. The marks left, accompanied by the tracks of their feet, form a line of evenly spaced sets of paired holes, representing the upper and lower halves of the bill as it is pushed into the mud. Other distinctive feeding signs that you may also stumble upon are the scything marks left by Shelduck sifting for *Hydrobia*, or displacements in the mud made by puddling with their feet to stir up food.

Wading birds make a living probing the mud and sand for invertebrate food – this line of holes shows where a Dunlin stitched its way along.

Above: *Dunlin will methodically pick food items such as insects, marine worms and small crustaceans from the shore.*

Left: *Shelduck feed on invertebrates and algae living and growing on the surface, usually harvested by side-to-side sweeps of the bill, which leaves a very clear and distinctive pattern.*

Pecked holes in wood

Woodpeckers are the largest bird carpenters, and there are three species in the UK and a further seven species on the Continent. All are equipped with specialised equipment in the form of a sharp and powerful bill and protective head gear, not to mention highly modified tail feathers, feet and claws that are all designed to enable these birds to rip asunder the wood fibres of trees.

They do this for two reasons: first, to access and eat the many insects that also live in and feed on the wood; and second, they chisel and chip away with great precision in order to create their own nest cavities, an ability that really does set them apart from other birds. In so doing, they benefit many other woodland animals, from bats to squirrels and other birds.

So, if you see a hole in a tree, you can be pretty sure that it was made by a woodpecker. The only other woodland birds that excavate their own nest cavities are Willow Tits and, in Scotland and continental Europe, Crested Tits. Obviously these small birds don't have the robustness of the woodpeckers. They tend to concentrate on really soft, rotten wood, particularly old tree stumps, so they often nest close to the ground. A pair of birds works together, removing fragments of wood and carrying them far from the nest.

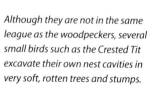

These are nesting holes or speculative holes made by a Great Spotted Woodpecker – it's difficult to know which without climbing the tree.

Although they are not in the same league as the woodpeckers, several small birds such as the Crested Tit excavate their own nest cavities in very soft, rotten trees and stumps.

Feeding signs The beak of a woodpecker is quite robust and in profile looks like a chisel turned on its edge. When a woodpecker is feeding it may get lucky and reach a grub with an exploratory peck, leaving a hole taller than it is wide, but at other times the bird repeatedly hammers away at a spot, resulting in damage to the surface of the wood. More often than not this can be seen at a distance and looks quite neat, but up close the edges of the holes are quite ragged. If it's a fresh hole there will be evidence of wood chippings immediately below.

Woodpeckers also make small holes when feeding; pock marks and chiselled holes show where a bird has been accessing grubs beneath the bark.

Occasionally woodpeckers, particularly Great Spotted, engage in a habit known as 'ringing', which is when a bird creates a ring of 'wells' spaced out around the trunk of a tree. The birds will frequently revisit these sites to drink the sap exuded from the wounds in the bark.

Nest-holes The nest-holes of woodpeckers are quite easy to identify as they are usually perfectly round apertures (although the hole of the Black Woodpecker, not a UK species, is usually more oval), with a diameter that varies between species. Not only are they the only birds that can truly excavate a hole in a tree, but they do it with such precision that their neat work should be almost instantly recognisable. The only real challenge left for the nature detective is to guess which species made the hole.

Rarely recorded is the 'sap-sucking' behaviour of the Great Spotted Woodpecker, which leaves rows of neat holes in thin bark.

Dead wood is softer and usually much easier to excavate than sound timber, and most species make the most of this and concentrate on dead timber if they can. Both the Great Spotted and Black Woodpecker, however, can and will tackle the wood of healthy trees.

The perfect nest site is as high as possible in a tree that is still living, so the surface of the wood has integrity and support, but with a touch of rot in the heartwood which makes for easy digging. The location of the hole is usually high off the ground and on the side most sheltered from the prevailing elements. In hilly terrain, south-facing aspects are preferred.

Woodpeckers create more than one nest site in their territories, presumably to use as roost sites too. They also make exploratory holes, and it is not uncommon to find the beginnings of a hole that has been abandoned – either because the wood was too hard or some other factor was not to the bird's liking.

Above and right: Look at the nice, neat chiselled nest-holes of both Black and Great Spotted Woodpeckers – typical workmanship of this family.

A guide to nest-holes made by birds

Species	Hole shape and dimensions
Black Woodpecker *(Dryocopus martius)*, not a UK species	oval – 1150 x 1000mm
Green Woodpecker *(Picus viridis)*	oval – 75 x 65mm
Great Spotted Woodpecker *(Dendrocopos major)*	round – 55mm across
Lesser Spotted Woodpecker *(Dendrocopos minor)*	round – 35mm across
Willow Tit *(Poecile montanus)* /Crested Tit *(Lophophanes cristatus)*	round – 25mm across

Arthropod holes

Holes smaller than the diameter of your little finger (less than a centimetre), no matter what they are dug into, will almost certainly have been made by an insect or other invertebrate. Many species create burrows, either as a retreat and permanent home or as a nest site. Some also make exit holes that are only used once as the animal emerges from a dormant stage in its life cycle, as in the case of a subterranean pupa.

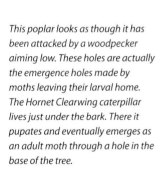

This poplar looks as though it has been attacked by a woodpecker aiming low. These holes are actually the emergence holes made by moths leaving their larval home. The Hornet Clearwing caterpillar lives just under the bark. There it pupates and eventually emerges as an adult moth through a hole in the base of the tree.

Tiny holes in the soil

The huge number and diversity of invertebrates obviously gives us an equally high number of possibilities when it comes to the process of matching a sign to the maker. However, there is a surprising number of hole- and burrow-making spineless operators out there that do have a recognisable modus operandi, so while we may not be able to nail an animal down at a species level, we can certainly have a good guess at this.

Holes made by invertebrates in the soil may come with adornments such as debris, silk or mucus, and there may or may not be evidence of some kind of spoil. As ever size and shape can give us some clues, but if you thought you were straining your eyes and your dedication trying to identify the holes of mammals, then these little spineless wonders will really test you.

Exposed soil such as that found at the edges of paths or at sites of erosion is a great place to find the holes of many sun-loving insects.

These perfectly circular front doors belong to the veracious predatory larvae of the Green Tiger Beetle.

Unadorned holes

So you're looking at a perfect portal into the underworld; how on Earth do you identify who made it? As always context has as much to do with it as size and shape.

Bare soil is a rare commodity in nature, and if it does occur, it's usually a temporary thing. Shores, cliffs, dunes and the edges of lakes and rivers are all providers of natural areas of exposed soil, and our footpaths also provide bare soil environments. These are all places where small animals can create their burrows.

Tiger beetles The neat, rounded holes made by the larvae of tiger beetles (we have five species in the UK) are frequently found on the edges of paths. They are the entrances to neat and uniform vertical shafts in which the beetle larvae live. The size of the hole changes as the larva progresses through its various moults and becomes increasingly bigger – the hole of a fully grown larva will be around 5mm across.

The holes may appear empty, but shine a torch down into the depths and you may just make out the twinkle of an eye or see some movement. If you gently push a little loose sand into the hole and patiently wait, you may be greeted with a curiously odd

and flattened head that acts as a spring-loaded excavation tool (it'll fling the sand and debris back out at you), a door to plug the entrance of the hole and an insect death trap.

These beetle larvae are voracious predators – they sit in their doorways and wait for their prey to amble past. Their numerous eyes, arranged around the fringe of the head disk, allow 360-degree vision, and their jaws and lightning quick reflexes enable them to capture their prey. If you see the dry and empty husks of past dinners in the form of dead flies, beetles and ants lying discarded in the vicinity of the holes, then you can be fairly sure that tiger beetle larvae are present.

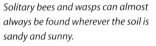

Solitary bees and wasps can almost always be found wherever the soil is sandy and sunny.

Spend enough time watching these holes during the spring and summer and you'll most likely see the makers coming and going, and maybe even excavating new holes, by dragging and flicking away sand from the burrow entrance.

Bees and wasps The majority of bees and wasps are solitary and don't live in busy, highly organised colonies. Instead, they quietly go about the business of making a nest, which usually comprises individual cells into each of which a single egg is placed complete with provisions. If it's a wasp, some unfortunate insect or invertebrate will be provided, but if it's a bee, the vegan option is taken and the egg is provided with pollen or nectar. Some species use natural cavities, while others dig out their own.

As a rule, the holes of these insects are not quite as tidy as those of tiger beetles; the entrance is often less uniform and smooth at the edges, and if you peer into it, the tunnel is rarely straight and varies in width along its length. The majority of adult bees and wasps dig their holes quickly, then rush to stuff them with eggs and food. Unlike tiger beetles, they are not building a permanent home, but merely constructing a bunker of sorts to safely contain the developing young.

The hole of a solitary wasp or bee is also called a cell. The female lays one egg in the cell, leaves food for the larva, then seals off the hole.

Any small hole could easily belong to one of the many species of solitary bee (more than 200 in the UK) and wasp (about 2,400). Some may create a spoil heap or even seal the hole when they are not present. Others back out of their hole and with rapid kicking motions of their legs fling the excavated dirt to the four winds leaving no visible trace. Several of the larger sand wasps (*Ammophila*) scatter, rake out and even carry away any excavated debris. For reasons unknown, some of the solitary wasps occasionally abandon the bodies of their prey nearby, which can be a big clue as to the identity of the hole maker (see chart below).

Solitary wasps and bees usually dig holes in the ground, but will also tunnel in wood, branches and hollow reeds.

Hole-in-the-ground-nesting solitary wasps

The wasps	Prey
Spider wasps (pompilids)	Spiders
Small spider hunters (*Miscophus*)	Spiders
Various sphecids wasps	Grasshoppers and crickets
Various digger wasps (*Alysson, Crossocerus, Diodontus, Gorytes, Psen*)	Shield-winged bugs (Homoptera)
Various digger wasps (*Astata, Dinetus, Lindenius*)	Other bugs (Heteroptera)
Various digger wasps (*Bembix, Crabro, Crossocerus, Lindenius, Mellinus, Oxybelus*)	Flies
Cavity-living potter wasps (*Ancistrocerus*), weevil wasps (*Cerceris*), *Entomognathus, Gymnomerus, Methocha*), mason wasps (*Odynerus*)	Beetles
Sand wasps (*Ammophila, Podalonia, Pseudepipona*), cavity-living potter wasps (*Ancistoderus*)	Caterpillars of moths and butterflies
Digger wasp (*Cerceris*), beewolves (*Philanthus*)	Ants, bees and wasps

Identifying the insects that make these holes is a specialist skill in its own right.

Odd holes

A collection of holes of varying sizes, some elongated where several have joined up or collapsed into one another, sometimes with maybe a trace of fine excavated soil nearby, are nearly always the workings of ants. Once they've put down tools and moved on, they often leave these mysterious perforations behind them.

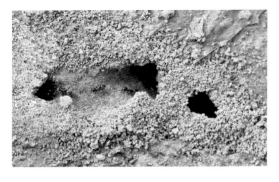

Less defined than those of solitary bees and wasps are the holes made by ants. Usually they are not as uniform in shape.

Adorned holes

If a hole you are looking at isn't literally just a hole but has certain embellishments around it, such as a spoil heap or some debris, maybe even traces of silk, here are some pointers to help you work out who the owner is.

The earthworm is one of the most numerous of the burrowing animals. There are loads of different species of soil-dwelling worm, but only a few of them give away their presence with a cast. They can be broken down into four main groups or ecotypes, but it's the anecic worms that actually live in burrows in the soil. A worm cast has passed through the cylindrical body of a worm as it digs, and if it's next to a hole this probably belongs to those worms that make permanent vertical burrows in the soil, such as the biggest worm in the UK: *Lumbricus terrestris*. These worms are plentiful under nicely balanced and unimproved pastures and lawns, which is why Badgers, Hedgehogs, Moles and other wildlife also like these areas.

The worm cast is a well-known adornment and a giveaway that the burrow is just below the surface.

Worms will also at times of plenty create quite elaborate middens; these depend on what dead or dying plant material is lying around on the surface. A worm will reach out of its burrow and grasp with its mouth any organic debris, such as moss, small sticks and leaf fragments, and pull it into the burrow to consume later.

A hole near a dropping is a good sign that you've found the burrow of one of the dung beetles, the most common of which is the Dor Beetle.

Dor Beetles have a varied taste when it comes to dung. One here has been busy recycling sheep droppings.

In the autumn, when there are lots of big leaves lying around, these worms drag entire leaves into the entrances to their burrows. The leaves are rolled up neatly and look like tiny cigars that have been bunged down holes in the grass. This aeration process is excellent for the soil and the health of your plants.

Pungent holes

Other animals whose burrows are commonly encountered include various adult beetles. While many species of ground beetle make a hole to hide in, others are much more industrious, and the most impressive and frequently seen holes are constructed by those incessant recyclers of unpleasant things, the dung beetles. Probably the most common are the bumbling Dor Beetles, which are black with polychromatic purple highlights. They make neat round holes about 8–10mm across, usually sited close to dung. Being one of the less fussy varieties of beetle, the dung can belong to almost any animal, though they prefer the dung of herbivores. I have even seen them dragging bits of Fox dung containing the remains of their own kind deep into their chambers. The surface hole leads to a vertical shaft that splits into others, at the end of which nursery chambers are created in which chunks of dung are placed for the developing grubs. You may also see holes of the Minotaur Beetle, which is particularly fond of Rabbit droppings, and the Rhino Beetle, which likes cattle dung and is found in the south of the UK and on the Continent.

Mini-volcanoes

Little volcanoes of soil that spring up, again in areas of warm, bare terrain or very short grass, are probably the work of another family of solitary bee, known as the mining bees. These little bees belong to the *Andrena* genus, and we have about 80 species in the UK. One of the larger ones, the Tawny Mining Bee, is usually fairly apparent during the spring, mainly because it prefers sunny, short lawns. A bee usually has its hole in the centre, while the solitary wasps that make spoil heaps tend to push their spoil out in one direction, so the hole is to one side of the excavated material.

Left: *Mining bees, dig holes where the ground is exposed or the grass is short – you can just make out the entrance hole at the top right.*

Below: *Ants make little 'volcanoes' of spoil around a central hole – usually this spoil is very uniform in particle size and is dry.*

Ants create similar-looking spoil heaps that consist of uniform and fine particles, but are much flatter in cross-section than the heap of a mining bee.

Different species of ant have very specific habitats and nesting habits, and it is possible (though beyond the remit of this book) to recognise a species by the shape, style and position of its workings. Ants like sunny spots and in the wild and in gardens, many species use stones as a kind of storage heater. Spoil heaps near paving slabs are usually signs that ants have been at work.

Cone-shaped dents

Cone-shaped depressions in dry and fine, sandy soil are the mark of a very ingenious insect. The Antlion is, as its name suggests, an extremely efficient predator of ants. It is the larva of a lacewing-like insect (sometimes called a Doodlebug) and though quite rare in the UK – it is only found in a few coastal localities in the southeast, Norfolk and Suffolk – it is much more common on the Continent. Antlions are fascinating and may start to spread with climate change.

The odd-shaped larvae of an Antlion sits at the bottom of the trap with just its mandibles and eyes showing. If an ant falls into the trap it will flick sand at it to bring the unfortunate insect within grasp of the jaws.

In a few parts of the UK and on the Continent – small, conical dents may be found. These are the ingenious ant traps constructed by the larvae of the Antlion or Doodlebug.

The distinctive conical pits, usually in colonies, are made by the larvae in areas of fine, sandy soil, and while there is no hole involved, the pits are very obvious once you've tuned in to what they look like. Their size varies depending on the age of the larva in residence, but a large pit is no more than 25mm across the top from lip to lip. The larva sits buried at the bottom waiting for an unsuspecting ant. When one stumbles close to the lip of the pit, it flings sand particles at it, knocking it in. When the ant comes into reach of its ludicrously long jaws it is grabbed and dragged to its doom, only to re-emerge again as a dry husk, which is then flung out of the pit. You can carefully scoop out a larva with a spoon if you want to have a close look (it will freeze and look just like a small pebble), before replacing it where you found it.

A beautiful elegant adult Antlion is completely different from its aggressive, dumpy and ugly babies.

Left: *If in doubt about who made this heap of fine vegetation, twigs and needles – get up close. These massive mounds found in woodlands are the homes of wood ants and play an important role in maintaining optimum environmental conditions within the nest.*

Massive mounds

Many ants create much bigger mounds than the ones described so far, for example the massive thatches made by wood ants from pine needles and wood chippings, found in forest glades. Some can be over a metre high and a couple of metres across at the base, and during periods of activity in spring and summer it should be fairly obvious whose hill it is by the presence of seething masses of ants crawling about on its surface. Ants that make these hills do so as a way of controlling the temperature of the nest, and they move their brood up and down to whichever spot suits their development best.

Meadow ants make smaller hills as they are made mainly of soil particles. As in the case of wood ants they are often permanent hills and can persist for years. You may mistake these grassy lumps for old Mole hills, but they usually have a good cover of meadow grass and other vegetation growing over them. In fact, these grassy hillocks often look like the perfect place to park your bottom if you are on a picnic. Pretty soon, however, thousands of tiny yellow-orange ants will come pouring out, clearly displeased that you've sat on their tenement. These hills are actually quite distinctive once you've got your eye in and often exist in groups. In Europe, they can be indicators of a good unimproved meadow.

Above: *These little yellow-orange ants are Yellow Meadow Ants, one of the most common ant species in Central Europe.*

Below: *Yellow Meadow Ants form long-lived colonies that in undisturbed pasture form a strange undulating landscape of humps and hillocks.*

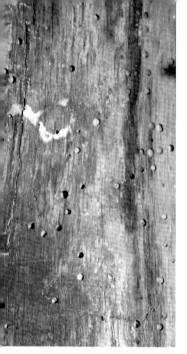

Holes in wood

Earlier in the chapter we saw how wood is used by birds; it is also used by a whole host of other animals, plants, fungi and bacteria as food or as a safe and insulated place to nest or roost. The most obvious signs of use are holes in wood – the golden rule is that an animal going in shoves any sawdust out behind it whereas an animal that's emerging doesn't.

Boring bugs

Small holes in wood are usually made by the larval stages of a range of insects – generally those of various beetles and a handful of specialised moths and wasps.

Most of the holes you will find will be perfectly round, tiny perforations, and will have been made by the insects emerging from the piece of wood in which they grew up. These are exit holes, and other than a little wood dust there will be little else in the way of clues. It is possible to narrow down or eliminate some species by looking at not only the diameter of these exit holes, but also the type of wood, the part of the tree the wood originated from, the approximate age of the timber and whether it is still alive (see pages 148–149).

Many insects make holes in wood for various reasons – these are the emergence holes through which the Death Watch Beetles exited.

In roof spaces where furniture beetles are attacking the rafters, you may find a light sprinkling of dust. If there is a large amount of sawdust, however, then the furniture beetles and their larvae may themselves be under attack. Chalcids – little parasitic wasps – sometimes prey on the developing larvae by entering their tunnels and kicking out the loose sawdust backwards through the exit holes.

A view into its room. Here a cutaway of a Longhorn Beetle's larva tunnel shows not only the grub in situ busy chewing through the dead wood, but also the fine dusty droppings or frass.

Mighty moths

Moths may seem too delicate to take on the hard stuff, and their caterpillars seem hardly any better equipped for chewing through wood. Having said this, there is a handful of species that are wood-chomping specialists.

The clearwings mostly tackle woody plant stems, but the two largest members of this family have larvae which feed under the bark and into the wood of large trees, normally members of the willow family. Their emergence holes are around 10mm in diameter.

Above and below: *Several moth caterpillars live within the stems and trunks of woody plants – the largest is the Goat Moth larva, which only becomes apparent when it emerges from the wood, leaving a characteristic hole, with pupa skin in place, as well as a distinctive smell – often described as like that of a billy goat.*

It is the Goat Moth that is a true wood turner. Its enormous caterpillars leave 20mm emergence holes – one of the largest insect emergence holes you are likely to see. They are often low down on mature trees, usually willows, poplars and oaks, and there may be several other signs present including the remains of the pupa case, which if fresh will be left sticking out of the hole, frass, coarse sawdust, the presence of silk and, in very fresh examples if you get down and give the hole a sniff, you might just get the whiff of billy goat and understand how this moth got its common name.

The Goat Moth is becoming increasingly scarce, and it is well worth recording any instances you have for suspecting its presence and letting your local moth recorder or Wildlife Trust know of your findings.

Carpenter bees

On the Continent and occasionally in the UK, a rather spectacular, solitary bee cuts its own cavities in dead wood. The biggest members of this family, looking like huge black bumblebees with an iridescent purple sheen, are unmistakable. They create very large and neat holes that are 10–12mm in diameter with a chamfered edge to the lip. These bees are solitary, but they will form colonies where the wood is of the right consistency. When the carpentry is fresh there is usually evidence of sawdust and wood fibres below the opening.

Carpenter bees chew holes in wood in which to nest.

A guide to commonly found insect holes

Shape of hole	Dimensions	Type of wood/sign	Species
Round with jagged edge	20mm	Moist but dead wood, usually willow or poplar. Evidence of frass, sawdust, silk, pupal case and even odour	Goat Moth *(Cossus cossus)*
Oval	15mm	Willow/poplar and aspen	Poplar Borer *(Saperda carcharias)*, a kind of longhorn beetle
Oval	Larger than 15mm	Willow	Musk beetle *(Aromia moschata)*, a kind of longhorn beetle
Round with jagged edge	About 10mm	Mainly in willow; may be evidence of frass, sawdust, silk and even pupal case	Hornet Moth or Lunar Hornet Clearwing Moth *(Sesia apiformes)*
Neat and perfectly round	10mm	Heart and sapwood of conifers only	Wood wasps (Symphyta)
Rounded, often opens through bark	5–8mm	Conifer bark and sapwood	Pine Sawyer *(Ergates spiculatus)* a kind of longhorn beetle
Rounded, often opens through bark	5–8 mm	Mainly in the roots of dead and dying trees	Tanner Beetle *(Prionus coriarius)*
Oval	6 x 3mm	Softwood with bark on; tunnel full of wood dust with pale and dark particles	Violet Longhorn Beetle *(Callidium violaceum)*
Oval	6 x 3mm	Sapwood of softwoods; tunnels are full of uniform-coloured wood dust and cylindrical sausage-shaped frass	House Longhorn Beetle *(Hylotrupes bajulus)*
Irregular and oval	6mm	Feeds on damp softwood timber	Wharf Borer *(Narcerdes melaura)*

Pine Sawyer

Wood Wasp

Shape of hole	Dimensions	Type of wood/sign	Species
Rounded	3–5mm	Oak damaged by damp, lens-shaped frass is obvious to the naked eye	Death-watch Beetle (*Xestobium rufovillosum*)
Roundish but with a ragged edge	1–2mm	Damp dead timber with very coarse wood dust that feels gritty	Wood-boring weevils (*Pentarthrum* and *Euophryum*) – larvae and adults
Round	1.5–2 mm	Eclectic taste in hard and softwoods; prefers sapwood; burrows along the grain; dust is a little gritty between fingers; cigar-shaped frass; shallow burrows	Common Furniture Beetle or Woodworm (*Anobium punctatum*)
Round with jagged edge	2mm	Softwood with bark present; burrows mainly in the bark; light and dark, bun-shaped pellets	Waney Edge Borer (*Ernobius mollis*)
Round	1.5–2mm	All woods, but only occurs in the wild. Burrows are deep – a pin will go in a long way; this distinguishes it from Furniture Beetle	Ambrosia beetles (Platypodidae and Scolytidae)
Round	1mm & less	Associated with Furniture Beetle holes	Chalcids – parasitic wasps that prey on the Furniture Beetle grubs
Round	1–1.5mm	Sapwood of oak; very fine, talcum-powder-like dust; needs high starch content, so very old wood is not attacked	Powder Post Beetle (*Lyctus brunneus*)
Round	1.5mm	Found only in Ash and emerges through bark. Dark wood dust can be seen if bark is peeled off	Ash bark beetles (*Leperisinus varius*)

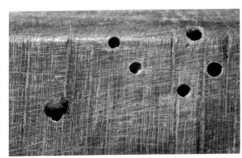

Common Furniture Beetle

Lunar Hornet

Wood carvings

Flick the bark off a dead tree and you will sometimes be rewarded by some of the most beautiful wood carvings in nature – these ornate and often symmetrical designs are left by the grubs and females of bark beetles. The adults are small, unassuming and easily overlooked little brown things.

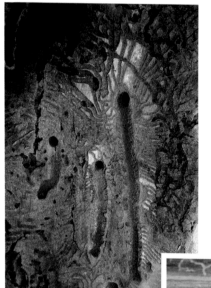

A female beetle bores through the bark and gouges out a mating chamber in the surface of the cambium or sapwood. Once she's met the beetle of her dreams, she heads off under the bark creating a deeper and thicker groove called the egg gallery. As the female digs she makes small niches at regular intervals along the tunnel, and into each of these she lays an egg. In time each of these eggs hatches and the grub heads off at a given angle away from the groove made by its mother. Cleverly, the grubs never bump into each other and always eat through fresh wood. As a grub progresses through the sapwood it grows, so that the radiating veins of the design get wider as it moves away from the egg gallery.

On the surface no more than a few holes are visible, but lift the bark and a complex arrangement of larval galleries is often revealed.

The shape, size and arrangement of these galleries is often specific to the species that made them. In this example the Maple Ips Beetle has been at work.

Each of these larval galleries ends in a chamber slightly wider than the feeding groove, where the grub settles down to pupate. When ready the new generation of adult beetles emerges through the bark, creating a distinctive pattern of 'shot holes'. This emergence pattern, the direction of the egg gallery, whether across the grain or with it, as well as the angle and number of larval tunnels and, of course, the species of tree, can all give us clues as to which species of bark beetle was involved.

Other holes and cavities

Fairly frequently I find evidence of holes and burrows belonging to various solitary bees and wasps, which have their entrances stuffed with debris – sometimes leaves, sometimes mud – and in many instances where these holes are in the ends of plant stems, or in loose masonry and mortar, it is quite difficult to ascertain whether the holes are natural or excavated. In most cases the answer is often a bit of both.

Leaf-cutter bees nest in tunnels in wood, often using those excavated by others.

Mason bees, particularly the common European Red Mason Bee, specialise in nesting within the tube cavities found in plant stems, holes in mortar and even the exit holes of large wood-boring beetles. They are very noticeable in sunny spring weather as the bees provision their cells, each divided from the other in the 'stack' by mud. Once complete each nesting hole is sealed with a thicker plug of mud. Common Leaf-cutter Bees are another noticeable common species, frequenting gardens, and they make similar nests.

There are far too many other species of solitary bee and wasp to mention, but many of them nest in cavities and holes that fit their individual requirements. Some only nest in plant stems or abandoned snail shells, while others are a little more flexible in their preferences. Nest-lining materials vary, too, according to the species, but often the only way to be certain of an identity is to catch the adult insects and use a specialised book to work them out.

The mason bee is another cavity nest builder, and will often use existing hollow stems or emergence holes of other insects.

Many well-known social bees and wasps also utilise natural cavities, including all the common bumblebees, which seek out disused small-mammal burrows. Species such as Hornets and other traditional tree-cavity nesters set up shop anywhere that fits their needs – a wood-lined cavity, insulated from extremes of temperature and sheltered from inclement weather, such as a roof space or garden shed, is often all that is required.

Marine wood

In coastal areas, wood is just as desirable to other animals for food or shelter as it is inland. Two coastal wood borers have fantastic names: the gribbles and the piddocks (boring piddocks at that).

Gribbles are tiny crustaceans that look like rounded woodlice, and at about 4mm long they are easy to miss. The combined efforts of thousands of these little wood eaters, however, can be quite impressive. Gribbles bore fine little tunnels into soft wet wood, feeding as they go; each gribble burrow is only about 2–3mm in diameter. These tunnels run just under and parallel to the surface of the wood, and every now and again a gribble makes a ventilation shaft back to the surface. A piece of timber that has been attacked by gribbles looks like a sponge. Although the animals bore into sound surface wood, in time this crumbles away and they start on the next layer. It is said that soft wood pilings can lose more than 2.5cm a year in diameter from the actions of these little marine animals.

This little crustacean – the gribble – is responsible for recycling driftwood, but will unfortunately also turn its attention to piers and pilings.

If the holes seem much wider (about 12–15mm), then you are probably looking at the work of a strange little mollusc called a shipworm. They are rarely seen as they spend all their lives in their burrows, but if you could exhume one it would look like an odd worm with a crash helmet on.

In fact shipworms, along with the closely related piddocks, abuse their shells by using them not as protective abodes but in exactly the same way you might use a drill bit. The sharp and hard shell is rammed and twisted into the wood, allowing the mollusc to work its way through all but the hardest of hardwoods.

The gribble is responsible for the fine spongy quality of many bits of wood that have spent time in or near saltwater.

The piddock is a tough little snail that uses its shell like a drill bit.

The holes left by shipworms literally become the shells because as they burrow into the interior of the wood, shipworms line the tube they create with calcareous porcelain. This smooth but hard lining protects the delicate worm-like body of the mollusc and is often evident where the burrows are exposed in shipworm-riddled timber. A complete shipworm burrow often has a hardened valve or palate, which forms an attachment for the mollusc at the surface and can be opened and closed, allowing the animal to flush the burrow with water or close it off if it becomes exposed at low tides.

There are several species of piddock in Europe, which have recognisable shells. They still use them as a drill bit but, unlike the shipworms that feed on the wood particles as well as doing a bit of filter-feeding, piddocks use the wood simply as a refuge and create quite large holes.

The Wharf Borer is a beetle which, though occurring inland as well, makes its best living at the coast in wood that has been exposed to salt water. This large beetle's larvae work their way through wood creating burrows and galleries. When they emerge as adults their exit holes often have a characteristic oval shape.

The shipworm is not a worm at all, but a mollusc with a body too big for its shell. It lines its burrows with a hard calcium compound and uses its shell to drill its progress through the wood.

Small holes in sand and on the shore

Sandy and muddy shores are usually rich in resources for animals that make a living filter-feeding because food is brought in on every tide. What they lack, however, are places to hide both from predators and from the sun and wind, so most animals that live here have no choice but to disappear beneath the surface of the sands.

Just like their terrestrial counterparts, lugworms produce a squiggly cast at one end of their U-shaped burrows.

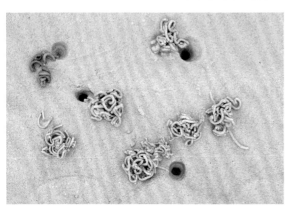

Our coastal environments are places for tunnel diggers and burrowers. The trouble for the nature detective is that there are so many mud lovers out there that the various etchings and hieroglyphics left on the surface by those in residence below can be a little confusing.

It's the burrows made by worms that are usually the first ones to be noticed, especially as some resemble those made by species found under your lawn. The wiggly casts made of sand and fine silt are mainly produced by **lugworms**. The worms themselves don't live in vertical burrows as do the earthworms in your garden, but rather in a U-shaped home. These burrows are permanent (the worms may live for more than 10 years), and the worms move backwards and forwards within them. The cast is left by the rear end of the worm, and if you look around each cast you should see a shallow impression that is often easier to see when the sun is low. This marks the head of the beast and is made when the worm sucks in new sand to process for organic material.

A small depression in the sand is the only visible sign of a cockle once it has burrowed under the surface. One of its circular siphons, used for breathing and feeding, is clearly visible here.

When it comes to unadorned holes and diggings, things get a little trickier. Sometimes all that gives away the presence of a beast below is a simple dent or depression that could have been made by anything from a sea potato to a small clam or cockle.

At low tides on some muddy beaches, the oval or keyhole shapes made by razor shells can be seen. These are shaped by the siphon that the animal sends to the surface when it's covered by water at high tide.

You may come across the strange star-shaped etchings made by filter-feeding molluscs belonging to the tellin family. At high tide these animals send skinny little siphons to the surface where they quest about in the sediment like roving vacuum-cleaner tubes, hoovering up any organic debris. It is this activity that creates the radiating spokes left in the sand at low tide. These animals also give away their presence by the washed-up shells you can find along the shoreline. To see the animals themselves, you would need to dig deep as they live 20cm or more below the sand's surface.

Chinese Mitten Crabs, an introduced species now widespread in the UK, have dug these burrows in the river bank of the Thames in London.

Further up the beach, you may find neat oblong holes, especially around a strandline rich in debris. These tend to go straight down, but usually only for a centimetre or so. They are merely a temporary abode to get the owner, one of the many species of small crustacean, often referred to as sandhoppers, out of the life-threatening effects of the sun and wind. They can cement the particles together to give some kind of structure to their homes, and some species will on occasion backfill the entrances with sand. With a gentle bit of excavating, it is usually possible to find the owner.

Other animals, from spiders to ground beetles, also find refuge in burrows higher up the beach, but they usually give away their ownership by the presence of tracks or, in the case of spiders, some kind of silk lining.

The pleasures of poo

So you've got something in front of you that looks as though it's been produced by the nether regions of an animal. It may make kids snigger and most parents run for the antiseptic wipes, but the nature detective will want to know which species produced it.

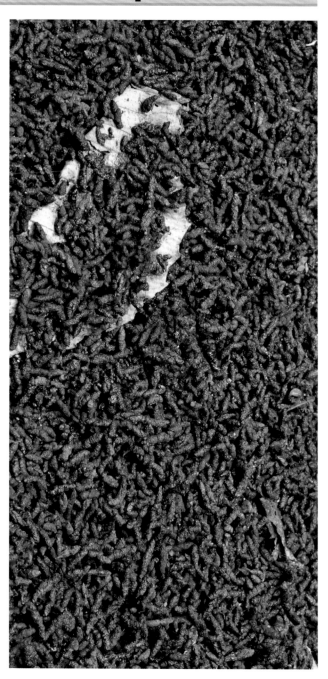

Bats mostly feed on insects and as a result their droppings are dry and crumbly.

🐾 Pellet or dropping?

First, you need to be sure that what you've found isn't a pellet (see page 187). Pellets are produced by most predatory and scavenging birds and even a few songbirds. They generally tend to be very uniform in shape and appearance, without the tapered, twisting and sculptural look of a mammal dropping. So if you've come across an object that consists of grey fur, feathers, beetle cases or bones you've probably got a pellet. Pellets also tend to have large items, such as long bones, feather shafts, etc, embedded in them in a random fashion, and they don't smell as strongly as droppings.

The first thing to check is the size of the deposit, which is directly related to the diameter of the anus and therefore to the size of the animal. Problems occur when domesticated animals get into the mix, especially as dogs and, to a lesser extent, cats and sheep occur in different adult sizes. The following summary of the size and description of different dropping categories will give a beginner a good start.

First things first – have you got poo or a pellet? This Barn Owl pellet looks very similar to a Fox dropping

Fox droppings are highly variable, but usually they are elongated and slightly twisted and pointed at one end.

BEGINNER'S GUIDE TO POO

Tubular – these chunky ones may come from the backsides of any of the carnivorous mammals from Badgers to bears.

Pancakes – cow family or other species with stomach issues.

Tapered and teardrop – cats.

Twisted threads – small mustelids like martens, Stoats and weasels.

Large peas – smooth and round; belong to Rabbits and hares.

Shiny and oblong – if not oblong then often with a nipple at one end or cut off at an angle; belong to deer.

Fried eggs: white with a dark solid within – most songbirds.

Curled cigarette ash – game birds and woodpeckers.

Whitewash – carnivorous birds, such as birds of prey, herons and owls.

Pencil lead – various rodents.

Sprinkles or rice grains – bats.

Ball bearings – large caterpillars and other insect larvae.

Tiny dark dollops – flies.

Tiny white dollops – spiders.

Dust – many other small insects.

Digestive differences

A basic understanding of the digestive processes of different animals will help the wildlife tracker to develop a deeper knowledge of the animal in question. So let's go on a trip through a typical digestive system. It's essentially a series of hollow tubes that run through the body, starting at the mouth and ending at the anus. On its convoluted journey, food is crushed, jiggled around, fermented and pummelled in various ways, so that nutrients needed to supply the body with energy and to enable the building of cells are extracted en route.

Food passes into the system via the mouth or beak; the beak plays a relatively minor job in food processing, while the mouth of a mammal, being armed with teeth of various designs, can tear, rip, chew and mash food in all manner of ways before it heads down the oesophagus to the stomach. Most mammals have a single chambered stomach, although the ungulates have stomachs divided into three or four chambers – they mainly feed on plant material, which is difficult to digest without the help of a gut fauna of trillions of bacteria. So the chambers are there to house these little helpers, to store food and to ferment it to extract as many nutrients as possible.

Birds, on the other hand, have a 'crop' that acts like a holding bay for the food before it passes down to the stomach (you can often tell if a bird such as a hawk or pigeon has a full crop just by looking at the base of the neck – if it's full the bird looks rounded and inflated, if it's empty the bird, conversely, looks deflated). Food is then trickled into the stomach, which is composed of two parts: the first part is where the digestive juices are added and the second is the gizzard, a tough-walled and highly muscular chamber, which works like a mill and grinds up and processes the food. This is often helped by grit and gravel deliberately consumed by the bird. A Turkey, for example, has been known to grind to bits 24 walnuts in 4 hours and turn steel pins and blades to dust in 16.

Ungulate stomach chambers

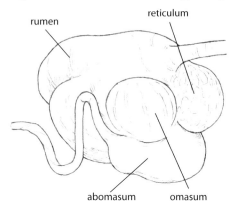

reticulum

rumen

abomasum   omasum

An ungulate digestive tract has a stomach divided into three or four chambers.

bird digestive tract

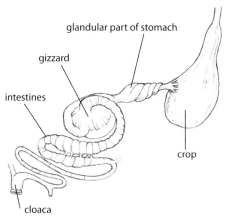

glandular part of stomach

gizzard

intestines

crop

cloaca

The bird digestive tract often has a crop and a gizzard for grinding food.

The turds of birds

Bird droppings come in roughly three categories: 1) highly liquid and white; 2) rounded, twisted and semi-solid; and 3) compressed, solid and cylindrical.

The white liquid waste tells us that this Cormorant has been eating a lot of protein.

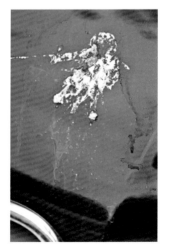

Birds excrete their food waste and urine together in droppings. The white is the equivalent of mammal urine and this makes bird droppings easier to identify.

Dropping details

Unlike mammals, which urinate and defecate through different orifices, most birds excrete their solid food waste and their urinary products from a shared holding bay known as the cloaca.

When we look at the dropping of, say, a pigeon or sparrow, we can see two different colours: a dark portion which represents the food waste from the gut and a white liquid or paste which is the equivalent of mammals' urine and is the nitrogenous waste. In birds, this waste comprises urates which are not toxic, unlike urea in mammals, and therefore they don't need to be flushed from the body with loads of water, which is why you never see a bird urinating. So if the dropping has white in it, then it came from a bird.

The high visibility of a bird dropping is the main reason why young nest-bound songbirds produce their waste in tough little mucus bags called faecal sacs, which are collected by the adult birds and either swallowed or discarded well away from the nest and the attention of any would-be predators.

Whitewash

Kittiwakes, like many seabirds, don't really care much for cleanliness and simply poop over the nest edge, leaving a distinctive whitewash beneath their shelf.

Unlike mammals, carnivorous (predatory and scavenging) birds do not let their waste pass all the way through their body. The indigestible bits – the bones, fur, feathers and hard body parts of insects and crustaceans – get to the second part of the stomach, the gizzard, and here they are squashed together with grit. Anything that is not digestible is formed into a neat pellet; this goes back the way it came and is regurgitated. Because this process is unique to carnivorous birds it means that there is little or no dark material in the droppings. A white splash of urates is highly conspicuous and is useful for finding and identifying the nest sites and roosts of both birds of prey and also birds such as herons, cormorants and all manner of seabirds.

This white stripe reveals the passing of a Raven.

Herons produce a white wash, because of their high protein diet.

Kestrels are small falcons and therefore let their mutes drop straight down unlike the hawks, which project theirs backwards.

Hawks often squirt their droppings out backwards in spectacular fashion. The falconry term for this is 'slicing', which perfectly describes that arc of effluent as it leaves the bird and forms a white stripe some distance from the bird's perch. Falcons and owls, on the other hand, drop their waste known in falconry as a 'mute', straight down. A Kestrel's perch or Peregrine's eerie is often quite obvious, and when the droppings have dried they are known as 'chalk'.

WHEN A MUTE SAYS A LOT

One of the best ways to find the roosts of owls (once you've confirmed you've got owls in the area by listening out for them after dark) is to search for their mutes. The densest vegetation or canopy cover, or a lone group of coniferous trees in a deciduous wood are good places to start looking. Woodland owls, such as Tawnies, almost always roost on a branch huddled up close to the main trunk – if so, their droppings tend to be visible as pallid vertical streaks around the base of the trunk. These almost seem to glow in the dim conditions under the canopy and more often than not will be accompanied by pellets and maybe a feather to help you identify the species.

The classic 'semi-solid fried egg' bird dropping was produced in this case by a pigeon.

Semi-solid fried egg

This describes the archetypal bird dropping that is produced by the majority of birds, including all the passerines (the smaller songbirds and perching birds). This is the classic 'fried egg' of urates with a dark, often slightly more solid deposit of the guts' waste products somewhere in the middle.

The droppings are sometimes not just black and white, especially if the bird in question has been feeding on berries of one kind or another. In the autumn, fruits of various trees and shrubs become a staple food for some species, and flocks of birds systematically strip

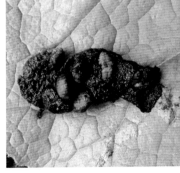

As is sometimes the case with mammals, it is possible to identify what the bird has been feeding on. This Blackbird has clearly been on the berries.

Below a Wood Pigeon roost, the green droppings show that these birds have been indulging in greenery, almost certainly a local cabbage crop.

bushes and trees of their bounty. Have a look beneath a depleted bush and you will see that the dark part of the dropping takes on the purple and red pigments of the fruits. You may also find the indigestible seeds and stones of the fruit.

A very distinctive dropping that had me foxed for a while was

this gelatinous dollop (left) that I found in midwinter stuck to a wall. I noticed many similar droppings on fence posts, branches and tree trunks that led me to conclude they must be from a bird. Then the penny dropped: Mistletoe. These were the droppings of thrushes that I had seen feeding on Mistletoe berries, but because the berries look neat and white and not slimy, I hadn't made the connection. In fact, it is this fruit and the penchant of a particular bird species for it that gave the Mistle Thrush its name.

Looking like weird jelly eggs, this is the dropping of a Mistle Thrush that has been feeding on Mistletoe – the seeds remain intact protected in their slippery cases.

WARNING

There is always going to be an element of variation in texture that can depend on the age of the dropping and the diet of the bird that made it – sometimes an older dropping that would have been semi-firm when fresh can appear solid after exposure to the elements!

Solid nuggets – fibrous faeces

Many birds that feed on predominantly hard and fibrous food lack a wet component in their droppings, so if you examine them closely with a hand lens you should be able to discern the bird's diet: from husks of grass seeds and fibres of plant stems and leaves to the pulverised remains of insects.

Game birds have a highly fibrous, plant-based diet and produce fairly firm, dry droppings, particularly in the winter when the food quality is pretty poor. Sometimes they can be so dry you could be mistaken for thinking they are mammal droppings, but a fresh one will almost always have a white 'cap' of urates at one end.

Grouse droppings are almost pellet-like in form, J-shaped and round in cross-section, with a pale grey to white end. The birds leave a pile where they have spent time resting or roosting; if the droppings are dry and scattered around a small area you have probably found where the birds have been feeding or lekking.

A Scottish naturalist once taught me that incubating females can also be identified by their droppings. An incubating bird simply doesn't get the opportunity to defecate as frequently as normal. When she does leave the nest to feed she gets rid of what is known in the grouse business as a 'clocker', which is larger in both diameter and length due to the quantity of material and the enlarged cloaca.

Top: *These are the fibrous droppings of Rock Ptarmigan in snow in Scotland.*

Centre: *Sometimes it is hard to see the white urates – as is the case with these fibrous Canada Goose droppings.*

Bottom: *These are Red Grouse droppings. The diet of a Red Grouse mainly consists of heather.*

A selection of game bird droppings

Name	Size	Description
Red Grouse (Lagopus lagopus)	10–25mm long, 6mm in diameter; clocker, see page 165, is 50mm long, 20mm in diameter	They occur in various shades of brown depending on diet. They generally have a very fine, crumbly texture due to the diet of heather and other ericaceous shrubs.
Black Grouse (Tetrao tetrix)	10–25mm long, 10mm in diameter	Same as Red Grouse but fractionally larger.
Hazel Grouse or Hen (Tetrastes bonasia)	10–25mm long, 6mm in diameter	Similar in size to grouse but contains material from birch or alder.
Ptarmigan (Lagopus muta)	10–25mm long	Not dissimilar to those of other small grouse; habitat is the big clue to identity.
Capercaillie (Tetrao urogallus)	50–70mm long, 20mm in diameter	Clocker is similar to the dimensions of a thumb, usually of a coarse texture, with evidence of pine needles.
Common Pheasant (Phasianus colchicus)	20mm long, 4–5mm in diameter, when dry	When feeding on fresh material they look like little 'pats'.
Grey Partridge (Perdix perdix)	10mm long, 2–3mm diameter	These are a similar shape to Pheasant droppings, but about half the length and smaller in girth.

Size comparison of Red Grouse and Grey Partridge droppings

Red Grouse

 I 6mm diameter

10–25mm

(Illustrations approximately to scale)

Grey Partridge

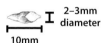 I 2–3mm diameter

10mm

A Great Spotted Woodpecker dropping; these birds feed on insects, fruit, seeds and nuts.

Ants in their scats

In open, grassy places the hills and hummocks created by meadow ants are regularly tapped by Green Woodpeckers – unlike in other woodpeckers, more than 90 per cent of their summer diet is made up of ants. You will often find the distinctive neat, tubular droppings deposited by Green Woodpeckers on the tops of these ant hills. They are an ashy grey colour, 4–5mm in diameter and around 10mm in length. Break them open and you will notice that the droppings simply crumble into a dark reddish-brown dust. This dust is composed of the hard and crispy exterior skeletons of ants, and if you look under a microscope you will see their legs, thoraxes and heads.

Mammal droppings

Basically, the bigger the droppings, the bigger the mammal that left them. Many of us, however, especially beginners, are not actually aware of the sizes of different animals because we do not encounter them on a daily basis.

Right: Here, a Stone Marten has conveniently chosen a stone on which to deposit its dropping – like many mammals martens place their droppings up high and at nose height of others, so they get noticed.

Size

The more time you spend tracking, the more likely you are to get your own first-hand experiences, which is how you accumulate field knowledge. The other thing is simply to refer to the sizes of droppings given in a book, stretch out a tape measure and imagine the size of the animal. You quickly get to realise that Badgers are not the size of bears, and that Foxes are smaller than Alsatian dogs.

Carnivore, herbivore or both?

So while the size of the dropping and the animal has narrowed your search down a little, the next thing you need to work out, by breaking open the dropping, is what the animal has been eating. Is it a herbivore, a carnivore or an opportunistic omnivore?

Left: If the diet is rich or the Badger isn't feeling territorial, it will deposit a dropping whilst foraging. In this case the Badger has been feeding on sloes and other berries.

The herbivores

These are the specialised plant eaters, the vegetarians whose diet is made up almost entirely of green things or food derived from plants. Because animals that graze are processing fairly low-nutrition food in the form of grasses, they have to eat vast quantities of it to supply their energy and nutritional needs, so the more that goes in, the more that has to come out at the other end.

Texture With such a high-fibre diet it's not that surprising to learn that much of the material that goes in comes out still fairly recognisable. The texture varies between species and, of course, depends on what kinds of plant material have been eaten. Break a dropping open and have a close look, and you will be sure to find plant fragments.

You will be familiar with the fewmets of deer and sheep – scatterings of neat little rounded pellets (see page 169) that are produced when the diet is dry and the animal is feeding on mature, tough plant stems, bark and leaves. But give the animal an abundance of fresh spring grass or unfurling leaves, and the droppings turn to mush.

Right: The fresher and greener the diet, the more runny and amorphous the dropping. This is very representative of a deer dropping in the spring and summer.

Red Deer pellets or fewmets – typical of the winter months.

Deer and their fewmets Deer droppings can take many forms, depending on what the animals have been eating, from loose and scattered pellets, suggesting a dry, fibrous diet of twigs, acorns and bark, to an amorphous clump, which can look like a cowpat but usually looks like a small rippled loaf. This indicates that the deer have probably been grazing on grass, browsing fresh leaves or eating windfall fruits.

A deer defecates on average about 13 times a day, and each dropping is composed of roughly 75 pellets. This may come in useful if you are ever surveying deer numbers – how often you encounter pellets can give you a pretty good idea of what the population is.

Large herbivorous mammal droppings

It can be quite difficult initially to work out which species of deer a dropping belongs to as the droppings are so variable in colour and form. Size is the best indicator, and in the case of deer and other ruminants you will need to take into consideration the size of the pellets as well as the overall bulk.

Rabbit and hare droppings can look superficially similar to those of deer, but on closer inspection you will see that they are much more rounded, and that fibrous material can be seen on the outside; fresh deer droppings have a black/brown, almost glossy coating, giving them a much smoother appearance.

Chinese Water Deer like marshy habitats and eat lots of moist greens that bind together their separate dropping pellets.

Muntjac Nearly spherical black shiny pellets (although shape can vary enormously), 0.5–1.3cm in diameter. Often deposited in piles of more than 100 pellets; in high-density populations these are often deposited at favoured sites with territorial significance.

A coin can be a handy tool for size comparison in the field. Roe Deer pellets are best identified by their size.

Chinese Water Deer Separate pellets in a cluster and pointed at one end, 1–1.5cm long, 0.5–1cm in diameter. Usually almost black in colour and deposited in piles.

Roe Deer Small droppings, 1–1.4 x 0.7–1cm in diameter; shiny, nearly black and glossy when fresh; cylindrical pellets often pointed at one end, with the other end rounded. Deposits 17–23 groups of pellets a day in summer, more in winter.

Sika Medium-sized droppings, 1–1.5 x 0.8–1.2cm in diameter; glossy black pellets; one end flat, indented or rounded, the other pointed; similar to Roe and young Red Deer.

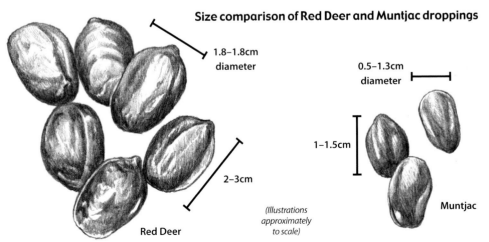

Size comparison of Red Deer and Muntjac droppings

1.8–1.8cm diameter

0.5–1.3cm diameter

1–1.5cm

2–3cm

(Illustrations approximately to scale)

Red Deer

Muntjac

Fallow Deer pellets loosely pressed together in clumps.

The larger, more rounded pellets of Red Deer in the winter.

Fallow Deer Medium-sized droppings, 1–1.5 x 0.8–1.2cm; oval shape, similar to those of Red Deer; black changing to brown. Usually pointed at one end and indented at the other; like Red Deer, if feeding on food with high water content deposits a congealed 'crottie'. Daily defecations: 22–28 in summer, 14–18 in winter.

Red Deer Large, acorn-shaped droppings called 'fewmets', often pointed at one end, rounded or slightly concave at the other; 2–3 x 1.3–1.8cm; initially black and shiny, gradually becoming duller and more dark brown. If feeding on lush herbage they are softer and the fewmets stick together as a pat or 'crottie'. Daily defecations: 24–29 in summer, 19-25 in winter.

Reindeer The pellets are similar to those produced by Fallow Deer in size and shape, but very dark. In the summer the colour gets lighter and the form is much looser as the diet becomes wetter and richer.

Elk In summer with plenty of lush food the droppings look like a kind of wrinkled up pat; in winter the droppings are drier and form clusters of large, shiny pellets. At 3cm long and 2.5cm in diameter, they are unmistakable. They can be almost spherical with a slight point, or lozenge shaped.

In summer Reindeer droppings are light coloured and fibrous; however, habitat and vegetation ultimately influence consistency and colour.

Wild Boar Although a bit of an odd one out in this section, its droppings can be confused with those of deer by the beginner. The form, colour and consistency vary according to diet; most frequently the droppings look like elongated sausages about 10cm in length and 7cm in diameter. Composed of many discs; when dry, they often break up into multiple parts, looking like a collection of misshapen fibrous golf balls. They are often deposited on runs and tracks and rarely in foraging areas.

Sheep/goat Deposited in piles and can be separate pellets or aggregations, depending on diet. Size and shape depend a lot on breed and can overlap considerably with many deer species and therefore cause confusion.

Top left: *Sheep droppings – similar to a pile of large peas.*

Top right: *The fibrous and pancake-like dropping of a Wild Boar.*

Bottom left: *A typical wet cowpat deposited in a field.*

Horse/pony We all know what these look like: distinctive piles of very fibrous or irregular nuggets of around 5–8cm in diameter.

Cow/Bison A runny pat which once dried out reveals the fibrous nature of the grass-based diet.

Bottom right: *Horse manure contains lots of fibre typically gained from grazing on pasture.*

The round, smooth droppings of the Rabbit are easily recognisable.

Hares and Rabbits

These animals belong to the lagomorph family, and instead of chewing the cud, they simply pass their food through a second time. Once the food has passed through the first time it is defecated as a wet, soft, green-brown pellet called a cecotrope. It is then eaten again by the animal for another run through the digestive tract. This unusual form of behaviour, known as coprophagy, is necessary to extract the little goodness there is in difficult-to-digest grass and is particularly important for the absorption of sufficient vitamin B12. The droppings have an almost biscuit-like smell to them.

These are weathered Rabbit droppings that have been exposed to the elements.

Rabbit droppings that are dark have a low-fibre content.

Rabbit droppings are pretty easy to recognise: they are roughly spherical nuggets, about 1cm in diameter, produced one at a time and clearly composed of dry fibrous plant material. They are left in obvious places: on the tops of stones, logs and tussocks to create scented signposts for other Rabbits. Their presence is often associated with closely cropped 'lawns' of grass, shallow scrapes, diggings or burrows, which is handy for identification.

Brown Hares are essentially big bunnies and, as might be expected, produce bigger pellets – some 1–1.5cm in diameter. Unlike Rabbits, you never find huge territorial heaps. You may find small groups where a Brown Hare has been feeding, or scattered pellets if it has been moving through.

Mountain Hares are smaller than Brown Hares, with smaller droppings – about 1cm in diameter. There should be no real confusion as the habitats that the animals frequent are so very different. Mountain Hares are only found in truly mountainous areas, while Brown Hares inhabit lowlands.

Hare droppings are very similar to Rabbit droppings, but slightly larger.

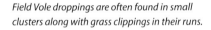
Field Vole droppings are often found in small clusters along with grass clippings in their runs.

Rodent droppings

Field Vole 6–7mm long, 2–3mm thick and green when fresh; often deposited in association with 'runs' in grass and grass clippings.

Bank Vole Elongated yellowish-green pellet, very similar to Field Vole's.

Water Vole Small, cylinder-like droppings, 7–12mm long and 3–4mm thick with blunt ends. They are often deposited in 'piles' that act as territorial markers, and are always near points where the animals enter or leave the water. Colour is variable when fresh: they often have a dark greenish tint and are quite mushy. They dry out when older and can be snapped in half, usually revealing bright green concentric circles.

NB Vole droppings are similar to those of mice, but tend to be much smoother and more rounded.

Mice droppings, unlike those of voles, have a certain musty smell to them.

Wood Mouse and Yellow-necked Mouse Elongated dark pellets 5–8mm long. They have a gentle smell to them, which is hard to describe but has been likened to wet newspaper.

Apples in storage that have been discovered by Wood Mice – plenty of incriminating evidence, including droppings and tooth marks.

Brown Rat droppings are much larger than those of any other rodents – their elongated pellets are often quite wet and smelly.

Harvest Mouse Tiny pellets less than 3mm long; the likelihood of finding them is slim unless inside an old nest.

House Mouse Very similar to those of Wood Mice but slightly smaller, about 7mm long. When fresh they have a distinctive musty smell, with a hint of ammonia.

Brown Rat Often deposited in groups, along runs and in favoured feeding places; they tend to smell pretty grim, like something rancid and rotten. They vary in texture depending on moisture content and type of diet, but most frequently are large, dark pellets, with some fibrous content, pointed at one end and around 12mm long.

Black Rat Droppings rarely occur in groups and are a little smaller and narrower than those of Brown Rat.

Squirrel (Red and Grey) Short and almost spherical – 5–8mm long and 5–6mm thick, flattened at one end and pointed at the other. Rarely seen unless in snow or at a squirrel table, such as a tree stump or fallen bough covered with food remains. They have a fresh, almost sappy smell to them.

Flying Squirrel The droppings of this squirrel from northern continental Europe are usually encountered beneath the nests and are often yellowish in colour with a length of 1–1.5cm.

Beaver A bit like those of hares, rounded and about 2.5–3cm in diameter. Unsurprisingly, they look like balls of sawdust and float! Rarely encountered because they are most often deposited in water.

Muskrats often share their feeding areas and toilets.

Edible Dormouse Oval pellets, 1cm long and 0.5cm wide; they vary in colour depending on diet and are often deposited in piles.

Muskrat Droppings are dark green, brown or almost black. They are slightly curved and cylindrical, and about 1.3cm long and 1cm in diameter. They can be found floating in the water, along shorelines, on objects protruding out of the water and at feeding sites. The animals may repeatedly use these spots, and more than one Muskrat may use the same spot.

The shape of Coypu droppings is key to their identification.

Norway Lemmings feed mainly on sedges, grasses and mosses.

Coypu This semi-aquatic rodent from South America was introduced to large parts of Europe. Its droppings are scattered around feeding areas, often close to or floating in the water. They are brown to green in colour, fairly soft with a fine ridged texture, about 5cm long and 1.3cm wide, and have a 'spindly' look to them.

Norway Lemming Where this rodent occurs in areas of northern tundra and heath, the droppings can be found in large masses. Neat, smooth pellets with rounded ends, 0.3–0.8cm long and often pale in colour.

The carnivores

Carnivores sustain themselves on a more nutritious diet than herbivores – the hard work of converting plant material to animal matter has already been done by the animals they prey on or scavenge. They tend to produce less faecal material and it often smells pretty pungent. Their droppings will either contain the indigestible fragments of their prey – feathers, fur and bones may all be detectable – or may be a chalky colour from the calcium phosphate of ground-up bones.

Why does carnivore dung smell? A dropping is made up mainly of water (about 75 per cent) combined with substances that a mammal's body cannot break down or simply needs to get rid of, including indigestible material from the diet, bile (which is made up of dead blood cells from the liver) and various bacteria.

Foxes are omnivores; they can eat a wide range of animal and plant matter.

THE SOCIAL NETWORK

Carnivores lead complex social lives, often laying claim to territories, and are famous for using droppings as 'signposts' – status updates that allow them to communicate without being present, very much like social networking. So the scat in this case is a precious commodity and is placed with great care and meaning.

Glandular secretions from specialised anal glands are sometimes incorporated into scats and are apparent as a strong odour, or at other times can be seen: for example, as the clear, yellowish, jelly-like substance produced by the Badger.

Odour can reveal all sorts of things, such as relatedness, age, dominance, sex and reproductive potential, and because it fades as a scat weathers it gives a time frame to the scat.

Badger droppings are more than a biological function; they are a social signpost, too.

The distinctive odour of carnivore dung is down to bacterial action in the gut which recycles and breaks down proteins producing the substances which smell, including indole, skatole, the sulphur-containing thiols and the inorganic gas hydrogen sulphide.

Below left and right: Fox droppings vary in shape, colour and consistency depending on diet. The droppings on the left indicate that the animal has been eating fruit, while the one on the right shows that it has scavenged sheep.

The one single substance that the human nose is more sensitive to than any other is skatole; it makes evolutionary sense for us to be repelled by skatole as droppings are a source of bacteria (many of which could be harmful), so by staying away from them we eliminate the risk of picking up disease.

Fox Usually a black deposit with some animal content visible, but extremely variable depending on diet – sometimes full of berries, sparkly and crunchy if dung beetles have been on the menu or a runny slurry if earthworms have been consumed. Twisted and pointed at one end, often connected by fur and feathers, but equally frequently found in a broken cluster of several sections. 'Foxy' smell when fresh; older droppings can be hard to distinguish from those of domesticated dog. Foxes also deposit their droppings on 'landmarks' such as Mole hills, tussocks, branches and stumps, which dogs rarely do.

Dog The size depends on the size of the dog breed. Mostly don't contain bone, fur or feathers, so little internal texture will be evident. Due to the lack of fibre, they are more sausage shaped than the droppings of Foxes and not twisted. If you see a soft, brown mush and detect a very unpleasant smell, it's usually dog.

Left: A Fox has eaten a bird – but you will notice that Fox droppings are similar in shape and diameter. They have a foxy smell, which is a dead giveaway.

Raccoon Dog Quite difficult to tell apart from the droppings of other carnivores. About 5–8cm long and 1cm in diameter, twisted, usually with evidence of fur, feathers and other non-digestible remains at the surface.

Above: Dog droppings rarely have any fibrous content, despite being variable depending on the breed.

Wolf Since the Wolf is effectively a large wild dog, it should come as no surprise to discover that its scat is pretty much like that of a dog, combined with the texture of Fox. Large, dark-grey scat with a tapered, twisted look, containing fibrous remains of the diet, usually fur, with fragments of bone. Often positioned in socially significant places.

Badger An opportunistic omnivore whose catholic diet is reflected in the variety of forms of droppings. Although often looser than those of dogs and Foxes, they can range from a runny slurry (quite frequently in many pasture areas as earthworms make up the bulk of the diet), and a rich purple when feeding on blackberries to a crunchy polychromatic appearance when beetles have been eaten. Although occasionally deposited randomly and singly, more often than not they dig a shallow pit in which to make each deposit. A collection of these pits, usually on territory boundaries or near the main sett, is known as a latrine and serves a social function.

Above: Badger droppings are as variable as the animal's diet – these dark, firm droppings suggest a diet of beetles.

Right: In this case the Badger has been eating various berries, including sloes and cherries. In autumn this type of food is plentiful.

This Otter spraint reveals the diet you might expect – fish and amphibian bones in a dark black, oily mass.

Otter The association with water is a dead giveaway, and the dropping, called a spraint, is often deposited as a scent-marker on conspicuous waterside objects, such as boulders, tree stumps and roots, or at river crossing points, around bridge foundations or anywhere the Otter leaves the water. In coastal locations this can also include favourite freshwater bathing spots. The form of the spraint can be variable, from a small blob or smear to a fully formed cylinder of material. When fresh the spraints are often quite black and tarry, and contain fish and amphibian bones, as well as distinctive fish scales and otoliths. They have a scent that has been described variously as like 'summer meadows' and 'fresh hay'.

Mink scat, often found near water, are much smellier and unpleasant compared with those of the Otter.

After a little weathering, all that remains of an Otter spraint is the hard stuff; the fine fish bones and vertebrae are very evident.

Otter spraints may smell musty but are by no means highly pungent and repulsive to the human nose, unlike Mink scat.

Sometimes a jelly-like glandular secretion is deposited with the dropping, no doubt containing further olfactory information intended for other Otters. Older droppings that have weathered may take on an ashy appearance as the black matrix leaches away, leaving just the fine bones and scales.

Mink Often a tapered cylinder, 5–8cm long and about 1cm in diameter. Found in the same sorts of places as those of Otter and can sometimes be confused. Mink tend to have more of a penchant for small mammals and birds, giving the droppings a more cylindrical and twisted shape. Scent, however, remains the easiest and best way of determining whether an Otter or Mink has passed by – Mink scat smells particularly pungent, even repulsive, and in no way could ever be described as pleasant.

Rarely encountered unless near the den site, Stoat droppings can be found in heaped piles.

Stoat Scat is twisted and fine, about 4–8cm long and 0.5cm wide. Rarely encountered except around den areas (where they can be present in a large number) or at the scene of a binge feed, such as a raided bird's nest. Normally contains fur and feathers.

Least Weasel Rarely encountered and almost indistinguishable from Stoat's except smaller and finer – 3–6cm long and twisted.

Polecat 7cm long and 0.5cm in diameter; twisted cylinders, like those of many other mustelids, with a tapered point at one end. Colour and texture vary depending on diet – from black and loose if feeding on amphibians to twisted and fibrous with fur and feathers – and a characteristic musty odour when fresh. Usually deposited in latrine sites associated with a den.

Polecat droppings have a strong unpleasant odour.

Pine Marten 4–12cm long and about 1–1.5cm wide. Fresh droppings have a faint fruity aroma to them. Texture and form vary depending on the marten's diet. Often strongly twisted like a spring, with a grey and hairy appearance reflecting the staple diet of small furry mammals; less twisted if the animal has been eating insects, berries and flowers. Scat is deposited as a territorial marker in fairly obvious places, such as rocks, edges of paths and forest rides, tree roots, stumps and fallen boughs.

Pine Marten produce long, twirly and twisty droppings, which are often placed in prominent places along paths.

Wolverine The largest European mustelid produces the largest droppings at 15cm long and about 2cm in diameter. They contain a lot of fur, have a slight twist to them and are deposited randomly.

Beech Marten Similar in size to those of a Pine Marten, with a twist but never tightly coiled. Often deposited at latrine sites where they accumulate and have a strong musty odour. Often much darker in colour than Pine Marten's droppings and always contain fur, feather and bone.

Brown Bear Large, blunt-ended, sausage-shaped masses can sometimes be found in the wilder parts of Europe. About 8–10cm in diameter with some evidence of indigestible items such as seeds.

Above: Bear droppings vary as much as the diet of this omnivore. Droppings range from long, sausage-shaped deposits to large, formless piles.

Wildcat Difficult to separate from those of feral domesticated cats; tend to be deposited on conspicuous objects. Colour and texture depend very much on what the animals have been eating. 6–8cm long x 1.5cm wide.

Domesticated cat Domesticated cat droppings are difficult to separate from those of the Wildcat – however, the location of the droppings helps in identification, and domesticated cats' droppings smell foul, are often soft and lack fibre.

Lynx Long and straight with a slight twist (18–25cm) and tapered at both ends; often with evidence of fur, feathers and large pieces of bone.

Wildcat droppings are remarkably similar to those of the domesticated cat – be careful interpreting.

Insectivorous mammals

The droppings of insectivorous mammals, such as bats, shrews, desmans, Moles and Hedgehogs, are rarely encountered with the exception of bats and Hedgehogs because they share our homes and gardens.

Bats Bat droppings are generally tiny dark pellets that look a little like those of mice in shape and size. They are also fairly inoffensive with very little in the way of smell detectable by the human nose. To be sure that they are bat droppings, simply rub a dropping between your finger and thumb and it will just crumble to dust because it's made up of many tiny fragments of insect cuticle. A mouse dropping, on the other hand, will just squash and smear; if you try this, I suggest you wash your hands afterwards. Older mouse droppings simply become as hard as bullets, whereas older bats' droppings crumble even more easily than when fresh.

Bat droppings can be found below roost sites and regular feeding perches.

Bat droppings are usually detected at sites that are frequently used, such as roost sites and places which are regularly used as feeding perches. In a roof space roost accumulations occur directly below occupied areas and also outside entrances. You do, however, need to have a licence or to be with someone who has in order to enter loft spaces that contain bats.

With about 52 species of bat occurring in Europe, 16 of which are native to the British Isles, it is impossible to identify all species by their droppings, but a few generalisations can be made. Like other mammals, the bigger bats, such as the Noctule and Greater Horseshoe, tackle bigger prey than do smaller bats and as a result have bigger droppings that contain bigger fragments of prey. If you look at a bat dropping under a microscope you will be amazed at how many insects it comprises, which is a clear indication of just how important a habitat rich in insects is to bats.

Bat droppings can build up in regular locations. These were found under roof tiles.

The droppings of bats are composed of tiny hard indigestible parts of their diet; they crumble to a fine dry powder, unlike those of mice.

A guide to a selection of bat droppings

Species of bat	Particle size	Dimensions – length and diameter	Texture and notes
Common Pipistrelle (Pipistrellus pipistrellus)	Fine	7–9 x 1.5–2mm	Smooth and elongated pellets, often found in loft spaces.
Brown Long-eared (Plecotus auritus)	Medium/ coarse	8–10 x 2.5–3mm	Knobbly, can look like a shelled peanut in shape. Found below roost sites in roof spaces, also at regular feeding spots.
Lesser Horseshoe (Rhinolophus hipposideros)	Fine/ medium	6–8 x 1.5–2mm	Little oval pellets, often with complete bits of insect present.
Greater Horseshoe (Rhinolophus ferrumequinum)	Coarse	9–13 x 2.2–2.7mm	Large beetle-wing cases often found near droppings in feeding roosts.
Noctule (Nyctalus noctua)	Medium	11–15 x 3–3.5mm	In tree cavities or bat boxes.
Daubenton's (Myotis daubentonii)	Fine	8–9 x 1.8–2.3mm	Uneven in shape although smooth in texture; can seem a little wet when fresh.
Serotine (Eptesicus serotinus)	Coarse	8–11 x 3.5–4mm	Often oval in cross-section.
Natterer's (Myotis nattereri)	Medium	8–11 x 2.3–3.3mm	Often contain complete bits of insect wings.
Barbastelle (Barbastella barbastellus)	Medium/ coarse	8–11 x 2.1–2.7mm	Smooth or knobbly, often in three segments.

Full of insect bits, the dropping of a Hedgehog is about the same size and shape as an adult human's little finger.

Hedgehog If you find a little blackish deposit about the width and length of your little finger on your patio or lawn, more often than not it will be the dropping of a Hedgehog. These black and shiny droppings, usually around 4–5cm long and 1cm in diameter, are deposited at random during the nocturnal wanderings of the animal, often under bird tables (where they pick up scraps) or on lawns. They are twisted with rounded ends, which distinguishes them from the droppings of members of the cat and dog families; they also don't have a particularly bad 'nose'.

If you were to tease the droppings apart you would see masses of compressed insect and invertebrate remains (this is what makes them sparkle like jewels), such as beetles, earwigs, millipedes and slugs, which is why Hedgehogs are gardeners' friends. When an animal has been scavenging on carcasses its droppings will often appear wetter and contain bone fragments and fur.

It's rare to find reptile droppings unless you're in the tropics. If you pick up a Slow Worm, the chances are that it will poop on your hands and the resultant mess is very much like a bird dropping.

Reptile droppings are very similar to those of birds, with a white and darker portion.

Reptile droppings

A dark package of waste material with a little yellow or white patch of pale urates is the archetypal reptile dropping be it lizard or snake, a combination that is similar to birds (see page 159), which are basically just warm-blooded reptiles with feathers. You may stumble across a dropping on a rock or wall, or even under a sheet of metal that may obviously belong to a lizard or snake – as always, size and the context of the habitat may give you some clues.

Insect droppings

Invertebrates are the most numerous animals on the planet – we have about 21,000 species of insect in the UK alone, and they are out there right now chewing their way through leaves, stems, roots, fungi, carrion, dung and even each other. As always, what goes in must come out. Invertebrates produce huge quantities of waste and in the process play a massively important role in recycling nutrients back into the soil. You would think that we would notice their waste more than we do. Yet being able to identify insect signs, however subtle, is an important skill for anyone remotely interested in plants.

Small, dark amorphous blobs pretty much sum up most medium-sized insect droppings – some, however, are distinctive, especially when seen with feeding and other signs.

Frass of caterpillars can often be found beneath where they have been feeding.

Frass I've always been quite fond of the word frass, which refers to semi-solid insect droppings. It comes from the German word *frasz*, which is derived from *fressen*, meaning 'to devour, to eat as a beast does'; here, of course, it refers to the end product of this devouring process!

Because insect droppings are so small and ephemeral, you are most likely to find them in enclosed spaces where they have had a chance to accumulate and become noticeable. I know what grasshopper frass looks like only because I've raised grasshoppers in captivity, but realistically the chance of finding one of these elongated, sharp-ended spindles in the field is unlikely – they simply vanish into the tangle of vegetation. However, frass may be found in nests of larvae living together communally inside plant stems, galls, seeds or rolled leaves.

The specialised diet of the Goat Moth results in droppings that are like sawdust, unlike the extruded pellets of regular caterpillars.

Caterpillars are often incredibly well camouflaged, but sometimes their frass gives them away. One of the more obvious examples are the fancy-shaped droppings of Privet Hawk Moth caterpillars. You may spot these on suburban pavements beneath overgrown privet hedges – you would then have a high chance of finding this spectacularly large insect. Gardeners who grow brassicas will be familiar with the slightly mushier frass produced by Small White and Large White Butterfly caterpillars.

In fact, anywhere there are leaves, stems or fruit being nibbled there will be frass.

In oak woodlands in spring you can even hear the frass pellets of numerous tortrix moth caterpillars falling like dry rain and hitting the dry leaves on the woodland floor as the insects gorge themselves on the newly emerging oak-leaf buds.

Some caterpillars have realised somewhere along the evolutionary line that their droppings can give them away to predators and have developed a bristly flap, with the unlikely names of anal comb or anal fork, to ping the frass as far from their feeding places as possible.

The larvae of the Lily Leaf Beetle wear their excrement to deter predators.

Beetle larvae, however, leave the frass where it falls; in many species the consistency is one of slight tackiness so the dropping sticks. In fact, some leaf beetle larvae (Red Lily Beetle and Tortoise Beetle) and a few caterpillars, too (White Admiral Butterfly), will actually stick frass to their own backs and become tiny mobile dung heaps. This is a brilliant way of hiding and putting off predators at the same time. So if you see a mobile dropping it's worth a closer look.

Wet spots You will probably have noticed what is often described as fly 'dirt' on window ledges, and this is the liquid waste excreted by the numerous flies that find themselves trapped in our homes. The darkish colour seems to depend on what the species is and what it's been feeding on.

Any house-proud homeowner will be familiar with the dark spots of excrement produced by flies.

Spiders also excrete an all-in-one liquid waste largely consisting of chemicals called guanine and uric acid, both of which very quickly crystallise to form chalky little spots. These can range from a yellowish colour to white or clear liquid and can often be found directly below their lairs.

After emerging from the chrysalis, the built-up waste products of metamorphosis are secreted as a bright red or pink liquid called meconium.

Messy meconium A butterfly, moth, beetle or fly emerging from its pupa or chrysalis will get rid of liquid waste, known as meconium. You can sometimes see this as a red or white substance splashed on vegetation. I once witnessed a mass emergence of Painted Lady Butterflies from a patch of thistles that had been annihilated by the caterpillars only weeks earlier; the vivid red liquid was so evident that on the leaves at the site it looked like a murder scene.

A Black Garden Ant feeds on the honeydew secretions deposited by a Black Bean Aphid.

Dark sooty mould has formed on the honeydew left by Rose Aphids on rose leaves.

Honeydew This sweet substance is actually the liquid waste of a huge family of insects, known as aphids, among them those well-known house and garden plant pests the Greenfly, Blackfly and Whitefly. Probably the most frequent experience of this for most of us occurs when we park a car under a tree infested with aphids and it becomes coated in a sugar rain that is hard to remove. Being sap-feeding bugs the apids simply plug their sharp stylets into the circulatory system of the plant through which sap flows under pressure. This means that they don't even have to suck and the sap simply pushes right through their bodies, the aphid taking out what it needs en route. In the countryside, black sooty mould growing on leaves and vegetation covered in honeydew is a clear sign that aphids are somewhere above. Ants and social wasps are often present, too, as they find the sweet honeydew irresistible.

Bubbles en masse Plant hoppers are another plant-sap-sucking bug; their nymphs use their waste to form fairly conspicuous bubble masses that keep them hidden and safe. The partially digested sap is whizzed up by a pumping movement of the abdomen tip working like a pair of bellows. As the abdomen works backwards and forwards, a special pair of downward-pointing plates traps air bubbles in the sticky excretion and this soon hides the nymph from sight but, conversely, makes it more obvious to the nature detective.

You can see the process for yourself by simply wiping away the bubbles from a nymph with a wet artist's paintbrush and waiting for the insect to feel vulnerable and cover itself up again. Not often does the wildlife tracker get to meet the animal that makes the field sign, then watch it create another to order.

Below: The stringy droppings of snails and slugs are often a giveaway sign of who has been predating your garden plants.

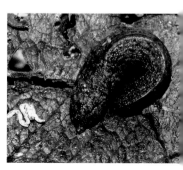

Above: *Cuckoo spit is the frothy excrement that is blown out of Leaf Hopper nymphs' bottoms in the form of protective bubbles.*

Coiled ropes Several invertebrates produce coiled 'ropes' of faecal material, but the most commonly seen are those produced by various species of slug and snail. The gut of these animals ends close to the breathing pore, which is situated on the right-hand side of the mantle. The two orifices are not always visible as the mollusc can voluntarily open and close them to help preserve water. The droppings, which look like badly coiled ropes, are simply deposited as the slug or snail goes about its wanderings.

The colour of these coils is very much dependent on what the animal has been eating – green if live plant material has been consumed or black/brown if the mollusc has been dining on dead leaves or scavenging.

This Budapest Slug has recently deposited a white stringy dropping.

Earthworms are a sign of a healthy garden and soil – a gardener's friend.

Earthworm casts contain the decomposed organic matter that has been processed by worms; the casts add nutrients to the soil.

The worm's turn

The other group of animals that produces long extruded waste products, of course, the annelid (ringed or segmented) worms. Whether a soil-eating earthworm (clittelate) or a beast that consumes sand or marine mud (polychaete), the digestive outcome looks like sculptural piles, referred to as casts. They consist of pretty much what the soil or sediment is that the animals are consuming minus a few of the important ingredients. It's all good stuff, too, because even though it's been through the worm's gut it still contains loads of goodness: about 65–70 per cent organic matter remains, and what's more this has been brought to the surface and stabilised as a slow-release fertiliser for the plants that have their roots here. This circulation of nutrients within the soil is often very evident when worm casts are formed on bare soil, because a cast is more often than not a totally different colour from the soil on which it sits.

Sand Mason Worms have left this mass of sandy-coloured casts on a beach in Norfolk.

Pellets

If you find a pellet, which is basically a lump of compressed fur, feathers and bone, and want to test your nature detective skills, there's a double challenge: to work out which species produced it, then to dissect the pellet and identify the prey species it contains. Bear in mind that it is illegal to disturb certain UK species at their nesting sites. Please do not be tempted to go and collect pellets from active sites.

Caught throwing up a treasure trove of information, this European Bee-eater is one of many species of bird that expel the hard and indigestible artifacts of their diets in the form of a pellet.

🐾 Pellet producers

We tend to assume that birds of prey, especially owls, are the only bird types that produce pellets, but many other birds share this regurgitatory habit – it's just that the large raptors expel more noticeable pellets, on average about twice a day.

Owl pellets are sought after by mammalogists as much as by ornithologists and wildlife detectives because they tell us what small mammals are in an area more effectively than any live trapping survey. This in turn is an indicator of the general health of the habitat.

For example, Water Voles made up only 3 per cent of the contents of Barn Owl pellets near an overgrown waterway in Yorkshire, but after the banks were cleared and managed the figure rose to 28 per cent.

An amazing case study in the 1980s of an owl that regularly hunted a waterway in Durham showed that Water Voles made up about 25 per cent of its diet. Then the number of Water Vole remains in the pellets started to crash until they reached a low of just 1 per cent. What this single owl's pellets had recorded was the escape of Mink into the countryside and their catastrophic predation on Water Voles, which in this case had effectively removed them from the owl's menu.

The Redwing – the smallest member of the thrush family – eats fruit, berries, insects, worms, snails and slugs, but regurgitates hard seeds and any undigestible matter in the form of a pellet.

Owl pellets also show that the birds eat shrews, which are difficult to live trap. Biologists in the Republic of Ireland were once sorting through the pellets of Kestrels and owls when they made an exciting discovery. Some bones they didn't recognise were later identified as those of the Greater White-toothed Shrew, a species hitherto unknown in Ireland.

A long-term study of the bones in Tawny Owl pellets revealed that Moles were occasionally turning up, and in some populations

Not just owls, but many other carnivorous birds produce pellets, including Kingfishers.

making up a significant proportion of the bird's small mammal diet. Interestingly, this was occurring only between the months of May and October, which is when Moles come to the surface more regularly than at other times of the year, a fact that was previously unknown. Why they do so is a question yet to be answered.

Birds of prey have a muscular two-part stomach, which compresses and forms the solid indigestible remains, such as fur, bone and scales, into a ball which is then moved back into the first section of the stomach, where it can sit for several hours. A bird that is producing a pellet cannot feed until it has regurgitated the pellet back up the oesophagus and out of the mouth. Short-eared Owls form a pellet after every 30–90g of food is consumed.

Bird pellets never seem to smell unpleasant and this is one of the main ways to distinguish them from the droppings of medium-sized carnivores, such as Foxes and Badgers (see Chapter 6). Pellets are usually fairly symmetrical, and are often found below a roosting or nesting site where there may be other clues such as the 'whitewash' of droppings or the odd feather.

Some birds, such as Barn Owls and herons, have regular perches and often large accumulations of pellets can be found below them. Other birds, such as Tawny Owls, tend to move their perches around, so you are less likely to find more than three or four pellets in one go. I nearly always get lucky finding gull pellets in short, tussocky grass above beaches and on spits, areas often chosen for their isolation and security at high tide.

Pellets can build up underneath regular roost sites or perches.

What kind of pellet?

The look of a pellet and what it contains depends on what the bird has consumed and how strong its digestive juices are – the pellets of the crow family are very loose, those of gulls are usually tight clusters of fish bones, scales and fragments of crab carapace, and those of Barn Owls are neat consolidated masses.

Pellets can tell you not only what's been eaten, but also who's been doing the eating – diet, colour, size and shape are all important. These very oval pellets belong to a Barn Owl.

Barn Owl pellets give a clear indication of what a bird has been eating, as many of the bones remain undigested and skulls tend to be in good condition. Tawny Owls, on the other hand, tend to crush the skulls of their prey, so you'll need to apply all your detective skills to work out what the species was. Other bones, however, such as pelvic girdles, can clinch the ID if the head didn't make it.

The hawks and falcons make your job harder still because they butcher and decapitate their prey, and their digestive processes are so strong that all but the biggest chunks of bone are dissolved. All you are left to work with are a few fragments of fur and feathers and, if you are lucky, a handful of teeth. With a microscope of at least x100 magnification it is possible to start recognising the species of mammal from the shapes and distinctive textures of individual hairs.

HEALTH AND HYGIENE

It is always worth bearing in mind the possibility of mistaken identity with a mammal scat and the ever-present risk of salmonella, so usual common sense should apply when handling pellets, i.e., wash your hands afterwards. If you are going to dissect a pellet, they can be sterilised with a blast in a microwave.

Identifying pellets

A pellet is a time capsule representing a day or night of hunting. An awareness of size, contents, shape, texture and of course where a pellet was found will all lead you down the right path of identification. From a single pellet it is possible to identify what has been feeding in the area and of course what it has been feeding on.

Right: This Barn Owl pellet may look uninteresting on the surface, but break it open and you are highly likely to find Field Vole remains.

When pellets get old the fine stuff such as fur and feathers decomposes, leaving a graveyard of bones. These vole skulls are below a regularly used Barn Owl nest box.

One important factor in determining which species regurgitated a pellet is **size**: think Eagle Owl versus Scops Owl. **Contents** can also give us some useful clues as some birds consume very specific types of food. Are there complete bones within, or just fragments, and how are they arranged in the pellet, randomly or aligned along the length?

It is worth making a note of **shape** and **texture**, too; some birds, such as the Barn Owl, Hobby (when it's been eating insects) and Kestrel, produce distinctively shaped pellets. Some are smooth and shiny, while others are bristly and fibrous with the contents on display close to the surface.

Finally, there is the **location** – I cannot emphasise enough just how important other signs are to the identification of your pellet. The habitat, and the presence of droppings and feathers can all give valuable clues. In one case I rushed off home to analyse a pellet but returned, none the wiser, to the gatepost where I had found it, only to be met by the scowling expression of a Little Owl.

The bigger the owl, the bigger the gullet, and the larger the prey that fits in and the bigger the pellet that comes out. This is all reflected in this Eurasian Eagle Owl pellet.

Owls

Owl pellets are usually quite solid, dark grey or brown castings containing numerous complete bones (long limb bones and skulls) in a matrix of finer material such as fur and feather fibres.

Eurasian Eagle Owl This is a huge bird and unsurprisingly gives us one of the world's largest and most unmistakable pellets, about 15cm long and 4cm in diameter. They are fun to dissect because of the range of prey taken: the remains of large prey such as Rabbit skulls are quite common, but equally you could find any bird, mammal, lizard, fish or amphibian that the Eagle Owl can catch. The pellets are often found near regular roost and nest sites, or below cliffs and quarry faces.

Barn Owl The pellets of Barn Owls are quite often discovered because the birds frequently nest and roost in outhouses and agricultural buildings. When fresh, the pellets are dark, glossy and dense with an almost varnished appearance. They are 3–5cm in length and 1.5–4cm in diameter, with a rounded blunt appearance.

Barn Owl pellets are very distinctive, grey and rounded. They are probably one of the most frequently encountered pellets due to the bird's association with buildings.

Pellets nearly always contain the same or similar species, such as Field Voles and shrews, which are the commonest prey items, preferring open grassy areas. Wood Mice and other surprise species may turn up. The hard items are usually contained within the interior of the pellet and are rarely visible on the surface.

Tawny Owl pellets are most likely to be found beneath trees with good cover. The owls like roosting in dense ivy or in old conifer trees – these are good places to look for the giveaway white droppings and of course pellets.

Tawny Owl This is the commonest owl species throughout most of its European range, so its pellets are quite often encountered near wooded areas and gardens. Another good place to look for pellets is below dense conifers where the birds frequently roost. Pellets look more elongated than those of Barn Owls, and are 2–5cm long but only 1–2.5cm in diameter. They are grey coloured and have an uneven and untidy look to them, often with bones and other matter protruding. They contain mainly small rodents, but bird, frog and lizard remains are also quite common. Urban Tawny Owls have been found to have a higher proportion of birds in their diets than rural birds. (Be careful not to confuse the pellets of this species with mammal droppings as they do tend to have a narrower end.)

Short-eared Owl Pellets are slightly neater, longer and wider than those of Tawnies' – 2–8cm long and up to 3cm in diameter. The species prefers open grassland habitats and uplands, and its pellets are most often found beneath prominent perches such as posts, but this owl also roosts and perches on the ground. The pellets often contain bones of Field Voles and shrews.

10   11   12   13   14

The main reason why Short-eared Owl pellets are difficult to find is because it is a rare bird.

Quite difficult to separate from the pellets of Tawnies, this is the lumpy production of a Long-eared Owl.

10   11   12   13   14   15

Long-eared Owl The pellets are of a similar size – 2–5cm long and about 2cm in diameter – to those of Tawnies, though they look more elongated, and share the same sort of irregular shape. Long-eareds prefer to roost in dense conifers.

Little Owl Produces little rounded pellets (ranging from 2 to 4cm in length and 1–2cm in diameter) that match its diminutive size. Its diet of principally small invertebrates such as beetles and worms, and occasional small mammals and birds, gives the pellets a very distinctive look and texture. The owl's mainly invertebrate summer diet makes the pellets quite delicate – they crush down into a powdery consistency in almost the same way large bat droppings do – and also gives them a black or dark brown colour. Being a diurnal species, if you've come across a collection of fresh pellets the chances are that the owl will be somewhere nearby. In winter, the owls feed more on small mammals. Pellets can be found below regular perches such as fence posts, and in holes in buildings and trees. The species has a preference for open parkland or fields interspersed with mature trees. There maybe some confusion with Kestrel pellets, but the thin bones in a Kestrel casting will have been eroded by partial digestion; in a Little Owl's they remain intact.

Little Owl pellets are best looked for under regularly used perches and roosts.

Little Owl pellets nearly always contain the remains of beetles and, of course, they are much smaller than the pellets of other owls.

Other owl species on the European continent

Northern Hawk Owl Pellets are small and in summer are likely to contain rodent bones, but in winter they are more likely to contain bird remains, such as grouse or Ptarmigan.

Tengmalm's Owl This bird's small irregular pellets (3.5 x 1.5cm) contain signs of small mammals and birds that are often visible on the surface.

Eurasian Pygmy Owl Small pellets that are on average 2.8 x 1.2cm in size, which are likely to contain the bones of small birds such as thrushes, crossbills, and Pied Flycatchers, and the remains of small mammals, fish and insects.

Northern Hawk Owl

Tengmalm's Owl

Eurasian Pygmy Owl

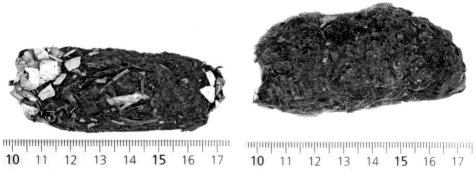

Great Grey Owl

Snowy Owl

Great Grey Owl A large owl that regurgitates large pellets on average 7.5 to 10 cm long, which are grey in colour and compact.

Snowy Owl Large pellets, 5–15cm long and 2–4.5cm in diameter, quite loose and irregular in shape, and contain fragments of Rabbit, small rodent and bird bones. These birds often swallow their own feathers, which are distinctive and easy to recognise in the pellets.

Other raptors

Hawks, eagles and falcons have very powerful digestive systems with a much lower pH than that of owls, so they do a pretty good job of digesting all but the most tenacious fragments of their meals.

Kestrel The small pellets (2–4 x 1–2.5cm) when fresh are an almost-perfect, if slightly squashed, teardrop shape. They are light grey and have a fine fibrous texture, reflecting the high proportion of small mammals and birds in the falcon's diet. Occasionally you will find small bone fragments and hard chitinous insect remains. They can sometimes be quite difficult to separate from the pellets of Little Owl.

Kestrels eat a surprising quantity of insect prey if it is available. Because of this it can be difficult to separate their pellets from those produced by Little Owls.

Peregrine Falcon The medium-sized pellets of Peregrines – 2–9 x 1–3cm – can be confused with those of several other raptors. They vary in colour but are nearly always made up of feather fibres.

Hobby Quite small pellets (2–3 x 1–1.5cm) with a more rounded look to them than a Kestrel's, though they can be confused if both have been eating small birds. The early-season diet of insects is reflected in the shiny remains of the exoskeletons of moths, bees and beetles. The pellets become more difficult to identify later on in the season when the falcons start to feed more on small birds; they will then contain feather fibres and bits of bird bone.

This is a Peregrine Falcon pellet. Usually birds of prey produce one or two pellets a day.

Merlin Pellets contain feather fibres and fragments of small bird bones. They are similar to Kestrel pellets, but slightly smaller, and are quite difficult to identify.

Buzzard The large pellets of these birds (4.5–6 x 2.5–3cm) are very rounded, with one end tapering more than the other. The variety of prey taken by this species is reflected in the different consistencies and colours of the pellets produced: very pale and fibrous if they've been scavenging on sheep carcasses; dark grey and fibrous if they've been eating Rabbits and other small mammals, and crumbly if they've been eating beetles and earthworms. If bones are present, they will have been partially eroded by the stomach acids (a useful way of separating the pellets from those of the large owls). Due to this variation the pellets are hard to distinguish from those of several other species of raptor, so other signs need to be present to confirm identity.

Buzzard pellets contain the bones of small mammals and can be found in open grassland and mixed woodland areas.

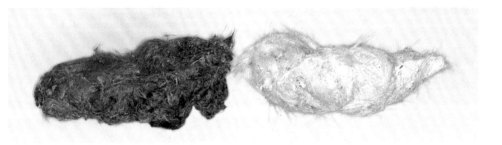

The Red Kite mainly preys on animal carrion such as sheep, Rabbits and birds, but will also take small birds, mammals and insects as live prey. The bones of all of these can be found in its pellets.

Red Kite Similar to Buzzard.

Sparrowhawk Its small pellets are rounded at one end and tapered at the other (2–3.5 x 1–2cm). They remind me of very small Tawny Owl pellets in their shape, but they lack much in the way of bone fragments. The feather fibres give the pellets an almost luminous, pale grey appearance on dark forest floors, where they are most likely to be encountered. Look for other signs, such as droppings and feathers, to confirm identity.

Sparrowhawk

||||||||||||||||||||||||||||||||||||||||||||||||||
10   11   12   13   14   **15**   16

Goshawk

||||||||||||||||||||||||||||||||||||||||||||||||||||||||||||||
10   11   12   13   14   **15**   16   17   18   19   **20**

White-tailed Eagle

Goshawk The pellets are a similar size to those of a Buzzard, but with more feather fragments, and are a similar shape to a Sparrowhawk's. Goshawks also hunt Rabbits and squirrels.

Eagles Large, hard-to-identify pellets (9–11 x 3.5–4cm). They are usually made up of a matrix of fur and feathers, containing bone fragments (those of White-tailed Eagles have been found with intact bird limbs). The presence of fish scales and bones is a reasonable indicator that the pellet belongs to a White-tailed, though this isn't totally reliable.

Harriers Small, rounded pellets which are very difficult to separate from the pellets of other raptors unless you are in a well-known haunt, beneath regular perches or at communal roost sites.

Osprey Loose pellets containing almost exclusively the bones and scales of fish.

Above: Collected around winter roosts sites, these harrier pellets contain lots of feather material, telling us that the birds have been feeding on small birds.

Osprey pellets are rare and crumble easily. Ospreys have a crop and therefore do not regurgitate their food as frequently as owls.

||||||||||||||||||||||||||||||||||||||||||||||||||||||||||||||||
10   11   12   13   14   **15**   16   17

Corvids

All members of the crow family can produce elongated but rounded pellets, and because of the birds broad tastes and opportunistic behaviour the pellets tend to contain the identifiable remains of all manner of materials from the husks of grain, plants seeds and pips, to fur, wool, feathers and bone, as well as other debris such as stones, string and plastic. They can be very variable in size depending on the quantities of indigestible materials that have been consumed. Their loose structure, the variety of remains and a definite musty smell can at least help to separate pellets of this family from those of raptors.

Raven pellets tend to be below or on high rock outcrops and cliffs, and you often find pellets under rookeries. It is, however, extremely hard to identify the pellet of a Carrion Crow.

Raven Pellets are very variable in size (5–8 x 2–3cm), but tend to be much bigger than the pellets produced by other members of the crow family. Their equally variable colour and contents reflect the opportunistic scavenging lifestyle of this bird. They can contain anything from wool to Rabbit fur, small bones and even bird rings.

Look for Rook balls beneath rookeries; they are often fibrous and contain vegetable matter.

I watched an upland crow produce this pellet, which glinted in the light due to a large beetle content.

Carrion Crow Pellet size (3–7 x 1–2cm)

Rook Pellet size (3–4 x 1–1.5cm)

Jackdaw Pellet size (2.5–3 x 1–1.5cm)

Magpie Pellet size (3.5–4.5 x 1–2cm)

Chough Smallish, dark and quite crumbly pellets, which contain a large amount (about 50 per cent) of invertebrate exoskeletons; the rest is seed and grain husks.

This Black-headed Gull is regurgitating a typical neat and smooth pellet. Pellets don't get much fresher than this, but they weather quickly.

Gulls

Herring Gull pellets, in particular, are frequently found because the species is a real urban survivor and happily co-exists with us in cities and coastal resorts. The size of gull pellets vary, as you might expect with the size of the bird, but most are compact and almost spherical, containing a variety of hard indigestible items. Birds that forage in fairly natural situations mostly feed on fish and molluscs; their pellets tend to be tightly woven with fine bones and fragments criss-crossing all over the place, and not aligned like the pellets of raptors. If they've been feeding on crustaceans, the pellets tend to be crumbly with obvious particles of shell, but if the birds have been feeding on fields or landfill sites the pellets will be much more crumbly and will contain husks of grain or indeed plastic, string and any item that could potentially fit into the beak of a scavenging bird.

Usually gull pellets contain fish bones and crustacean fragments, but when the birds have been feeding on fields, grain is not an unusual find.

Wading birds

Most birds that feed on shores and mudflats produce pellets of some kind that are particularly short lived and consist of gritty material and small organic items. They blend in so well with their habitat that they are easy to miss. Many waders are of a similar size, which makes identifying their pellets quite difficult. You really need to see a bird bring up a pellet to be sure of a correct identification.

I first became aware that waders regurgitate the indigestible residue of their diet while fishing off a pier that was habitually used as a high-tide roost by a small 'gang' of Turnstones. These charismatic little shorebirds spend much of their time foraging for small molluscs, worms and crustaceans along the shore. Because these prey are incredibly small and fiddly to process and the Turnstone is up against the clock to forage between the tides, digestion takes place when the tide is in and the pressure is off. Any hard crunchy stuff can then be regurgitated. This is exactly what I witnessed happening from time to time. On investigation of the birds' roost site after they had departed, I found small, sandy dollops of loose grit, containing fragments of shrimp, worm jaws, bits of barnacle and mollusc shells.

Wading birds, such as the Green Sandpiper, produce small, smooth, grainy pellets, usually made of excess mud, grit and tiny fragments of their prey; these pellets are a rare find.

What's in an owl pellet?

Small mammals make up the bulk of the diets of these super-efficient hunters, so it's useful to be able to identify their remains and to be able to pick up on any rare and surprise prey species. Let's start with skulls, which are the biggest bones you are likely to come across.

It's almost a science in its own right. Investigating what is in an owl pellet is very revealing and quite addictive.

Insectivores

Skulls and jaws with continuous rows of teeth belong to various species of shrew. Their skulls are small but relatively long and thin, and look quite bird-like. Shrew teeth have discoloured, orangey-brown 'tea-stained' caps to their sharp and pointed teeth. Size and tooth shape are the clinchers when separating the Water Shrew (the largest species), Common Shrew and Pygmy Shrew.

If you are looking at pellets from birds on the European continent, the Scilly Isles, Ireland and the Channel Isles, you may find other species of shrew. The white-toothed shrews are recognised, not surprisingly, by their white teeth, but in all other aspects their skulls resemble those of the other, more common and widespread species. The Lesser White-toothed Shrew is found on the Isles of Scilly, Jersey and Sark, while the Greater lives on Alderney, Guernsey and Herm, and in the Republic of Ireland.

Moles also turn up, and their skulls look superficially like those of shrews, but are bigger and bulkier, though still elongated. The teeth, however, are white, and Moles have prominent canine teeth, whereas the teeth of shrews all seem to run at the same height from the axis of the jawbone.

Bats are rarely taken by owls, but do turn up from time to time in their pellets. They can be recognised by a short, squat skull and mandible complete with sharp white teeth – those in the front of the jaw don't protrude forward as in shrews and Moles. Interestingly, the red coloration in shrew teeth is actually caused by the presence of iron, which makes the teeth hard and sharp. Shrew teeth have more than 10,000ppm (parts per million) of iron, whereas the white teeth of a Mole or any other mammal only have 70ppm.

Small mammals

Mice and voles make up the majority of raptor diets and therefore turn up frequently in pellets. There is a big gap between a rodents' chiselling incisors and the cheek teeth, which makes the skulls and jaws of these animals instantly recognisable.

The best way of distinguishing voles from mice is by having a good look at the cheek teeth. Both types of animal have three teeth in each jaw, but the shapes are different. If you look at the horizontal grinding surfaces you'll notice that voles' teeth have a zigzag edge to them whereas the edges of mice teeth are rounded.

If you don't have any loose teeth in your sorting dish, you can gently pull them out of their jaw sockets with a pair of forceps.

With care and attention to detail it is possible to identify most of the unfortunate animals down to species level, given the right books and information.

Mice have rooted teeth, complete with little rounded cusps, whereas voles' teeth look like little blocks of enamel with a corrugated surface.

If you pull the teeth out of a vole's jaw you will see slots, which run along the axis of the jaw. Bank Voles have three slots, while the root cavities of Field Voles (the Barn Owl's favourite) blend together to form a single continuous groove. Field Vole teeth have little in the way of separate roots, with ridges and furrows running from the top to the very bottom of the root. Bank Vole teeth have a root-like structure and the ridges do not run all the way down them. Water Vole teeth sometimes turn up and these look like much bigger versions of Short-tailed Field Vole teeth.

The most common prey in most owl pellets is rodents – look for the large and orange incisor teeth.

If you apply the same dentistry skills to the jaws and teeth of mice, you will immediately notice that as the teeth come out of the jaw they leave neat little rounded holes. The patterns left by this closed-root system are diagnostic. Wood Mice and Yellow-necked Mice have six root holes (the latter are rare in pellets, and the longer lower jaw is the best guide – anything over 16mm), Harvest Mice have seven root holes and House Mice have five root holes. The incisors are also notched in House Mice, which separates them from all others. Larger molars with ten root holes indicate that rat was on the menu, although often it's the juveniles that are taken.

If you notice four teeth in the jaws you've got a dormouse skull. This will also have a little hole in the corner of the jaw angle on the lower jaw.

Rabbit

Young Rabbits sometimes turn up in owl pellets, and the teeth and bones of adults may be evident in Eagle Owl pellets and those of other large raptor species. Rabbit skulls are big, and the cheek teeth have a groove that runs down the length of the side of the tooth, with two oval cusps.

Least Weasel

Least Weasels sometimes turn up in pellets and look distinctive with their large size and large canines.

Birds

The skulls of birds regularly appear in pellets, but because they are very thin and lightweight they are rarely preserved intact within a pellet. Without teeth, you have to rely on a good fragment of the beak to confirm identity. The beak should give you an indication of what kind of bird was taken: long and narrow could be Blackbird or Starling (the latter has a slightly downward-bent beak); short and thick is probably a kind of finch or sparrow.

Other bones

Bird bones are usually very thin – almost see-through – compared with those of mammals. In cross-section they are either hollow or filled with a spongy-looking substance to keep them light in weight for flight. There are a couple of other signature bird bones that may show up, such as the sacrum and the sternum, which are fusions of bones.

Fish bones may turn up from time to time in Tawny Owl pellets.

Mole

Big, flat, almost plate-like bones, usually accompanied by other short and squat bones, are the robust front-limb bones of Moles.

Frogs and toads

Amphibian bones are thin and double-barrelled in cross-section. If you find these, look out for a strange T-shaped bone (some refer to it as a cross), which is the floor of the skull.

Fish

Scales will be present, and the bones will have a typical jagged and needle-like look to them. The vertebrae are distinctive, too, with a smooth concave surface at each end.

DISSECTION OF A PELLET

Dissecting a pellet will enable you to work out in detail what a bird has been eating. It is best to start with an owl pellet. Owls swallow their prey whole. They do not have a crop and have a weaker digestive process compared with other birds. Because of this a considerable portion of their food is regurgitated and the remains of their diet are better preserved than in the pellets of other birds. I am using a Barn Owl pellet in this example. If you're having trouble finding an owl pellet, you can now even buy one on the Internet.

1.

If the pellet is large and firm you may need to soak it for a few moments until it has become less buoyant and sunk. Then carefully remove it to a shallow tray of water or a weak solution of disinfectant. You will need forceps or tweezers and a dissection probe. Cocktail sticks are also handy.

2.

Begin to gently tease apart the pellet using the probe and forceps. You will quickly see that the background packing material is actually the fine grey fur of mammals.

3.

Feathers may also be evident if the bird has been feeding on its smaller relatives. However, be aware that sometimes a bird of prey will also consume its own feathers when preening.

4.

Separate out the bones. If you are going to keep the bones for future reference, I would recommend transferring them to a weak peroxide solution (such as very watery bleach) for half an hour. Then place them on a kitchen towel to dry. Needless to say, take care when working with acid substances.

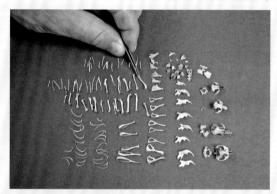

5.

Sort out the bones, starting with the upper portions of small mammal skulls. Try to match these to the lower jaw mandibles and pretty soon you'll get a good idea of the identity and the number of victims taken by the owl on its feeding foray.

6.

Also look out for teeth, scapula bones, and claws and other odd items; reptile and amphibian bones occasionally turn up, as do the remains of fish and the beaks of birds. It is helpful to group together finds by size.

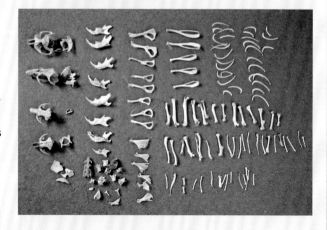

Occasionally, pale caterpillars or hairy insect larvae turn up as well; these are nature's recyclers of keratin and are the immature stages of clothes moths, and Museum and Carpet Beetles.

If you want to keep the bones, you can either bottle them in specimen tubes, with a dried silica pouch, or mount them with glue on a black board.

Dead things

Finding a dead animal can often be a real challenge for the nature detective in terms of working out whether the individual died from natural causes or was killed by a predator. Scavengers of all types and sizes will quickly start the recycling process and this, of course, doesn't make your task any easier. Each group of predators, however, has a particular modus operandi that can help you narrow down the investigation and point the finger at 'who done it'.

A dead animal immediately launches many questions – what killed it? How did it die? Is this where it happened or has the body been moved? What's been eating it? Has it been scavenged or killed? It's the nature detective's job to try and piece together the story.

🐾 Birds on birds

A pile of feathers scattered around a prominent post, rock or ledge may well suggest that a bird of prey has taken a victim. Pay attention to the habitat in which such a 'plucking' post is situated, and the size and type of prey that the remains belong to, as these are all clues as to who has been operating in the area. If it's windy and exposed you may have to do a bit of feather following before you find the plucking post. Sometimes you may find only a big 'puff' of feathers, without any other signs, and this is likely to be the place where the bird was struck and killed.

Above: *When birds hit on other birds like this male Sparrowhawk has – it's about the feathers. The species of prey and a few other details can give you the answers.*

Right: *This is the butcher's block for a Sparrowhawk that has used it as a convenient perch to pluck and feed on a smaller bird.*

After making a kill and if it isn't feeding young at a nest, a bird of prey will carry its prize to a nearby secure perch to process it. It will first decapitate the victim and eat its brain. It will either rip the skull apart, leaving fragments and the beak, or swallow the head whole. It will then move onto the breast meat and body cavity contents; often all that remains of a kill are feathers and feet.

If a carcass has been left, look for little triangular notches made by the raptor's beak in the sternum. The bird of prey begins by ripping away any large feathers and those of the breast before entering the body cavity.

In more open environments such as salt marshes, beaches and cliff tops, dense patches of feathers can be attributed to the Peregrine Falcon.

Guess who's been to dinner

A plucking post in a woodland setting could be used by either of the woodland hawks: Sparrowhawk or Goshawk. The Sparrowhawk is far more common and widespread than the Goshawk and will more often than not take smaller birds, although a big female may take doves and pigeons. The Goshawk takes small prey, but is more likely to routinely target larger birds such as Woodpigeons and doves.

A post, boulder or hummock with the feathers and legs of numerous species of small bird in an open moorland setting is likely to be the plucking post of a Merlin, but it could also be the work of a Kestrel, particularly in rough grassland and field margins.

Harriers tend to be fairly habitat specific and use a different plucking site after each kill. Hen Harriers frequent heather moorland and Marsh Harriers are associated with wet areas, but the fact that they take small passerines, as do Kestrels and Merlins, makes these birds very difficult to distinguish from each other by kill evidence alone.

Peregrine Falcons are birds of big skies and open vistas (and cities now); remains of birds, particularly pigeons found on ledges, cliffs and other such open spaces, are likely to be their work.

These are by no means hard and fast rules – there are exceptions. I've found Peregrine feeding remains in woodland near a quarry where the birds were nesting, and I've seen Sparrowhawks plucking prey from field hedges and suburban gardens.

FEATHER DAMAGE – BIRD OR MAMMAL?

If a bird of prey has feasted on the carcass of another bird then feathers will often have a pinch, crease or split along their length. Mammals use their sharp carnassial teeth to cut through feathers, leaving the rachis (shaft) neatly sheared through. Their saliva also causes feathers to clump together in masses.

Large numbers of feathers with no sign of damage or any other body parts point to some kind of trauma.

Individual feathers with no obvious damage have probably been naturally shed by the owner.

The remains of a Little Tern on a beach not far from a nesting colony – question is who did it?

Birds on mammals

Normally very little or nothing at all is left when a predatory bird has fed on a small mammal. Most small to medium-sized owls leave no evidence of their meals, as they usually manage to jam the entire prey down their gullet in one go. Larger owls take larger prey, such as Rabbits or adult rats, which they tear into chunks and swallow pieces whole until most if not all of the meal has been consumed. They sometimes leave behind a little fur and maybe a limb or two, but not much else.

No chance of finding any feeding remains in this situation – Barn Owls swallow their prey whole.

It can be very difficult to separate the kill of a bird from one that has been subsequently worked over by scavengers such as Foxes. Buzzards, eagles and Goshawks tend to tug out beakfuls of fur before making the first penetrating plunge with their beak, and when the bird has been able to take its time the body will be surrounded by a halo of hair, fluff and fur. A large meal may take many hours to consume, and the bird may revisit it for several sittings, a process which, depending on the hunger of the bird, can leave nothing but the skin and a few indigestible body parts.

Smaller mammals, such as young Rabbits and rats, can be tugged almost inside out by a Buzzard's beak, leaving the skin looking like a discarded furry sock. A Rabbit or squirrel body in a woodland, maybe draped over a log or stump, is probably the work of a Goshawk. Other clues such as pellets or more likely the 'slice' of the bird will help. Sparrowhawks tend to excrete a pure-white dropping which is squirted some distance backwards away from the kill, while the Goshawk's squirt, which can be up to 150–200cm from the kill site, is a little more yellow. A large kill that a hawk has worked on for some time is often surrounded not only by a decorative ring of fluff, but also by radiating spokes of whitewash.

Butcher birds Shrikes are unusual in the sense that they are relatively small passerines that prey on small mammals and invertebrates. Because they lack the strength in the feet of other, more typical 'birds of prey', and also because they often require a store or cache of food, these birds create larders where prey is either wedged in the forks of suitable bushes or trees, or impaled on thorns.

The Goshawk and other birds of prey will tackle large prey and spend some time working the carcass unless disturbed. During this protracted feeding they often leave other clues for the detective.

The sorts of prey species taken depend on the species of shrike. The Great Grey Shrike is a large bird capable of tackling prey such as small mammals, amphibians and rodents, although beetles, caterpillars and grasshoppers also are taken.

The smaller Red-backed Shrike tends to tackle invertebrates and is inclined to impale its prey, while the Great Grey is more likely to wedge its food into place.

A strangely decorated thorn bush, complete with impaled beetles, small birds and mammals, is the unmistakable signature of the Great Grey Shrike also known as the 'butcher bird'.

Mammals on birds

The clearest sign that a mammal has been on a bird kill is the presence of feathers that are sheared clean through at the base. If you watch a Fox feeding, it will often use the side of its mouth to chew through anything tough, behaviour that leaves clumps of neatly sheared feathers stuck together with saliva. Foxes also sometimes leave their scat in situ.

Mammals usually leave evidence of crushed bones and even teeth marks in the bones, so that overall the carcass can look much messier than the kill of a bird of prey. If the kill is fresh, the musty and pungent scent of many mammals, especially Foxes and Badgers, may be detectable.

Mammals on mammals

Small mammals are the perfect mouthful, so most 'mouse-size' meals are consumed in their entirety leaving no trace for the tracker, with the exceptions of Moles and shrews. You'll often see a shrew carcass at the side of a path, perfect in every way except for slightly wet and ruffled fur where it has been mouthed by its killer. Shrews use flank glands to mark their runs, and the substance they secrete is repulsive to the taste buds of many mammals and even some birds of prey. The predator presumably kills and then abandons its meal when it realises how distasteful it is.

These clusters of pigeon feathers, clearly pulled out together, sheared off at the base and stuck together with saliva, are almost certainly the work of a Fox.

Shrews have pungent glands on their flanks, which many mammals find distasteful. This is why you may often find just the decapitated body, or an abandoned shrew carcass.

Mustelids The weasel family usually kills with a swift bite to the back or side of the neck or head, and if an animal drops its prey while carrying it to another location a close inspection will show very little other damage, just puncture wounds and saliva-soaked fur in the area of the bite.

Although Badgers usually take small invertebrate prey, they love Hedgehogs and often leave nothing but a clean skin, like a spiky doormat. The stops of Rabbits are also a favourite hunting ground, and Badgers will eat the Rabbit kits on the spot leaving their little skins turned partially inside out, usually with the stomach and caecum left intact; Foxes will also do this.

Wolverines are the largest members of the family and often take large prey, overpowering it by leaping on it, and delivering bites to the back of the neck. Deer and sheep are too much for one meal, and so the Wolverine often butchers its prey and carry it away in pieces to bury it.

A Rabbit carcass with a wet neck or wound to the back of the head is classic Stoat killing sign.

Foxes eat almost anything, but a large meal will often be carried off and hidden or buried for later.

Fox Foxes take a range of prey – bites to the neck, nose and beak are all common signs of Fox predation. They often start by removing the head of their prey and carrying the rest off and burying it. Smaller meals, once the initial hunger is satisfied, buried in what is known as a food cache. Food caching is a very typical foxy thing to do as the Fox is a fairly slight predator, with a relatively small stomach (which can only hold a maximum of 10 per cent of the body weight). Removal of food keeps it safe from the attention of other opportunistic scavengers, so by pushing food into dense undergrowth or burying it underground the Fox can return to consume it later.

Food caches can sometimes be found in areas of loose sandy soil – look for areas of disturbed ground with shallow grooves where a Fox has heaped up material over the food with its muzzle. Sometimes wings, feet and bones can be seen protruding from the ground.

Foxes usually urinate on feeding sites, which gives a

very distinctive 'foxy' smell to fresh evidence. They often leave skin, fur and feathers; limb bones are stripped clean, but the feet and feathers are relatively untouched.

Foxes scavenge – this is all that remains of a lamb after a family of Foxes has finished feeding.

Wolves tackle large prey as a pack – the resulting scene is usually fairly obvious and is a messy assortment of tracks, scat and hair.

Wildcats Cats are much more delicate in their operations, and feral cats and Wildcats kills are difficult to tell apart. They usually start on carcasses in the shoulder region and pick leg bones clean. They rarely decapitate birds or Rabbits, but may turn them inside out as do by Foxes and Badgers.

The bigger cats, such as lynxes, tend to bite their prey in the throat to bring it down; otherwise, the feeding signs are similar to those of other cats, with the head and lungs typically left untouched. They will return to larger kills, sometimes partially covering them with vegetation and/or snow.

Scottish Wildcats are pure carnivores; they eat only meat. This one has dragged its Rabbit prey up an oak tree for undisturbed feeding.

Brown Bears occasionally tackle large prey, such as deer, using a combination of biting, usually on the head, and blows with the front paws to bring it down. Once dispatched, feeding usually starts with the softer underside and the offal. Bears invest quite a lot of time in covering the entire carcass with vegetation in between visits.

This Brown Bear is eating a Roe Deer. However, it also feeds on fruit, berries, nuts, roots and leaves.

CARNIVORE CANINES

The bite marks of a mammal may sometimes register well on a prey item, bone or shell, and it is usually the indentations or damage caused by the well-developed canine teeth that are most distinctive.

Taking into account the size variation between individuals of the same species and that the upper canines tend to be further apart than the lower ones, here is a rough guide to the distance between the teeth.

Mink *(Neovison vison)* 9–11mm

Scottish Wildcat *(Felis silvestris grampia)* 18mm

European Lynx *(Lynx lynx)* 25–35mm

Wolverine *(Gulo gulo)* 25–35mm

Fox *(Vulpes vulpes)* 26–30mm

Badger *(Meles meles)* 28–30mm

Wolf *(Canis lupis)* 35–50mm

European Brown Bear *(Ursus arctos)* 45–65mm

The Scottish Wildcat is a true carnivore; its canine teeth are specially developed for hunting, holding prey and stabbing flesh.

The remains of dinner

In this section we look at what is left at the dinner table once the main meal is over – nature's leftovers and plate scrapings. These can take many forms depending on the diet of the animal in question. It might seem difficult to decide if something has just died or has been naturally discarded, or whether you are looking at feeding signs. With experience, you will start to notice details, patterns and arrangements, which will give you a clue as to what happened.

Above: On closer inspection, this pile of debris turns out to be the remains of several crayfish eaten by a mink.

Fish remains near water that have been neatly chomped could be the work of either an Otter or a Mink.

Fishy tales

If you find a partially eaten fish close to water, then an Otter or Mink is almost certainly responsible. The head and the guts are eaten first, but in most cases every morsel of flesh is removed, leaving a spine, the hard parts of the head and the skin, which is often rolled backwards towards the tail where it rucks up, like a hastily abandoned sleeping bag.

Fish are taken by a variety of birds, too, and the remains of large fish with most of the flesh gone can be attributed to an Osprey if Ospreys are in the area. Herons sometimes kill large fish, then abandon them – look for single or multiple stab wounds caused by the beak of the bird.

Amphibians

Every spring throughout most of the northern hemisphere frogs and toads gather en masse to spawn. These noisy orgies of procreation draw the attention of predators, such as herons, Storks, Buzzards, Mink, Otters, Hedgehogs, Foxes and Badgers, among others.

Frogs are more palatable to most mammals as they lack the distasteful skin glands of toads and are eaten in their entirety by many animals, especially birds, which tend to spear them, then swallow them whole.

Signs of frog or toad predation are variable: usually the legs and heads are taken, leaving the skin, particularly of toads, and sometimes the spawn carried by females in the breeding season.

Foxes are the most likely predators in urban situations and will leave partially eaten frogs and dollops of spawn. Mink often kill many frogs, consume a few and cache the rest for later. A Mink will sometimes leaves bodies or parts of bodies stashed in piles in root holes or under sheds.

Occasionally, an Otter or Mink will take toads – in most cases both eat only the legs in a

The mass mating gatherings of amphibians in the spring are too much of a temptation for many predators, such as this Polecat.

process termed 'de-gloving', whereby they bite across the pelvis or lower back and pull the skin off the legs backwards, consuming the leg muscles. This is a horrible thing to stumble upon especially when fresh, as some of the toads may still be alive. I've also witnessed Buzzards feeding on toads, but again they usually rip out the insides leaving fragments of skin and feet.

Shattered shells

On land the most frequently encountered signs of predated molluscs are the shells of snails. A pile of empty cracked shells scattered around a rock, step, hard log or any other suitable 'anvil' is almost always a sign that a Song Thrush has been busy. These birds feed on snails at any time of the year, but when times are hard and the ground is frozen I've seen them working their way along garden walls, hedges and banks, winkling snails out of cracks and crevices, then taking them to a favourite anvil to eat.

Many rodents also eat snails, particularly Bank Voles, but Wood Mice, Brown Rats, Yellow-necked Mice and Field Voles are also partial to snails from time to time. If you find a collection of shells hidden away in a hole, underneath a piece of corrugated tin, in a bird's nest or under a log, it's highly likely that a small rodent of some kind has been using this as its lair. If you want to be doubly sure, have a look at the damage on a shell: a rodent nibbles its way into the hapless animal inside by entering through the coil of the shell, normally leaving the lip intact.

A common garden sight and sound is that of the Song Thrush – here it has returned to a favourite rock, or anvil, to smash the shells of snails.

The fact that these snail shells have all had the coil neatly nibbled out tells me this is the work of a Field Vole not a thrush.

Otters often take shellfish such as Swan Mussels, nibbling along the edges of the shell to access the animal inside.

Clamming up

Many molluscs are aquatic and can be found under the surface of water, mud or silt in both freshwater and saltwater environments.

Otters will take freshwater mussels and it is thought that they are responsible for some of the neat piles of shells found on some river banks. Shells have been found that look as if they have been nipped along their edges, but whether or not Otters have created these marks is uncertain. Measurements between the tooth marks on some of the shells are in keeping with the distance between the incisors of an Otter, so it is possible that only certain populations of Otter have learned the skills necessary to extract the molluscs inside and have then passed this knowledge on.

Mink take molluscs occasionally, but in the detailed studies carried out on these mammals they hardly feature.

Water Voles, like their land-based cousins, sometimes supplement their plant-based diet with molluscs. They access the meat inside freshwater clams by nibbling chunks out of the edge of the shell until they break through to the adductor muscle.

Brown Rats often regularly take molluscs of all kinds. Separating their work from that of other rodents is a challenge; you often need to take into account other signs and habitat. They are excellent swimmers and in some places, particularly in tidal areas, even make a habit of diving for their food. I have seen a large adult swim down to a river bed and emerge with a mussel or clam, which it has then carried off somewhere private to work on. A Brown Rat holds a mussel upright and nibbles away at one end until it breaks through the adductor muscle. You may come across evidence of this behaviour in the form of small middens of shells.

These leftovers are the work of Mink; the presence of Mink droppings confirms this. Crayfish remains are distinctive – note the white button-like gastroliths, or stomach stones, of these crustaceans.

Muskrat On the Continent, where there are populations of the introduced Muskrat, feeding stations complete with distinctive runs, droppings and other signs, often feature the shells of freshwater clams of which Muskrats are very fond.

Skilled oyster smashers Oystercatchers excel at catching and consuming molluscs of many kinds, mainly cockles and mussels. They have famously developed techniques for dealing with the rather specialised task of extracting a snail from its fortress. The pioneering work of ecologist John Goss-Custard, who studied the feeding behaviour of these birds, identified several different techniques used to tackle their prey. He found that the birds belong to three 'guilds', distinguishable from each other by slightly different shapes to the bill tip. There are stabbers, chisellers and hammerers, and they leave damage consistent with their methods of feeding.

Oystercatcher or mussel-killer, this bird uses three shell-opening techniques to get to the soft mollusc inside the shell: stabbing, chiselling and smashing.

Any shell with a localised area of damage could easily point to Oystercatcher activity. The hammerers are the least subtle of the bunch and create the most easily identifiable signs. They select a mussel from the rocks, usually targeting the fastest-growing individuals with the thinnest shells, then wedge the entire shellfish in a crevice or between its feet and bash into the ventral side of the mussel with its heavy blunt-tipped bill. This breaking and entering leaves the shell with a portion missing on the hinge side of the shell.

The chisellers usually work in situ over exposed mussel beds. When they find a suitable thin-shelled victim, they chisel their way through the valves on the opposite side to the hammerers, and this leaves a notch bashed out of the thinner edges of the shell.

The third group of Oystercatchers is the stabbers – most tend to be juvenile birds and females. They wedge the mussel on its side and stab their suitably thin and pointy beak ends between the valves, cutting through the nearest adductor muscle, then levering the shells apart. This behaviour leaves few if any signs – maybe just a little superficial damage to the ends of the shells.

The hammerers and chisellers also tackle that other 'hard hat' of the shoreline: the limpet. Oystercatchers tend to select species with the thinnest shells, such as *Patella aspersa*. They smash into them at the weakest point of contact, that is, on either side of the head where the foot muscle is at its weakest.

The fast-growing beak of the Oystercatcher (which grows three times faster than your fingernails) is a handy multi tool. Here it is being used to gain access and lever apart the valves of a mussel.

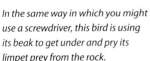

In the same way in which you might use a screwdriver, this bird is using its beak to get under and pry its limpet prey from the rock.

Cuttlebones

Those soft white objects looking like tiny windsurf boards washed up on many beaches are all that remain of squid and more often cuttlefish, which are larger and more obvious. We call them 'cuttlebones' because they are found inside the animals, but they are in fact specialised internal shells, made of calcium carbonate. So when the remains of these marine animals wash up on the shore, they are an easy source of calcium. Look closely at the soft white surfaces and you'll nearly always find strange little triangular pock marks; these are the impressions left by the beaks of birds, more often than not various species of gull.

Left: *This bivalve bears the evidence of the work of a driller killer – a smooth, rounded hole bored by the Necklace Shell.*

Bored shells

Gastropods (snail-like molluscs) are found on shorelines, but they have tougher and thicker shells than their land-living counterparts. It is quite common to find the shells of these and the valves of otherwise secretive burrowing molluscs with perfect chamfered holes that pass right through. These holes are made by other, predatory snails.

Many species have turned their scraping radula organ into a device that works just like a drill bit. It is often on the tip of an extendable proboscis that can bore a hole in a shell, in combination with an acidic secretion produced at the same time by an accessory boring organ, which is diverted from time to time into the borehole.

Cuttlefish bones are worth a look at as the beak marks of the birds that scavenged the softer flesh are often evident in the soft, white chalky material.

The entire drilling process varies depending on the thickness of the shell and the size of the predator, but in Sting Winkles it has been recorded to take 8–16 hours of alternating grinding and dissolving action – with much longer taken over the production of acid and enzymes (for every minute of drilling there are about 30 minutes of oozing). By this process these predatory are molluscs can gain access and grind their way through the toughest of shells.

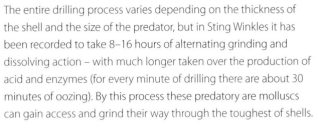

Dog Whelks simply crawl around a barnacle colony rasping the tops off to get to the helpless crustaceans inside, leaving nothing but empty shells still stuck to the rock.

Variation in the size of predator and prey means there will always be a bit of guesswork involved in identifying the predatory species.

Necklace Shell or Moon Snail This species is found on sandy beaches and specialises in feeding on burrowing bivalve molluscs. Its signature is a very neat hole about 2–3mm across, with a chamfered edge to it, tapering from the outside inwards. The hole is usually positioned near the umbo (knobbly middle bit of the shell).

Dog Whelk This is a scavenger, but it also actively preys on mussels and barnacles. It uses its accessory boring organ to scrape its way into victims, making holes in mussels and consuming barnacles alive. If the hole is in a mussel and the habitat is a rocky shore, the Dog Whelk is probably the culprit.

Sting Winkle This gastropod has a more eclectic taste and preys on a larger range of species than many of the others, but it is fond of cockles. A steeply bevelled drill hole of around 2mm is created by an adult snail.

American Sting Winkle or Atlantic Oyster Drill Introduced with American Oyster stocks and now a pest of commercial oyster beds. As their reputation and their names suggest these beasts love oysters (particularly the younger, thinner-shelled individuals) and are mainly responsible for holes in the valves of these species. Usually the hole is no more than 1mm across and less bevelled than that made by the Moon Snail.

The Sting Winkle makes a small bevelled hole in the shells of oysters.

The not-so-Boring Sponge

How does something so soft turn something as hard as a shell or a rock into a perforated labyrinth? Well, the answer is by the process of micro-erosion. The free-swimming larvae of this sponge settle on a shell (with or without an inhabitant) or a rock made of calcium. They start the process of chipping away minuscule fragments of the calcium with microscopic sharp needles called filopodia, in conjunction with etching chemicals exuded by the sponge to weaken the calcium. Bit by bit the solid substrate is scraped away, creating squiggly burrows and cavities in the shell or rock. The sponge then lives in these cavities, burrowing deeper and periodically sending a branch back to the surface.

A Boring Sponge has burrowed into and through the hard substrate shell of this scallop, leaving its characteristic riddled structure when the animal dies.

If the mollusc on which the sponge started work was alive it eventually perishes, not by the direct predations of the sponge but simply because its fortress walls have crumbled and can no longer protect the mollusc within. Shells or lumps of rock with a multitude of perforations are quite commonly washed up on shores.

Lots of smashed shells – often on promenades, could be the work of the ingenious Herring Gull.

Busting a mussel

If you find shells smashed to bits in areas of rocky habitat or even man-made concrete-covered areas you may have come across evidence of the cunning of birds such as gulls and Carrion Crows. Both have been seen to collect a bivalve, usually a mussel, and drop it from a height onto a hard surface. I have watched both bird types on several occasions lifting and dropping the same resistant mollusc, sometimes

up to 20 times, until finally a combination of gravity and luck has resulted in the shell becoming damaged enough for the bird to gain entry to the meat within.

A variation of this behaviour has been witnessed at several seaside towns where the local Carrion Crows have worked out that a car passing over a mussel does a very effective job of busting open the shell. So the crows regularly drop their prey into the road in front of traffic lights, then nip back when it's safe to pick up the scraps of their self-made road kill.

The uneven hole, the pushed in edges and the presence of yolk tell us instantly that this egg has not hatched naturally.

Predated bird eggs

A smashed bird's egg rests in the grass, seemingly a long way from any likely nest site – whose egg is it and what's it doing there? This is quite a common scenario for the nature detective to unravel as birds' eggs turn up frequently in unexpected places. Has it been carried away from a nest site by a parent bird, so it doesn't attract predators, or has it been dropped by a predator?

Smashed and grabbed

When an egg has been procured by predatory means, the signs are different from a naturally discarded eggshell, though in many cases the damage is so extensive that it can be difficult to interpret what has happened. In all cases, however, the invasion of the egg has come from a beak, talon or tooth pushing inwards. Although more often than not the eggshell is picked totally clean, if there are any contents present, you can be pretty sure you are looking at a predated egg.

This Coot egg has been grabbed by an opportunistic crow – note the single large hole.

Bird predators usually bash an egg in the middle and often make more of a mess and spill some contents. Mammal egg thieves are many, but once they've broken into an egg all of the contents are usually eaten. A Fox may crush an egg in its mouth and consume the bulk of the contents. It then drops the shell and returns for seconds.

Some smaller mammal predators make a neater job, biting their way through one end of the shell, but again the edges will be pushed inwards. If you are very lucky, the mammal predator may have left clear holes created by its canines. By measuring from the centre to centre of these holes, you can get an inter-canine distance.

Here a Fox is about to raid a Pheasant's nest. It will swipe the contents of all the eggs and leave a recognisable mess of crushed shells.

Occasionally, a very tuned in tracker discovers a complete buried egg – I've known them to turn up in the herbaceous border of a garden (stolen from a nearby chicken's nest), high up on a sandy beach, in golf bunkers and in loose soil. This is more often than not the sneaky behaviour of a Fox, who commonly carries away eggs from a site of bounty and buries them for later.

THE HATCHED EGG

When a new bird comes into the world it breaks out of its calcium carbonate confine either by pecking its way around one end of the egg with a tough little projection called an egg tooth, or by pecking in several areas of the shell, which eventually causes the eggshell to crack as the chick forces its way out. These techniques leave either a neat 'capped' egg (just like you might knock the top off a boiled egg), or one that has come apart in several irregular fragments. The main thing to remember is that any broken fragments will be pushed outwards.

Ignore the duckling – but if you found either the neat cap or the base of this shell away from the nest – you would be able to conclude that this egg hatched and wasn't eaten.

Piles of large yellow underwing wings are all that is left of the insects after bats have been feeding. Sights like this are often found under the favourite feeding roosts of bats.

Bat leftovers

The bat species that tackle large moths and beetles often discard the wings and wing cases of their prey, which are not nutritionally very valuable. Long-eared Bats are fond of moths and if they catch large specimens will quite frequently return to regular 'feeding perches' to dismantle them. These perches are sometimes shared with other individuals from the same colony, so dismembered wings, heads and other body parts can accumulate below.

Other bat species such as Greater Horseshoe also regularly use such feeding perches, but they tend to feed more on large beetles such as the Dor Beetle and Cockchafer. The places most likely to be used (or at least noticed by humans) are in open man-made structures such as barns and porches, but feeding perches can be found anywhere a bat can find privacy and shelter.

Zombie caterpillars

There are many species of parasitic wasp that lay their eggs in or on a living host species; caterpillars are the most frequently noticed target of these insects, and it is not uncommon to find a caterpillar still alive and surrounded by a mass of yellow fuzzy cocoons. The caterpillar is ultimately doomed by the ravages that numerous wasp grubs have had on its still-twitching body.

The insects that are most commonly responsible for this zombification are the braconid parasitic wasps.

The first time I witnessed this, Large White caterpillars were eating the Nasturtiums in my mother's garden. As a child I remember being both fascinated and equally horrified at the macabre spectacle as 28 maggoty little heads ripped through the skin of a caterpillar, then proceeded to bed down next to its saggy weak body to embark on the next stage of their life cycle: the transformation into pupae within the cocoons.

There are many thousands of species of these wasps and they attack a huge range of hosts. Cocoons surrounding a hapless host are quite a common signature of *Apanteles* wasps, while the efficiency of *Aphidius* wasps in attacking aphids (200–300 in a two-week lifespan) has been harnessed in the biological control

Below: *This parasitoid wasp is laying its eggs in an unfortunate aphid – the wasp larvae will complete their development within the host body, eventually leaving the aphid as an empty husk with a hole in it.*

Left: *This Cabbage Butterfly caterpillar has provided the food and protection for a generation of* Apanteles *wasps – the yellow fuzzy objects are the cocoons from which the adult wasps will emerge.*

of these plant pests. The characteristic signs in this case are the hollow 'mummies' of aphid bodies with a large hole ripped in them where the wasp larvae burst forth.

Ladybird Killer is what another little specialised braconid is known as (although around 25 per cent of ladybirds that harbour the *Dinocampus* wasp do amazingly survive the ordeal). An emerging wasp grub spins itself to the leg of a host ladybird and remains there under the guard of the zombie mum until the adult emerges. It is thought that the parasite gains extra protection from the distasteful nature and the associated warning coloration of the still-present and barely alive host insect. It is quite common to find the almost lifeless carcasses of these insects apparently glued to the spot on a leaf or plant stem.

A chrysalis or insect egg with a neat little hole in it (you've got to have pretty sharp eyes to spot this) has possibly been parasitised by another very numerous family of parasitic wasp known as the chalcids – these most commonly lay their eggs in the still-soft pupae of a variety of insects, but are most noticeable in those of butterflies. Look over any chrysalis attached to a wall or fence for a long time with a magnifying lens for the tell-tale exit hole. It was probably used by many more than just one wasp – sometimes more than a hundred can be found inside a single butterfly or moth chrysalis.

Fatal fungus

Furry flies or grasshoppers seemingly welded to the tops of grasses or even flowerheads usually point to the end product of a body takeover by a parasitic entomopathogenic fungus. It starts with a microscopic spore landing on the insect's body, then by various means invading and spreading through its tissues rendering the insect dysfunctional. Its final moments take it to the top of a plant stem, where the emerging sporing bodies stand the best chance of being spread by the wind.

A fungus has killed this adult grasshopper in its tracks. In its final moments of life, the grasshopper climbed higher up the stalk consequently spreading the deadly spores of the fungus.

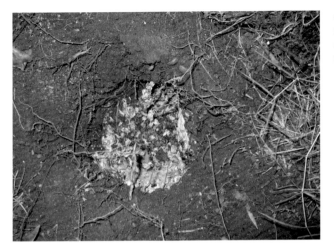

A Badger has dug out this wasp nest from the ground. Its coarse long hair will have protected it from the wasp stings.

Nest raiders

If you ever come across smashed up brood cells and combs, and numerous dead and injured bumblebees and wasps, this is likely to be the aftermath of a raid on a subterranean nest. This is nearly always the work of Badgers that feast on the grubs and, of course, any stores of nectar to satisfy their sweet tooth.

Ant nests can similarly come under attack from Green Woodpeckers – the hills of many species, from the grassy hillock nests of Meadow Ants to the densely thatched domes of Wood Ants, will be plundered. The attack usually doesn't kill a strong nest, but the damage does look pretty drastic from the outside.

Green Woodpeckers go with Yellow Meadow Ants just like Lions do with wildebeest – look at ant hills for signs of woodpecker feeding and the signature droppings that reveal the bodies of the ants within.

Natural objects and remains

Bones can turn up almost anywhere, and you may even be lucky enough to stumble upon a complete skeleton, which would allow a rare glimpse into the inner workings and mechanics of an animal. Sadly, though, it is much more likely that you will find a single bone, and the best you can do is try to work out who it belonged to and whereabouts it fitted in the skeleton.

You may or may not discover the story behind how this crow ended up here – but just knowing it was a crow is satisfying in its own right.

🐾 Boning up

Bones, for the most part, are like a tough internal scaffold that all the softer parts of the body are hung on. All vertebrates – mammals, birds, amphibians, reptiles and fish – have skeletons. The tough, growing, flexible portion is made of collagen and the other 50 per cent by weight is made up of a hard crystalline form of calcium called hydroxyapatite. This enables bones to resist the processes of decomposition and become a lasting memorial to their owners.

Below, left: Bones occur in different thicknesses and sizes, but they are all recognisable and identifiable if you are familiar with basic animal anatomy. This jumble of bat bones might look exotic, but really it's just a highly modified version of a standard mammal skeleton.

The problem with bones is that there are a lot of them. A human being, depending on age, can have more than 300, while a snake has a tally that can be double this. Osteology (the study of bones) is a fascinating science and could easily be the subject of a book of its own, but I'll endeavour to give you some basic tips. The skull is a gift and is the easiest object from which to get a positive identification. However, I'll start with the rest of the skeleton as this is more of a challenge and in many cases the head will be missing from the remains you are trying to identify.

These horse bones are much larger and chunkier than the bat bones on the left. However, if you study the bones of both animals, you will see many similarities in their skeletal structures.

This chapter includes the body plans of a classic bird, mammal, fish, reptile and amphibian, so that if you find a bone you'll have a better idea of whether it's a shoulder blade (scapula), leg bone, rib, pelvis, etc, and which type of animal it belonged to.

This is a deer carcass – the colour of the fur and the antlers tell us it's a Fallow and a buck. Working out the cause of death and who has been dismantling the body, however, is more of a challenge.

Mammal bones

The basic plan of a mammal skeleton (as seen above) is the same for all mammals. The main components are generally the same, but vary from species to species. At one end of a vertebral column is the skull, the protective casing for the brain. Further along, the ribcage extends out of the spine, which protects the major internal organs and supports the limbs for movement. The tail usually concludes the vertebral column, although not all mammals have a tail. The individual size, length and thickness of each of these parts varies between mammals according to their different lifestyles.

Common Shrew skeleton

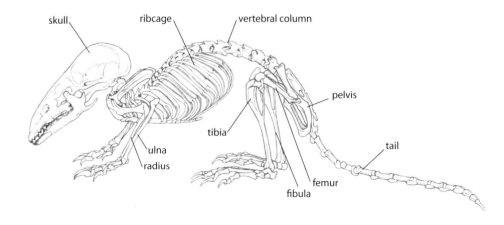

skull ribcage vertebral column pelvis tibia ulna radius femur fibula tail

Bird bones

In birds there are some characteristic bone clusters where groups of bones have been fused as a way of cutting down weight and increasing rigidity. For instance, the bones that make up the pelvis (the illium, ischium and pubis) have fused with a bunch of vertebrae to create an odd boat-shaped structure. Taking a look at a roast chicken carcass is a great way to learn about how a bird skeleton is put together and what the bones look like.

Birds have very few 'normal' vertebrae, and just a few in the neck and tail give the flexibility that is common in some of the more bendy mammals. Those in the middle of the back are fused together (to form a solid box

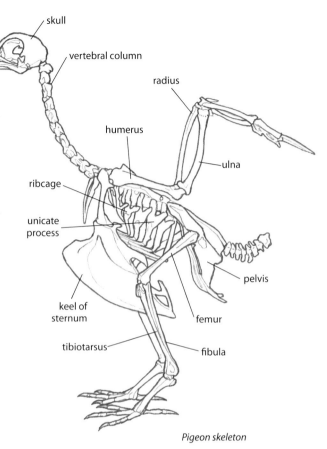

Pigeon skeleton

in the chest region which is needed to resist the stresses of all that wing flapping). Look at the ribs of a bird, too. They are very different from those of a mammal. They are flattened and have a backward-pointing structure called a uncinate

Beaches are excellent places to find skulls and bones. This partially desiccated gull is well preserved. However, identifying a gull from just its skull or a leg bone is not easy.

BONE TEXTURE

Bird bones are usually quite easy to identify because most species are adapted for flight and as a consequence the skeleton has been adjusted by evolutionary pressure to form a lightweight rigid fuselage. In cross-section most bird bones have a honeycomb appearance, with more struts and linkages near the joints and bigger air spaces away from them. These pneumatic bones are connected to a bird's breathing system. It's a neat way of creating strength where it is needed without adding too much weight – a technology familiar to the designers of aircraft, bikes and any other structures that have to be strong and light.

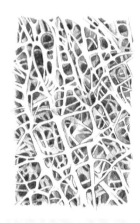

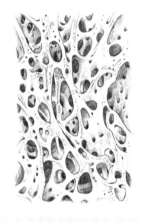

Bird bone   *Mammal bone*

The majority of fish have skeletons made of bone, and only a few species have cartilage skeletons. The spine is the main support structure for the swimming muscles.

process, which locks with the next rib behind it to again help form a protective box for all the organs.

The sternum forms a keel, to which the powerful flight muscles attach (this is the big flattened bone that sticks up from your Sunday roast and to the sides of which are attached the flight muscles that we call the breast of the bird), and the wishbone is also distinct, made from the same bones as our collar bone.

Fish bones

If you've ever tucked into a grilled trout, you will be acutely aware of just how fiddly the bones can be: lots of thin, almost wiry bones that get stuck between your teeth. Being animals of water, fish don't need the structural rigidity of animals that live on land. Water gives a lot of support, so even the bigger bones in fish skeletons are actually quite thin and delicate.

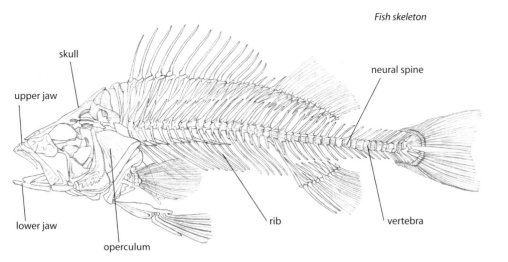

Fish skeleton

skull

neural spine

upper jaw

lower jaw

operculum

rib

vertebra

Incidentally, heads of fish tend to fall to pieces, so finding a skull is quite rare. More often than not the head may be represented by a toothy jaw, or you may find the operculum, which is the bony outer cover of the gills. The remaining bones of a fish rarely occur in isolation. If you've found one there are probably others, especially in places such as below the perches and nests of fish-eating birds and, for example, at the feeding sites of Mink or Otter.

When fish skeletons fall apart, or bones are found in pellets, recognising them is a challenging task, because they are so lightweight and delicate.

Also look for the characteristic vertebrae, with spiky projections of varying length, depending on which part of the spine they belong to and the species of fish. The smooth, concave interface between them is also very distinctive.

Additional clues are scales and large bony discs, sometimes with a little original pigment if fresh, or if old they bleach out to form glassy plates. Look at these through a hand lens and you'll see a pattern of concentric, ring-like ridges, which can be used to age the fish. Teeth may turn up, they are usually fairly simple, and some species have grinding pharyngeal teeth in the throat that don't look much like teeth, but their presence can help you identify the species.

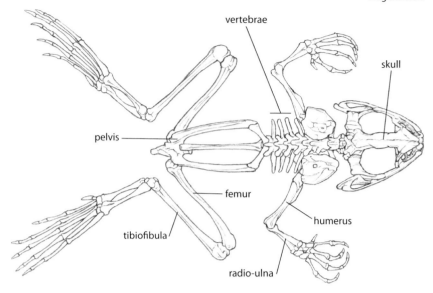

Frog skeleton

vertebrae

skull

pelvis

femur

humerus

tibiofibula

radio-ulna

Reptile and amphibian bones

The skeletons of frogs, toads and salamanders, including the skulls, are so fragile and light that they very quickly fall to pieces, so it's a difficult task to recognise any of their bones. Frogs don't have ribs; instead they house protuberances from the spine, unlike the pin-thin equivalents found in fish.

This dead Slow Worm has been partially eaten, revealing the top of its delicate long vertebral column.

The long bones of rear limbs are quite distinctive in all reptiles and amphibians, and do occasionally turn up in the pellets of owls (especially Tawny Owls which seem to have, a penchant for frogs). If you look at them in cross-section, they tend to have a groove that runs along their length, giving them a double-barrelled appearance. Frog-leg bones are usually much longer than those of toads.

Skeletal specifics

Now we've got an idea of the skeleton types and who has one, it's time to get down to more detailed investigations. How do we go about fine-tuning our understanding of the bones we've got in front of us? What can we learn about the animal when it was alive? What size was it? What did it eat? Could it hear well? Did it have a good sense of smell? In some cases we can even tell what sex it was, of course what species it was and the cause of death.

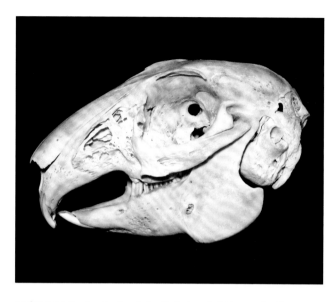

It often helps to visualise the skull with flesh on it. Add a couple of long, large ears to the top of this one and it clearly belongs to a Rabbit – the buck teeth and eyes not withstanding.

The sense of sight is important for this animal – would you have guessed this belonged to a cat? The distinctive sharp teeth and canines are missing in this specimen.

Head case

The skull in its simplest form is composed of two main parts: the cranium and a lower jaw. The primary function is as a 'brain box' to protect that most delicate organ, and it is also home to an animal's main sense organs: eyes, ears, nose and mouth. It can tell us a lot about the lifestyle of its owner. Just by looking at the shape and size of the skull, the form of its teeth and the size of its eye orbits (sockets) and ear bulla (bony shields), we can tell whether the animal was a predator or prey species, and which senses were most important.

If you look at the skull of a Rabbit, for example, you can easily deduce by looking at the large, spongy nasal cavity and the ear bulla, two roundish bubbles of bone at the back and base of the skull, that the senses of both smell and hearing are important to this mammal. Likewise, the large, forward-facing craters of eye sockets on a cat skull tell us immediately that the sense of sight is hugely important.

Because of its robust protective function, the skull often keeps its shape through death, so if you've got a relatively intact specimen and a good imagination you will almost certainly be able to identify the owner. A good way to practise is to visit a local museum and, without looking at the interpretation boards, have a guess at who the skulls belong to.

Above: Mouse skull – the distinct yellow pair of blade like incisors is evident.

Left: Cormorant – obviously a bird, the long, hooked beak says fish-eater.

Below: Mallard – it really looks like the animal that owned it.

A selection of various skulls demonstrates the ultimate in form and function. Once you've tuned into them and know what you are looking for it becomes very easy to narrow down the species based on the size of the skull, the shape of the teeth if they are present and of course the relative importance of the various senses by just a glance at this collection of bones we call the skull.

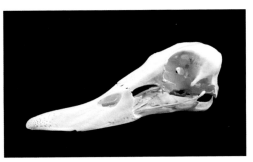

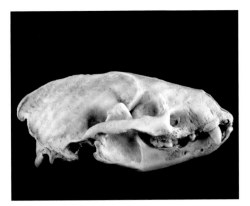

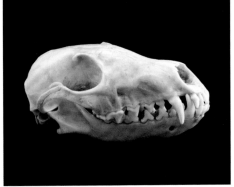

The large crest on the skull, solid and integrated lower jaw and canines say powerful predator, when in reality Badgers mainly feed on invertebrates. These family traits are probably for use in defending territories and fighting.

On this skull the long snout suggests that the sense of smell is important for this animal, while the teeth are definitely those of a meat-eater. It is a Fox skull. Foxes mainly eat rodents, but will also eat fruit and insects.

IDENTIFYING A SKULL

Things you can consider when you hold a skull in your hand are:

1. The teeth – their shape, type and number – should help you work out whether the animal was a herbivore, carnivore or omnivore.

2. The big cheek bones or ridges to which the main jaw muscles attach provide an indication of the shape of the animal's head and the power of its bite.

3. The shape and size of the snout (rostrum) indicate how important the sense of smell is to the animal.

4. The size of the eye sockets lets you know how important vision was to the animal. Eyes that are positioned on the sides of the head suggest a prey species that needs good all-round vision.

5. The shape and size of the ear bones (auditory bulla) tell you how important hearing was to the animal.

6. The size of the brain case gives you a clue as to the mental powers of the animal.

This skull can quickly be identified as a deer skull; it has no upper front incisors, and the molars are all of a similar size and shape for grinding bark, leaves and nuts.

Teeth

Experts can estimate the age of a Badger from its teeth. The teeth often display white patches of enamel wear, which increase with age.

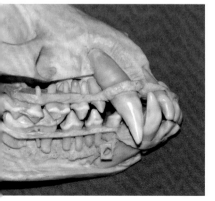

If a skull or a piece of jaw contains teeth, you can be sure you're looking at a mammal, fish, reptile or amphibian – teeth are too heavy for birds. Frogs have tiny teeth in their upper jaws only, including vomerine teeth which are in the middle of the upper jaw; toads, however, are toothless. Newts and salamanders are equipped with very fine and simple teeth that line the edges of both jaws, but they are so small that they are barely noticeable. Lizards, especially Slow-worms, are much more toothy than you might expect, but again their teeth are not obvious.

Mammal teeth are much more noticeable and useful to the nature detective. Their number, shape and variety can tell us how old the animal was and what it fed on, which helps identifying exactly what species it belonged to.

Mammal teeth can be incisors, canines, premolars or molars, and their number can be written like a code, known as the dental formulae. This code looks like this for, say:

a Badger	3.1.3.1	or a Roe Deer	0.0.3.3
	3.1.3.1		3.1.3.3

It refers to the number of incisors, canines, premolars and molars in one half of the head – the upper line refers to the upper jaw and the lower line to the lower jaw.

Incisors are the snipping and pruning teeth, and in Rabbits and hares the tooth number is reduced but the individual teeth are the most frequently used tools. In these animals the teeth are constantly growing and rely on being worn down by the continuous activity of feeding. Enamel is on the front of the tooth only and therefore wears down at a slower rate than the softer dentine behind, thus creating a self-sharpening edge. For a beginner the teeth of Rabbits and rodents can look similar, but look closely and if it's a Rabbit, tucked away behind the big teeth is another tiny set of incisors. Some animals, such as deer and sheep, only have incisors in the lower jaw and nothing but a tough gummy plate in the top jaw for them to work against.

The self-sharpening hardware in the mouth of a Brown Rat – typical of a rodent.

Rabbits are not rodents, but they have similar teeth for the slicing and biting of plant material.

Canines, also known as eye-teeth or fangs, are well developed in the jaws of meat-eaters and present in many omnivores. These are the big four teeth that make the gape of a dog or cat look so threatening. Their primary job is to grab and hold onto prey and help to hang on while the power of the head and neck muscles allow the animal to tear at its prey. Animals that tend to eat their

Left: *The canines are the signature of an animal that is designed to grip and hold meaty prey.*

Above: *A Fox skull shares family traits with Wolves and dogs.*

prey mainly whole or have to deal with dinner that is particularly slippery, such as seals and toothed whales (like dolphins), have lots of sharp, pointed teeth, although not all of them are canines.

Although canines are missing from the mouths of many herbivores, they do appear in some species – deer, for example, often have canines in the lower jaw, but these, known as incisiform canines, are cleverly disguised as incisors. In Muntjac and Chinese Water Deer the upper incisors are like tusks and take on the role of weapons in much the same way as do antlers in deer of more open habitats.

A row of flat-topped cheek teeth, not the flesh-slicing carnassials found in predators, immediately tell us this is a vegetarian – a Roe Deer in this case.

Premolars and molars Towards the back of the mouth are the 'cheek teeth', and there are two kinds: the **premolars** and **molars**. The shapes of these teeth vary according to what the animal eats, so they can be very revealing. Herbivores, which include animals that feed on seeds, nuts and fruit, use their flattened and often ridged cheek teeth as millstones, grinding up food before swallowing it. Most carnivores, on

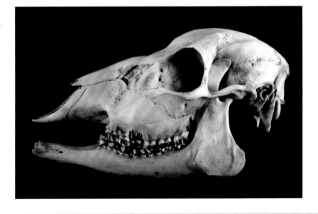

the other hand, need teeth that will slice effectively, and most of their back teeth have become ridged and sharp to work against each other in the same way as the blades of scissors. They are called **carnassials** and form a very effective set of meat shears.

Above: This is how you may find a skull when out on a walk. The jaw is hinged to the skull. Its size and shape, and the big crest of bone along the top, tell the naturalist that this belonged to a Badger.

Right: The fine, needle-sharp teeth of insectivores such as Hedgehogs are designed for holding and smashing up insect bodies.

Omnivores are somewhere between the two; animals like bears and Badgers have teeth that show both qualities, with sharp, ridged premolars and flattened molars at the back.

Insectivores, includings bats, shrews and Hedgehogs, all have sharp and spiky teeth that are perfect for gripping onto slippery or hard and shiny invertebrates.

Getting long in the tooth?

The teeth of mammals are embedded into sockets by a tough substance called cementum, and this is laid down every year around the root of the tooth. By cutting a cross-section through a tooth and treating it with various chemicals before applying a dye, it is possible under a microscope to see the growth lines that show when each layer of cementum was added. This occurs annually when conditions are good for growth and repair, and the lines can give us an accurate age in years. This is the dental equivalent of counting the rings on a tree stump.

Mammals can be aged by the number of teeth, and their wear and position. Just like humans, other mammals have a temporary set of 'milk' teeth before they are finally replaced by the permanent teeth. Young animals usually have a different tooth count from adults, and their teeth tend to be smaller and sharper. If you know the pattern of development for a particular species, it is possible to get some idea of the age of an individual by its teeth alone – see the box on ageing a deer (page 246). Assessing the age of medium to large carnivores is more tricky, as less work has been done on these species. All you can do is estimate whether the animal was old or young based on tooth wear and tear. A handy rough guide you can use is that there is an approximately 10 per cent loss of canine and incisor tooth height for every year of life.

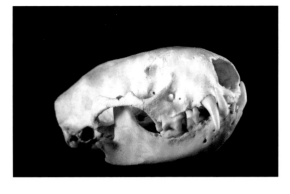

This skull shares many of the traits of a Badger skull, because it is a member of the same mustelid family. Its smaller size tells us this was a Stoat.

Fortunately teeth are rarely found in isolation, and the rest of the skull will provide further clues as to the age of an animal. In many animals like Badgers the shape of the skull changes throughout the first year, and there is a crest of bone that runs across the top of the skull (called the sagittal crest), to which the jaw muscles are attached, which gets taller and thicker as the animal matures.

The bones that make up the brain cases of all animals become more fused during the ageing process. In younger animals the sutures (the beautiful, ornate wiggly seams between these bones) are clear, but as an animal matures they close up and become less obvious. Other features of the skull also get thicker and more gnarly as the animal ages through a process called ossification.

This Wild Boar skull shows the grinding teeth of a herbivore with massive sharp tusks, or elongated, continuously growing teeth. Boars are omnivores and use their tusks as weapons for fighting.

AGEING A HERBIVORE...CASE STUDY OF A DEER

Young deer usually suckle for the first 3–4 months, but may suckle for longer. After 6 months the fawn's first teeth will have developed and it will have started to graze on vegetation.

Deer, like many mammals, have milk teeth that start being replaced at about six months. If you can see new teeth that look a little twisty erupting at the front of the mouth, in addition to working teeth already in position, then the animal is about six months old.

A Fallow Deer doe with a four month old fawn suckling.

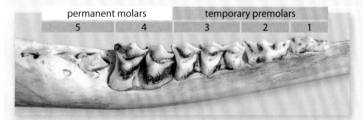

permanent molars		temporary premolars		
5	4	3	2	1

6 months

A deer under six months old does not have the full quota of adult cheek teeth, so a jawbone with four to five cheek teeth is that of a fawn (three premolars and one to two molars). The third premolar has three points or cusps on it.

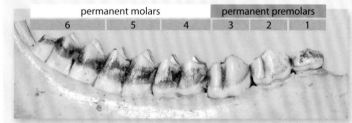

permanent molars			permanent premolars		
6	5	4	3	2	1

20 months

When the deer is over a year and a half old, all the adult teeth positions will be filled, so six cheek teeth are visible – the molars have erupted from the jawbone to the back of the mouth, and the premolars start to wear flat (in time these teeth will be lost and replaced by permanent premolars with two cusps instead of three). The new teeth have a sharp, ridged feel to them, as they haven't yet been ground down by use.

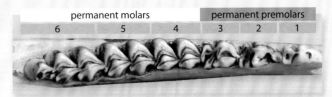

permanent molars			permanent premolars		
6	5	4	3	2	1

2 years

At about two years of age the animal is in its prime – the three cusped premolars have been replaced by two cusped permanent versions, and all the other premolars also have two cusps. The molars, particularly the first one, have sharp cusps with white enamel well above the darker dentine. The third molar at the back has a little wear.

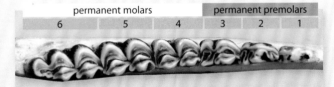

permanent molars			permanent premolars		
6	5	4	3	2	1

3 years

At three years of age, the cusps of all the molars start to show some wear and the dentine is now showing as much thicker bands in the teeth as they wear down. The last cheek tooth, the third molar, is now beginning to wear flat.

permanent molars			permanent premolars		
6	5	4	3	2	1

4 years

At four years old, all cheek teeth cusps are beginning to round off and become blunt, and the dentine of the first molar is now twice as thick as the white enamel.

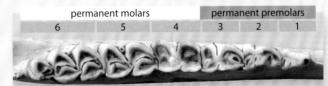

permanent molars			permanent premolars		
6	5	4	3	2	1

Over 4 years

Animals over four years of age show varying degrees of tooth wear. The first molar starts to wear flat and smooth or will become concave.

If an animal is lucky to reach nine years or over, the teeth are nearly all worn down almost to the gum-line.

GETTING YOUR SKULLS WHITER THAN WHITE

Naturalists often like to collect the skulls and bones that they find either as items of reference or for their intrinsic beauty. They rarely discover them, however, as bleached visions of perfection.

My favourite method of whitening skulls, called maceration, is a gentle way of allowing decomposition to take place. All you do is immerse the bones in a jam jar or bucket of water and let the natural bacterial action take place on the soft tissues. This creates a perfectly horrible smelly soup, with conditions of high nutrients and low oxygen perfect for the bacteria. If the water is warm the process is quicker: a Fox or Badger skull will take about two weeks in summer temperatures.

You will end up with a clean collection of bones with the added benefit that many of the tiny details, such as fragile inner ear bones, will all be preserved and revealed by careful sifting of the contents of your maceration container.

Rinse the bones well with fresh water and maybe even soak them in a little detergent and peroxide (gentle laundry bleaching agent), but never household bleach as this makes fine bones brittle and chalky. Then just leave the bones to air and dry.

Outstanding bills

If you find a complete bird skull, you should have no trouble identifying if not the species then at least the main group of birds to which it belonged. The beak will be a strong visual clue to the bird's identity and will also point to its likely diet. Unfortunately, a beak is often much more fragile than a jaw full of teeth and can easily be damaged.

Finding a complete bird skull is a gift and makes it easier to identify. This skull is either a Rook or a Carrion Crow.

Beaks are covered by a sheath of keratin known as the rhamphotheca, which contains the pigments and a few other clues such as serrations or, in the case of petrels, devices such as tubular nostrils. Sometimes this will still be present, but it often quickly breaks down or slips off the underlying bone.

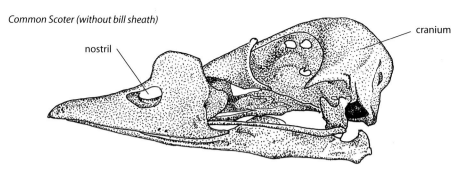

Common Scoter (without bill sheath)

nostril

cranium

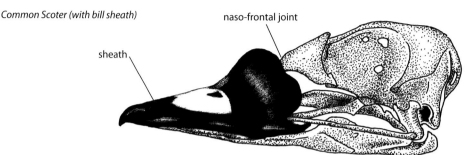

Common Scoter (with bill sheath)

naso-frontal joint

sheath

MARKS ON THE SKULL

The head is often the first target of a predator trying to knock down an animal, so a skull found following predation will have clues as to how the animal died etched into its surface.

One of the most common sources of skulls is road kill, and most victims of cars show the signs of a blunt-force trauma, which is a shattering of the bones radiating out from the point of impact. Animals that have been shot often have a neater hole with more concentrated damage.

The canine teeth of a predator are designed to concentrate the power of the bite and often inflict a neat hole or pair of holes. These can give you the diagnostic distance between the canine teeth of the predator and reveal its identity.

Birds of prey often tackle the head, and damage tends to occur towards the rear of the skull. It may show the triangular impression of the bird's bite, a sign often seen along the breastbone as well, as the bird has pulled at the flesh of its victim's chest and incidentally nicked the thin, flat bone in the process.

Bones represent a valuable source of calcium and other minerals, and it is quite common to come across bones, including antlers, that have been nibbled by mammals with the suitable hardware to do so. This leaves various neat diagonal, but straight, striations on the surface of the bone. The most common recyclers of bones are small rodents, Rabbits and squirrels. If you measure the grooves they make, the incisor width can be used to identify the culprits. Deer and sheep will also have a chew on bones, and deer will recycle their own antlers, which gives a distinctive angled appearance to the bone. Carnivores, such as members of the cat and dog family will also gnaw bones and in doing so leave grooves. As a rule cats bite down harder and leave deeper, narrower grooves and impressions than do dogs and Foxes.

Skins

All arthropods, those animals with an exoskeleton, as well as reptiles shed their skins periodically as they grow or the skins abrade. Often these empty husks are left behind, giving the nature detective some insight into their lives. In the case of reptiles and many invertebrates, their existence is so cryptic that you may not have been aware of the presence of these animals at all if it wasn't for these shreds of evidence.

Insects leave behind their various cases and skins when they grow or move on to the next stages in their lives.

Reptiles

All reptiles, including lizards, snakes, tortoises and turtles, regularly moult their skins; when they are young they do this quite frequently because they are growing rapidly, but the process tends to slow down in frequency as an animal matures.

The style of moulting and therefore the shape and quality of the skin left behind varies from species to species. Lizards, turtles and tortoises moult their skins in relatively small fragments, which are not obvious and only occasionally found.

Snakes moult larger sections of skin much more frequently. In some cases the entire skin is moulted, but more often when the snake attempts to scrape off the old skin, it will get torn into fragments, although these will still be much larger than those shed by lizards.

Snakes start their moult around the mouth, and by rubbing and moving the body against snags in their habitat, slowly peel the skin back along the body, effectively crawling out of their 'old' mouth. A good skin will be an impression of the entire body surface, including the caps that cover the eyes and the markings, albeit a paler version, so that it should be possible to identify the species.

As I've already mentioned, most lizards moult in bits, but look for the patterns of the skin on any flakes with small scales as these will almost certainly have come from the back or flanks of the animal. A lizard has belly scales that are bigger than the scales on the rest of its body – they will be arranged in rows of multiple oblongs.

Snakes, on the other hand, have belly scales that are much longer and wider than those found on lizards; each scale usually spans the entire width of the animal. The two most widespread and common species of snake: the Grass Snake and the Adder, both have strong keels on their scales. Adder scales have a slightly more rounded appearance and there will usually be some hint of the zigzag pattern that runs down the middle of the back. Grass Snake scales, by comparison, look like flattened rice grains and there is little evidence of any markings except a little blotching on the lower flanks.

Smooth Snakes are much rarer, and as their name suggests the scales on their backs and flanks are smooth and without the keel.

The Slow Worm leaves a sloughed skin that looks like a rucked-up old sock and could easily be mistaken for the skin of a snake, but the scales are smooth and rounded on the back, sides and belly, so are easy to identify.

Lizards such as this Common Lizard shed their skins in flakes, occasionally to be discovered by the lucky passer-by.

The discovery of a Grass Snake skin is much more likely than that of a lizard skin. Many snakes shed their skins whole or at least in large sections. Faint markings and distinctive scale patterns help to identify the species.

MOUNTING SKINS

Most skins are found in a dry and crispy state, and once the traces of natural lubrication have evaporated they become very delicate and brittle. However, there's one neat little trick that comes in very handy sometimes if you want to preserve any moulted skin, be it from a crab, crayfish, cricket, snake or dragonfly nymph. This involves simply rehydrating it – the easiest way to do this is to pop it into hot water and let the steam soften it up. Then, once the skin is pliable, you can gently remove it from the water and spread it out on a board. Snakes are very difficult to unroll but well worth the effort if you have a

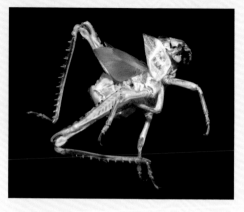

good specimen. With oodles of patience and a gentle touch the whole skin can be stretched out and dried flat, then mounted on a dark board to show up the subtle markings.

Similar procedures can be applied to arthropod skins – use a pointed cocktail stick and forceps to manipulate the limbs and skin into the desired position on a board then use pins to hold the limbs in place as they dry out. When thoroughly dry, the skin reverts to its crispy state and can then be scrutinised up close or preserved and mounted. This is very handy in particular for identifying dragonfly and damselfly species, as all the unique details of the nymphs can still be seen in the empty skins or exuviae.

1) Dried out nymph case

2) Rehydrate case in water

3) Pin case to board using tweezers

4) Mounted nymph case

Arthropods

I recently dismantled my old allotment shed and was amazed at how many empty husks of moth pupae and house spiders there were in it, not to mention the white dust of countless moulted greenfly skins. It was partly this experience that prompted me to include a brief section on signs that often go unnoticed.

All arthropods have an external 'skeleton', which is not made of bone but of a protein called chitin (this is reinforced in crustaceans with calcium carbonate); although tough when in use, it becomes brittle and fragile once discarded and doesn't last long.

Woodlice moult half at a time, here the front part is being shed first – usually this is eaten and recycled.

This outer casing provides the support to hold the body of the animal together, but a major downside to having the tough stuff on the outside is that in order to grow you've got to burst out of the case and start again. This is something that all crustaceans, insects, arachnids and myriapods have to do periodically – it's a process called ecdysis, and the vacant skins can be extremely useful to a naturalist.

When the time comes for an arthropod to bust out of its old tight skin it usually does it in one go, so that the empty hull left behind will represent the animal that once owned it. You might expect the planet to be covered in a kind of dry husky snow made up of these abandoned skins, but, in fact, in most cases the skins are immediately eaten, a case of reuse and recycle.

The metamorphic life cycle of a Peacock Butterfly

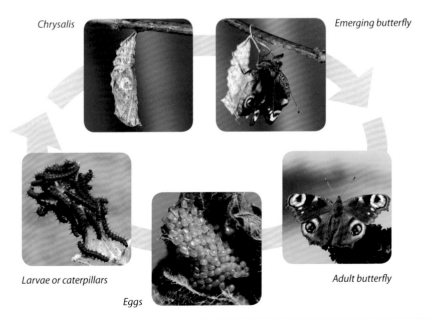

Chrysalis

Emerging butterfly

Larvae or caterpillars

Eggs

Adult butterfly

The empty husks of life

It's sometimes quite difficult to tell if the lifeless thing in front of you is something that has died or the empty husk of a moulted animal. For species that live out of the water, an empty skin is usually lacking in colour if it's a moult of an insect with an incomplete life cycle, such as a grasshopper or cricket, and resembles a crispy ghost of the previous occupant.

Sometimes you'll have to use your imagination and observational skills – imagine finding the empty 'light-bulb' – like pupal case without this Marmalade Hoverfly next to it.

Larval stages do retain pigments, but lose the shape – as they moult, they crawl out of a split just behind the head capsule and the skin is wriggled off and left abandoned. The most frequently encountered are the moults of caterpillars, leaf beetles and ladybirds.

The empty skins of dragonfly and damselfly nymphs can be found around the edges of freshwater bodies in spring and summer, usually attached to stems of plants that are emerging from the water. They are hollow and the split behind the head where the adult emerged is usually obvious, as are the white stringy linings to the trachea. Exuviae of other water-based insects are very similar, and moults that take place in the water can sometimes be found floating on the surface.

Crustaceans and myriapods also moult, but finding skins of terrestrial animals such as woodlice and centipedes is rare, mainly due to the moist environment they live in. Woodlice only moult half a body at a time, then usually eat the skin soon after, but you may find some very pale empty shells under logs and stones.

Marine species' moulted skins, such as those of crabs, are more difficult to separate from dead animals. Looking for the carapaces of moulted crabs on the strandline, however, can give the nature detective an excellent idea of what species are out there.

When a crab moults, its carapace splits along a fracture plane at the back and on the pincers, allowing the crab to pull its newly formed and soft body out of its old shell backwards. This is usually a very private moment as it takes several days for the new exoskeleton to harden, so the crustacean is vulnerable to predators. If you find what looks like a complete dead crab on a beach, have a look for the fracture plane at the back. If it's there you can lift up the top of the carapace a bit like the bonnet of a car, it will reveal a clean and empty cavity where the body once was.

Cases are also left behind during the transition from pupa or chrysalis to the adult stage of insects such as beetles, flies, butterflies and moths that undergo complete metamorphosis. When a pupa splits and the adult emerges, a life cycle is complete. Because the mouthparts of the emerging insect are so different from those of the high-consuming larval stage, the cases are often not eaten and are therefore readily discovered.

The exuviae (for that is what the empty skins are called) of dragonflies and damselflies can be found attached to vegetation surrounding ponds in spring and summer.

This is a Shore Crab moult. Crustaceans are the insects of the sea and grow by moulting in much the same way as their terrestrial insect counterparts.

The pupa is the last 'moult' in the lives of these insects and the remaining pupal case should contain all the information that you need to get a reasonable identification of the insect that left it. It is, however, a shame that there isn't a good reference book that covers all species.

Butterflies tend to leave their chrysalises in more open and exposed places than the moth equivalents, which are often buried or at least cocooned in silk and debris. Most species of butterfly have highly camouflaged chrysalises that are attached to a silken pad at the tip of the abdomen and dangle down, sometimes at an angle, with a little waistband of silk around the middle to hold them in position.

All of these pupae or chrysalises are termed obtect, which describes how the appendages of the developing insects inside are neatly pressed and contained within the pupae. Using a hand lens, you will be able to see the sculptured details of the insect inside. First find the head – the impressions of the eyes are usually fairly easy to see – then along the underside you'll see an elongated collection of grooves and striations, which represent the legs, proboscis and antennae. Across the back and wrapping

Each species of butterfly and moth can in theory be identified by its chrysalis. This is a Red Admiral chrysalis hanging from a nettle.

Right: *Many species of moth create a silk cocoon, in some species this is characteristic.*

Below: *Inside this 'skin' the final transformation into adult insect is about to take place – the empty husk will be left to tell its own story once the insect has emerged.*

around the middle are the smooth areas of the wings, with the imprints of the wing veins, and if the adult insect is about to emerge you may even see the colour of the wings underneath. The last segmented section, which can be quite mobile, is the abdomen.

Beetles and flies also emerge from pupae, and these can give forensic scientists information on how long a human body has been dead in situ and what sort of conditions it has been subjected to, based on the range of beetle and fly species that have fed on the corpse and completed their life cycles.

Most blowflies and several other flies have quite simple segmented caskets called pupariums, which don't show any features of the insect that will eventually emerge. Other flies, such as robber flies and craneflies, have much more typical pupae. In stagnant water it is also possible to find the pupal cases of various aquatic flies, from mosquito 'tumblers' to midges – they usually float and stick together on the surface.

Rarely appreciated, the sculptural qualities and intricate design of a robber fly's pupal case can be seen here.

Beetles have fabulous pupae that are, of course, as bizarre and varied as the adult forms of these insects. If you are lucky enough to discover one, you will see it is almost like a pale, slightly shrunken and sleeping version of the adult beetle, with wings, legs, eyes and jaws all very clearly evident on the surface. Unlike butterflies and moths, which in most species have all these component parts neatly pulled together, beetles, wasps and bees are known as 'exarate' because the legs, jaws and wings are all free and not closely pressed to the body of the pupa.

Beetle pupae are quiet detailed, with limbs and many other body details separate from the main body.

Pupae that are hollow, but have been parasitised, usually have an emergence hole that is fairly obvious somewhere on the surface; in most cases this is quite neat and in a position that isn't associated with a natural moult.

Feathers and fur

Feathers and hair quite often fall out and get left behind, giving the nature detective the task of trying to work out who they were attached to and whether they fell out as part of the natural process of moulting or were helped out by a predator.

Not all bird feathers are as easy to identify as those found in the wing panel of a Jay – but with a little understanding of bird topography you can make some educated guesses.

Two things can be learned from this scene – the identity of the bird – a Pheasant, and the fact that it was consumed (or at least plucked) by a mammal – probably a Fox judging by the size of the mouthfuls.

Found a feather?

Feathers are beautiful objects in their own right, and my fascination for them started as a small boy when I couldn't resist picking them up – a habit I've retained even to this day. I would stick them in my scrapbook and attempt to put a name to them using my observations. Some feathers are very obvious and are almost a signature of the species: for example, the speculum of a duck, the azure and black chequerboard of a Jay's alula feather and the tail feathers of a Pheasant.

However, it gets more tricky with body-contour feathers of some of the smaller birds; for even the most experienced ornithologists, these can be a challenge. It's a good idea to start by becoming familiar with the topography of a bird's body, and getting a feel for the landscape of feathers. You may then, for example, be able to identify the presence or involvement of a Jay not just by that

bright blue signature feather, but also by a tail feather or, if you're really good, a single breast feather. Again it's all about the detail – the more focused and tuned in you become, the more you will be able to read from the clues that are left.

Feathers can sometimes give us information about the health of their owners: a feather with stress bars along its length, for example, can tell us that the individual was having trouble meeting some of its nutritional requirements. Feathers can sometimes indicate the position of a roost or even that a nest has been predated – the possibilities are endless. For more information I can recommend *The Tracks and Signs of the Birds of Britain and Europe.*

The severed feather ends and the size of the feathers tell me this was a swan scavenged by a Fox.

A typical bird of prey.

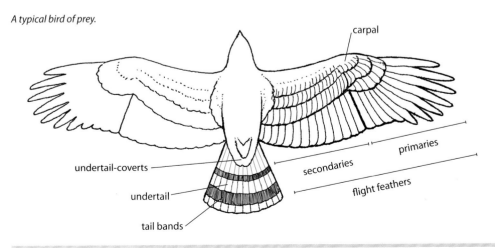

carpal

undertail-coverts

undertail

tail bands

secondaries

primaries

flight feathers

STRAIGHTENING A BENT FEATHER

A field notebook is very useful to have in your pocket for keeping leaves, flowers and feathers flattened and protected. If you've gone out without it and have found some interesting feathers and popped them in your pocket only to return home to find them in less than pristine condition, all you need is a kettle of boiling water to remedy the situation.

Hold the feather with forceps over the steam from the boiling spout of your kettle and the keratin will miraculously find its chemical memory and spring back to its former unbent shape.

Fur and hair

Often overlooked as a sign, animal fur falls out in small quantities during everyday wear and tear, so is useful to the wildlife tracker as an aid in confirming the presence of an animal in an area. It occurs in noticeable quantities in places where an animal has perhaps spent time scratching or grooming itself.

Distinct tufts of coarse hair are ripped out by moulting Fallow Deer.

Close scrutiny of the ground outside a Badger sett, bear's lair, Fox's earth, or even a Rabbit warren should reveal some fur. If it isn't apparent at first glance, you could try pressing a piece of clear sticky tape to the ground and you will soon see some.

Scratching posts and barbed wire fences are also good places to look, as they often effectively comb out the hair and fur of a mammal as it passes by. Two kinds of hair may be apparent: the outer guard hairs, which are usually relatively stiff and give the body a degree of waterproofing and windproofing, and fluffier finer hairs, which perform the task of insulating the body by trapping air and keeping it warm or cool.

The height and position of hairs removed from objects such as posts and fence wire will give you a clue as to the size of the animal. Hairs on the topmost wires normally belong to domestic cows or horses, but lower down the hairs of wild mammals may be caught, though be aware that domestic dogs and cats can leave hairs to cause a bit of confusion.

It's a classic – hair caught on barbed wire. Pay attention to the height at which the hair has been left on the fence, as this can give away or at least eliminate some of the previous owners.

Look for places where well-used paths and tracks go under, over or through an obstacle such as a wire fence or a stiff and spiky bush.

Fur can sometimes be found in clumps where it has been bitten or gouged out during a dispute over territory or a mate. You're most likely to find fur on the lawn after a domestic cat fight, but Rabbits will also do this and rutting deer often end up losing chunks of their coats during sparring contests.

Whose hair have we here?

Rabbits leave little clumps of very soft, short hairs, especially when they've been fighting. The under fur is pale grey, but look closely and you will see the guard hairs that are relatively more robust and banded with brown and black; the tips can be either colour, but are usually black giving the Rabbit's fur its grizzled appearance.

Badgers have very distinctive guard hairs, which are 1.5–4cm long, quite stout and wiry, and two-toned: white with a distinctive band of black that runs across the middle. Traditional shaving brushes were made from the guard hairs of Badgers.

Left: The soft grey underfur and distinctively coloured guard hairs of the Rabbit – are often shed in tufts while fighting or moulting.

Right: Look closely at hair with a hand lens and you'll often see details that identify the owner. Badger hairs have a grizzled appearance caused by a black band that runs through the middle of the guard hairs.

Left: *Red Deer hairs are hollow and coarse. From close up they have a crimped wavy shape to them.*

Right: *A clump of red fur has been caught on a barbed wire fence – the colour of this tuft says Red Fox.*

Deer hair is thick, hollow and very bristly, with a zigzag appearance. If you fold one of the hairs it will crease at the bend.

Fox guard hairs are often found on the lower rungs of barbed wire fences, where an animal has squeezed through. They are pale grey at the base and a uniform brown at the tips.

To identify other hairs the serious nature detective would need to get into the realm of forensics with the aid of a microscope that is at least x400 magnification.

Shrews hairs are X-shaped in cross-section.

Hairs under the microscope

By magnifying a hair you get a detailed look at its colour, the texture and scaling on its cortex (surface) and its medulla (internal structure). The medulla can be seen quite easily with a normal light microscope, but the scales and texture of the surface are much easier to see if you make an impression of the hair by using a thin film of warm gelatine spread on a microscope slide. Place the hair in the gelatine, let it cool, then peel it out. The textured impression will be left behind for you to look at, preferably at x400 magnification or above. Here are a few examples of the different characteristics of European mammal hairs under a microscope.

Dormice have much finer hairs than those of mice and voles and they are pale and sandy coloured. Under high power magnification they show a similar structure to Shrew hair.

Mice hairs have a groove along one edge and small jigsaw rough-edged scales on the surface.

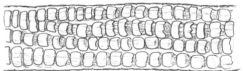

Rabbits have fine hairs with a large medulla and thin cortex. The medulla is filled with what looks like many wavy ladders running up and down the length of hair.

HAIR TRAPS

A tube trap attracts small mammals and, with a little extra help from sticky tape, persuades them to gently part with some of their hair. This is a technique mammalogists use to survey for the presence of certain small mammal species; with the use of a microscope it is possible to identify the species that are around.

1.
A tube trap is a simple device that can be made at home with a short length of bamboo or plumbing pipe, sticky tape and bait.

2.
Take a section of bamboo with a 2-3cm diameter and then cut two small slits either side of the open end, about 2cm deep.

3.
Stretch sticky tape between the slits with the sticky side facing up. Then bait the tube with peanut butter, or fruit, and place it either on the ground or, if surveying for small arboreal species such as Dormice, tie it to a tree branch.

4.
Any mammal attracted to the double bonus of food and a secure place to eat it, will then leave a sample of its hair on the tape for later analysis under a microscope.

Secrets in silk

Silk is a very special substance, a complex protein fibre that is produced by many invertebrates and put to a multitude of uses. Famously it is used to create snares and traps by spiders, covers for egg cases and cocoons. A structure made from this wondrous fibre will last long after an animal has finished with it.

Spiders have existed for millions of years and there is a wide range of spider web structures.

Made of silk reinforced with wood and bark, the cocoon of the Puss Moth demonstrates the surprising versatility of silk.

Cocoons

The most famous use of silk produced in nature, and one which we've exploited for our own fibre and textile industry, involves the cocoons made by caterpillars of various moths in the Saturniidae family, but almost all moths use silk in some way.

The nature and positioning of the cocoons is dependent on the species and is often very diagnostic. It can, however, sometimes be difficult to work out the differences between cocoons, egg cases and retreats, especially if silk is involved.

For most species of moth the cocoon is generally lozenge shaped, but some of the micro-moths and caterpillars of certain species of butterfly simply roll a leaf or some other vegetation around themselves, using silk to line and bind the building materials into something more substantial.

A Jersey Tiger Moth busy weaving its own sleeping bag.

Cocoons can be thin and flexible or thick and tough and, of course, anything in between. Those made by hawkmoths underground are loose-weave bags, which look a bit like fish net. The cocoons of Puss Moths are composed of silk bound with wood fibres, which together form a concretion that is so tough that a hammer and chisel are needed to remove them from the tree trunk or wooden post on which they have been built.

The cocoons of hairy caterpillars such as those of the tiger moths, Vapourer and Yellow-tail, are armed with an array of barbed hairs, which in turn are often coated with various toxins. These defended the caterpillar and now stand guard as a palisade of protection at this vulnerable stage of the life cycle.

The papery cocoons of Burnet Moths with the pupal case sticking out from the hole – tells us the moth has successfully emerged.

A close inspection of the surface of a mystery cocoon will reveal fibres of silk stitched by the caterpillar in its penultimate act prior to splitting and shedding its last skin to reveal the pupa underneath.

Although the majority of cocoons belong to moths, there are various other insects that also make them to protect their pupae. Occasionally, you may find the small (around 3mm), lozenge-shaped and papery cocoon of a lacewing. They use silk to make this structure and if you look closely you should be able to see the

Above: *Silk turns up in the most surprising of places; these little barrels just a few millimetres long are the cocoons of a parasitic wasp.*

Right: *Silk is usually associated only with spiders and moths, but sawflies also use silk to form their cocoons.*

Brown-tail Moth caterpillars are one of the more frequently observed tent weavers. Their large numbers, size and habit of spinning shelters out in the open make them easy to see.

strands anchoring it to the substrate. Sawflies make cocoons that are similar, but usually a lot bigger – at least 7mm long. In either case, if the insect has emerged, you will see that the top of the cocoon has been neatly snipped off by the adult jaws from within, leaving the cap attached.

The parasitic braconid wasps form little white, yellow or brown, rice-grain-sized cocoons that are often clustered together with the now dead or dying caterpillar or beetle host nearby.

Tents

Silk is also used to create much larger, veil-like structures under which life goes on protected from prying predator eyes and the elements. These are often what are called larval tents and they are spun by the caterpillars of several species. They are often white and show up clearly in bushes and trees.

In winter, caterpillars of moth species such as the Brown-tail, Yellow-tail and White Satin hunker down in their silken survival capsules to sit out the winter. Rare Marsh Fritillary caterpillars make similar larval tents, which are waterproof and can withstand winter flooding of their wetland habitats. These webs provide an excellent way of finding this species, as tracking the caterpillars is much more effective than finding the adult butterflies.

Silk draped around the tender tips of Common Nettles is also often the work of caterpillars. If they are dense and white and noticeable from a distance then the webs have probably been left by Small Tortoiseshell and Peacock Butterfly caterpillars. They are used as shelters, so that the caterpillars can get on with eating the leaves of the plant in relative safety, and the silken sheets can also act as sunbathing hammocks, where the herd of little dark-coloured caterpillars bunches up and bask in the sun (Marsh Fritillary caterpillars do this too).

As the caterpillars grow and consume the nettles, they move between plants, spinning a trail of silk as they go, which helps to keep the gang together. As they get older and larger, they disperse and build a different kind of silk tent – by biting out the main rib of a leaf they cause it to droop, then they use silk to bind and roll the leaf around themselves.

Often spectacular is the larval web of the Bird-cherry Ermine, a micro-moth that sometimes has population booms, when its work becomes noticeable. Its caterpillars sheath their host tree, usually a flowering tree, with a skin of white silk. At first they cover the leaves with webs and feed under their protective canopies. When the time comes to form their cocoons, they do so on the bark of the same tree. When they eat themselves out of leaves on one tree and move on to another, they leave a veil of silk in their wake.

In the summer most healthy nettle patches will show some silk workings by caterpillars, like these Small Tortoiseshell larvae– but the Peacock, Red Admiral, Comma and countless moths all make tents of some kind, too.

Bird-cherry Ermine caterpillars are prolific web spinners and silk flingers, often covering entire trees in a white cottony veil.

Some spiders also create a thickly woven shelter from silk, and some of the most noticeable structures are the 'nurseries' of the Nursery Web Spider. This leggy-looking spider bends over the tips of grasses and other tall plants and, using a very thick sheet of silk, incorporates these into a lair in which the adult spider keeps her egg sac and stand guard. The water spider *Dolomedes* creates similar dense white silken structures. The main difference between spider silken structures and those made by the caterpillars of butterflies and moths is that the latter usually aren't as clean – frass will be evident as dark speckles and there will be empty caterpillar skins, which look like tiny wrinkled-up socks, and evidence of leaf nibbling.

The only other time silk produced by caterpillars is conspicuous is when various species have parascended from the canopy of a tree, either in response to rough weather or predators, or to pupate below the surface of the ground litter; such descent lines are often simply straight silken affairs that are extruded as gravity acts upon the caterpillar.

Not just a means of trapping prey, this is the nursery of the Nursery Web Spider, which creates a protective tent for its eggs and spiderlings.

Probably the most ingenious use of silk is the highly evolved aerial spiral woven by the orb web spiders.

Silk–smiths and web design

Spiders are the masters of silk technology in nature and they all use it in some way at some point in their lives – even if they don't use it to snare food by making a web. Nearly all spiders trail silk as a dragline, allowing them to retrace their steps if they fall or are displaced, and just like rock-climbing humans will create periodic anchor points as they climb, the spider does the same with attachment points. These draglines can also be used to span gaps and to parachute to the next blade of grass or up into the sky for some serious far-reaching dispersal. A meadow full of tiny spiders all parachuting is quite a spectacle, especially if the draglines are backlit on a dewy autumnal morning.

More advanced are the prey-catching webs, and what is handy for the nature detective is that different families of spider and sometimes individual species make such distinctive and unique web designs. There are many kinds of silk and every spider can produce one or more of them. Here are a few of the most recognisable shapes and their makers.

Orb webs (the classic spiders' web) are made by several families of spider and can be further divided by their size, silk colour and decoration (and usually the spider itself, which will often be present). The garden orb webs are big and showy although quite plain, whereas the *Argiope* spiders often incorporate a thickened design in the middle called a stabilimentum. The long-jawed orb weavers tend to leave out the spiral in the centre, while *Zygiella*, which is frequently called the window spider, makes a small web with a slice of the spiral missing in one corner. *Meta* spiders make their orb web in a square frame of silk.

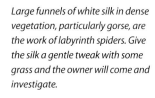

Large funnels of white silk in dense vegetation, particularly gorse, are the work of labyrinth spiders. Give the silk a gentle tweak with some grass and the owner will come and investigate.

Left: Linyphiid spiders construct bell or dome-shaped webs, creating a large surface area in which to catch insect prey.

Below left: This untidy mesh of blue-tinged silk around a defined lair is the work of the Lace-webbed Spider, which is most common in walls and on window sills.

Dome or bowl-shaped sheets belong to the linyphiid spiders.

Large funnel-shaped webs in bushes are the lairs of labyrinth spiders.

Lined tunnels with a mass of silk around the entrance are probably created by amaurobiids.

Lined tunnels with a collar of silk under debris could belong to *Coelotes*.

Below right: A female Coeletes atropos *spider often builds a tunnel-shaped web under logs or debris. This female is sitting inside its web.*

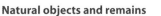

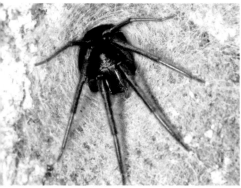

Above left: *One of the most ferocious and fascinating spiders. A tube spider weaves its abode in crumbly walls or neat holes with clear, long, straight radiating spokes of silk.*

Above right: *Spiders have woven a delicate mesh covering the tops of these heather plants.*

Bottom left: *The light, fluffy untidy sheets of silk in outhouses and cellars are the work of house spiders – there are several similar species.*

Bottom right: *A rather chaotic web of a Daddy Longlegs Spider.*

Silk-lined tunnels with radiating spokes/trip wires could belong to *Segestria* or tube spiders.

Irregular mesh sheets over and around the tops of plants are the work of the meshweb weavers from the Dictynidae family.

Lined tunnels or crevices, often in sheds and houses, with a large triangular area of silk leading from the entrance, are likely to be the untidy work of house spiders belonging to the *Segestria* genus.

Tangled, disorganised webs can belong to several species, but in the house they are probably the work of the Daddy Longlegs Spider, while outside they may well be created by any number of members of the *Theridion* genus.

Early morning is a good time to see abundant spider webs covered in dew. This field is covered with the webs of money spiders.

Watery webs

An aquatic spider and the caterpillars of several moths use their silk in much the same way under water as their more terrestrial counterparts, but you're unlikely to see the 'diving bell' of this spider or the cases and cocoons of the micro-moths without a deliberate search.

On lifting rocks in fresh water you may uncover the delicate webs of a group of caseless caddisflies, which spin hammock-like webs with great precision between stones and other objects in fast-flowing water. These usually accumulate silt and other debris, which increases the visibility of the structures. These caseless caddisflies are scavengers and feed on all manner of debris, including other animals that become trapped in the net; they also use the silk to knit a sock-like refuge.

The ingenious Water Spider spins a sheet of silk to form a diving bell underwater.

Found in the potting shed, this little cottony mound was probably the egg case of a spider – now long gone.

A Cucumber Spider sits guard over her large egg sac.

Egg sacs

If you find a silken structure that consists of a tightly woven sphere or a messy, amorphous ball that seems to be concealing something, the chances are it's the egg case of a spider. The many forms of egg sac include the beautiful silken vases of *Argiope*, the tiny suspended sacs of *Ero* and *Theridiosoma*, the small fried-egg-like masses made by some of the money spiders and the messy balls of the various house spiders.

Eggs en masse and egg cases

The structures that serve the purpose of containing and protecting young animals are many and varied, from eggs (not birds' eggs as we've already dealt with them) and egg cases to cocoons and blobs of jelly. They are often naturally robust, so some are left for the curious naturalist to discover.

These Emperor Moth's eggs are hatching. Like every species they have their own identifiable characteristics: colour, size, shape and habitat.

The smallest of the small

Invertebrate eggs can be single or clustered and may be encased in some way – they are almost as diverse in form and structure as the animals that lay them. Most eggs look like small spheres, ovals or skittle-shaped objects, and viewed close up they may display some beautiful and ornate sculpting and fluting. You will often need to employ all your detective skills to work out which insect left them. You can, of course, rear them to hatching and see what comes out, but that is the subject of another book.

Butterfly and moth eggs can turn up almost anywhere: usually on plants where they tend to be most obvious, but sometimes on other objects. Some eggs are laid in clusters, either neatly stacked

A mass of potential – this skittle-shaped egg cluster belongs to a Black-veined White Butterfly. It is typical of many butterfly species.

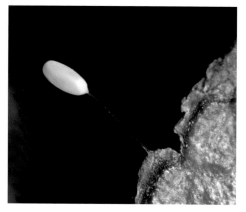

Above left: *This is the unmistakable and bizarre egg balancing on a bristle – a trick employed by the Green Lacewing.*

Above right: *Translucent, perfectly spherical eggs found in soil or under objects are most certainly those of a slug or snail.*

to form a mat or scattered in a more random manner, while other eggs are covered by leaves, droppings or even a shield of protective hairs. The eggs of lacewings, however, are placed on top of hair-like filaments and look a little like moss spore capsules.

The eggs of slugs and snails look like a collection of tiny crystal balls and are usually laid somewhere damp away from the drying effects of the wind and sun. If they are in the latter stages of development, you may even be able to see the little developing embryos inside, beginning to take on the form of the slugs or snails.

Egg cases

You can sometimes think that you've found an egg case, only to discover that it's actually a tight cluster of eggs, such as mosquito eggs that form dark floating rafts on stagnant water, or a structure resembling an egg case. I've often unravelled a silken shroud to find not the expected cluster of spider eggs', but a caterpillar or even an adult spider. It is best to make your own discoveries and that way develop your own knowledge base.

Bark Lice Their egg cases are visible as tiny 1–2mm-long white silky patches on the surfaces of bark and leaves.

Cockroaches Some carry their egg cases (or ootheca), some keep them internally and others deposit them. The case has a frothy texture and hardens on exposure to air.

Earthworms Their 1mm-long brown/yellow, pear-shaped egg cases are easy to miss unless, perhaps, you're digging through your compost heap.

Bark lice cover their egg batches with a little blanket of silk

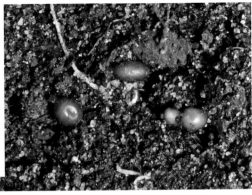

Leeches Their egg cases look similar to those of earthworms and can sometimes be found on leaves and twigs, and under stones in freshwater habitats.

Scale insects and mealy bugs These insects cover their egg cases with a fluffy white waxy secretion; sometimes the remains of the female's body are incorporated on top.

Above left: Some cockroaches carry their egg cases (or ootheca) with them, while others deposit them.

Above right: Small, lemon-shaped lozenges in rotting plant material or soil are the egg cases of worms.

Female mealy bugs lay their eggs in easily recognisable white fluff. The eggs hatch after about ten days.

Above: Leech egg cases are variable, from fibrous balls to little flat flasks stuck to the undersides of aquatic leaves or rocks.

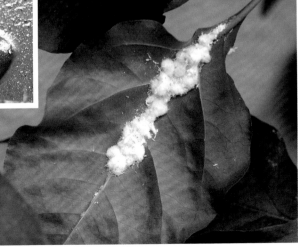

On the strandline

The strandline is the place where quite a few different and very distinctive egg masses turn up on a regular basis. One of the largest and most obvious are those of the Common Whelk, which often wash ashore after stormy weather. These pale yellow to white masses, called sea wash balls (apparently their abrasive and spongy properties made them handy for scrubbing down the decks of boats), are actually masses of masses – each lens-shaped structure is an egg case in itself containing up to 80 eggs. If the egg case is dry you can shake it and hear all the little dead whelks rattling about inside.

These familiar objects are the egg cases of the Common Whelk. Each is made up of lots of 'lenses', each of which contains numerous eggs.

Skates, rays and small sharks lay their eggs in protective cases – each one is species specific in its shape and colour. Therefore they are useful in surveying for the presence of these animals without even getting wet.

Smaller whelks live on rocky shores and you should be able to find the little yellow, skittle-shaped cases crammed into all manner of crevices and under overhangs.

The egg cases of sharks and rays are also very species specific and it is possible to get a really good idea of what is offshore without even getting wet. When fresh and wet, an egg case tends to look like a flattened leathery bag with a squarish shape. Each corner extends into horn-like projections, which can go on in some species to form stringy tendrils that allow them to become attached and tangled with weed when they are laid.

Small, caramel-coloured, vase-shaped egg cases with curly tendrils from each corner belong to small species of shark, usually dogfish.

Egg cases that are commonly referred to as mermaid's purses are much broader and darker as a rule, and have shorter horns at the corners – these belong to various species of skate and ray.

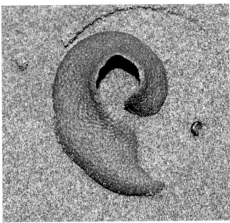

Clusters of black, grape-like, leathery eggs belonging to cuttlefish often wash up in the spring. However, probably the most bizarre and beautiful of all the egg cases are those produced by the Necklace Shell or Moon Snail – these almost look like wide, hammered neck torques constructed of sand grains. They are so delicate once dry that they don't last long, but while fresh the almost rubbery mucus that holds these egg masses together permits them to be washed up onto beaches where they can be discovered on the strandline.

Above left: Like a bunch of rubbery grapes, cuttlefish eggs are often washed up after spring storms.

Above right: This delicate structure is the egg mass of the Necklace Shell – a complex build of sand and mucus containing the eggs.

Gelatinous masses

Jelly, which is just water that has been trapped and held in place by other chemicals such as proteins, is a useful substance for protecting mollusc and amphibian embryos from predators, and for preventing dehydration.

If you've found clusters of numerous spheres, all stuck together in a disorganised mass, you will probably not need the help of this book to identify it as the spawn of frogs, and for most of Britain and Europe this is likely to be produced by the Common Frog.

It is worth looking at the way the masses are laid and the size of each clump, as well as the size of the eggs and the colour of the embryo within, as each of these details could denote a different species.

If the spherical blobs, with embryos centrally embedded, are stuck to plants, then you may have found some newt eggs. Newts normally lay their neat little eggs singly on the leaf of some submerged pond vegetation.

Below: We are all familiar with what frog spawn looks like – but it's often possible to identify species from the size and habitat that it has been laid in.

Amphibian eggs

Species	Size of egg Embryo/egg	Colour of embryo	Other notes
Common Frog (Rana temporaria)	8–10mm 2–3mm	Black/dark grey with a white spot on underside	Large floating clumps
Agile Frog* (Rana dalmatina)	9–12mm 2–3 mm	Dark brown with light underside	Small, free-floating clumps
Pool Frog* (Pelophylax lessonae)	7–8mm 1.5mm	Brown with cream underside	Laid in small clumps attached to water plants near surface
Marsh Frog* (Pelophylax ridibundus)	5–6mm 1.5mm	Brown with cream underside	Laid in small clumps attached to deep-water plants
Edible Frog (Pelophylax kl. esculentus)	7–8 mm 1.5mm	Brown with cream underside	Small, free-floating clumps
Common Toad (Bufo bufo)	1.5–2mm	Black	Eggs laid in two rows of strings
Natterjack Toad* (Epidalea calamita)	1–1.5mm	Black with white underside	Eggs laid in a single string
Smooth Newt (Lissontriton vulgaris)	3mm 1.5mm	Grey or brown	Eggs laid singly in folds of submerged plants
Great Crested Newt (Triturus cristatus)	4.5mm 2mm	Pale yellow-white	Eggs laid singly in folds of submerged plants

*These all have very specific habitats or limited distribution, so need to be checked thoroughly with distribution maps if suspected.

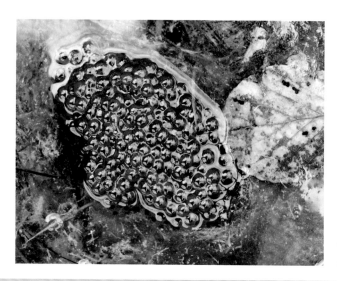

This small, tight clump is the egg mass of an Edible Frog.

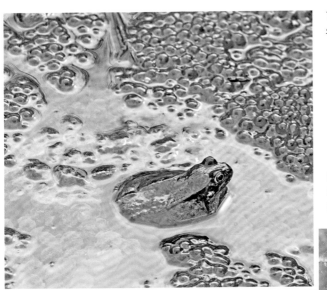

The most commonly seen amphibian spawn belongs to the Common Frog.

Below: The double egg lines within these strings of spawn are Common Toad eggs.

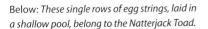

Below: These single rows of egg strings, laid in a shallow pool, belong to the Natterjack Toad.

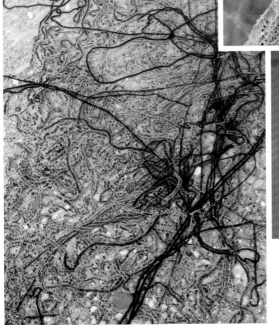

Above: Newt spawn is less obvious than that of frogs and toads, but look for the carefully folded leaves of pond weed in the spring and you may get lucky and see a sight like this Great Crested Newt egg – nearly ready to hatch.

Newt eggs are not to be confused with the egg masses of another couple of groups of aquatic animal: the snails and caddisflies. Many pond snails lay jellied eggs, and most are attached to the surfaces of submerged plants and other objects. If you look closely through a hand lens at an egg mass in the later stages of development, you will see that each of the dots is a perfect replica of the mollusc it will become.

The jelly masses of Great Pond Snails are common on waterweed and other submerged objects.

Nerite Theodoxus: 1mm-long capsules; eight embryos

Common Bithynia: 10–15mm-long on rocks

Great Pond Snail: Up to 50–60mm-long and sausage like; 300 embryos

Wandering Snail: 5–10mm and more rounded masses

Great Ramshorn: Up to 30mm across and oval; 70 embryos

River Limpet: 2–3mm-long spherical egg cases; usually four

Caddisflies also lay their eggs in gelatinous masses; the largest belong to the bigger species, such as *Phryganea*, which crawl back into the water to lay their ring-shaped egg masses on rocks and submerged vegetation. Many other caddisflies lay egg masses that vary in size and shape from mats to sausages. *Triaenodes* lay beautiful spiral-shaped masses on the undersides of floating leaves in ponds and lakes.

Looking like snail eggs out of the water, these are the eggs of a caddisfly.

Other easily overlooked gelatinous structures include the long and thin threads of hair worms, which get draped around submerged vegetation like tinsel around a Christmas tree, and the masses of delicate midge eggs.

On the seashore, you may come across the gelatinous masses of marine snail egg

These swirly masses of jelly are the egg strings of a sea slug, which look a little like silly string.

cases. I regularly find the little C-shaped, jelly-encased egg masses of Flat Periwinkles on seaweed.

Look out, too, for the gelatinous teardrop-shaped egg masses produced by several marine worms. The leaf worms create a very thin-coated green cluster that is anchored to seaweeds, but you have to look very closely indeed to see anything that resembles eggs inside. Lugworm egg cases are brown and tethered to the substrate. In rock pools at certain times of the year you may see some very strange and distinctive egg masses looking like pink, yellow or white silly string – these are created by the various species of sea slug.

In addition, the egg masses of Atlantic Squid turn up from time to time on shores, having been displaced from their natural holdfasts on the seabed. They look like creamy, banana-shaped lumps of jelly, each attached to the next at the base.

Occasionally seen washed up is a medusas wig, which is actually the egg mass of a squid.

Glossary

Bioregion An area defined by physical and environmental features with characteristic flora and fauna.

Brock A British name, with Old English language roots, for a Badger.

Cambium A delicate layer of plant tissue that gives rise to new cells situated between the phloem and xylem.

Carapace In chelonians, the upper part of the shell, above the bridge.

Carnassial A larger and longer tooth, than adjacent teeth, in carnivores adapted for cutting.

Cloaca A common chamber that the digestive, urinary and reproductive systems all discharge into, which opens to the outside.

Clocker The droppings of a female incubating grouse, larger than normal droppings because of her inability to defecate as frequently and enlarged cloaca.

Distal Concerning that part of an appendage furthest from the body.

Ecdysis The skin-changing or moulting process.

Ecoregion An area defined by its environmental conditions and processes determined by its climate, geology and landforms.

Exuviae The cast off moults of various organisms, such as the skin of a snake.

Folivore An animal whose diet consists largely of leaves.

Frass The excrement and refuse of leaf-eating or boring insects.

Gall A plant growth caused by the presence of a parasite.

Mole fortress An extra large and tall molehill often found in areas where there is a high water table or in areas prone to flooding.

Mutes The droppings of falcons and owls that are deposited straight down as opposed to squirted backwards.

Myriapod A class or subclass of arthropods with segmented bodies, at least nine pairs of legs and a pair of antennae.

Nymph The immature form of some insects, especially dragonflies and damselflies.

Ootheca The egg case of mantids and cockroaches.

Ossification The process of hardening or calcification of soft tissue into bone material.

Radula organ In some molluscs a tongue-like structure used for feeding.

Uncinate process A projecting hook-like body part often from a bone.

Acknowledgements

The Publisher would like to thank Julie Dando, Alice Ward and Jasmine Parker for their photo research, Wendy Smith for her copy-editing, Krystyna Mayer for her proofreading, Helen Snaith for the index, Julie Bailey for her support throughout the project and all our contributors.

Picture Credits

Bloomsbury Publishing would like to thank the following for providing photographs and for permission to produce copyright material. While every effort has been made to trace and acknowledge all copyright holders, we would like to apologise for any errors or omissions and invite readers to inform us so that corrections can be made in any future editions of the book.

Key t=top; l=left; r=right; tl=top left; tcl=top centre left; tc=top centre; tcr=top centre right; tr=top right; ct=centre top; cl=centre left; c=centre; cr=centre right; b=bottom; bl=bottom left; bcl=bottom centre left; bc=bottom centre; bcr=bottom centre right; br=bottom right

FLPA = Frank Lane Picture Agency; SS = Shutterstock

Half title AlexussK/SS; **title** verso Nick Baker, recto Eduard Kyslynskyy/SS; **6** Marcel Nijhuis/SS; **7** cl Nick Baker, r Tomasz Otap/SS; **8** Patrick Poendl/SS; **9** Graham Taylor/SS; **10** t Bryan Eastham/SS, b CoolR/SS; **11** Karin Jaehne/SS; **12** Nick Baker; **13** t, c, b Nick Baker; **14** t, b Nick Baker; **15** tl, tr, b Nick Baker; **16** tl, tr, b Nick Baker; **17** David Hughes/SS; **18** PeJo/SS; **19** Nick Baker; **20** t, b Nick Baker; **21** Nick Baker; **22** Nick Baker; **23** l David Dixon, c Carsten Medom Madsen/SS; **24** l Pi-Lens/SS, c trouvik/SS; **25** t Jill Reid Images/SS, cl T.Allendorf/SS, c P.Fabian/SS, b Anastasija Popova/SS; **26** c Vaidas Bucys/SS, b Wolf Design/SS; **27** c Rumo/SS, cr Rey Kamensky/SS, b Croato/SS; **28** t Photoman29/SS, b Guy J. Sagi/SS; **29** t bofotolux/SS, cl Lone Wolf Photos/SS, cr Elliotte Rusty Harold/SS, bl Rob Hainer/SS, br Menno Schaefer/SS; **30** t, b Nick Baker; **31** t Natali Glado/SS, c David Dixon, b Rebecca Nason; **32** c, b Michael Lawrence and John Ferguson; **33** t, c, b, Michael Lawrence and John Ferguson; **34** t, b Nick Baker; **35** tl, tr Nick Baker; **36** t Pi-Lens/SS, b Kurt/SS; **37** jps/SS; **38** t David Dixon, b Wolfgang Kruck/SS; **39** t Michael Durham/FLPA, c Art_man/SS, b SeDmi/SS; **40** t Volodymyr Burdiak/SS, b Eduard Kyslynskyy/SS; **41** t Nick Baker, b slowfish/SS; **42** tl Jasenka Luksa/SS, tr Bob Orsillo/SS, b Susan Montgomery/SS; **43** t Tom Reichner/SS, c Kelvin Pulker; **44** t CreativeNature.nl/SS, b Sascha Burkard/SS; **46** t Richard Schramm/SS, br scattoselvaggio/SS; **47** t Scott E Read/SS, b Nataliia Melynchuk/SS; **48** Menno Schaefer/SS; **49** t PRILL/SS, b Dennis Donohue/SS; **51** Foto Natura Stock/FLPA; **52** 72286210/SS; **53** David Dohnal/SS; **54** Jody/SS; **55** David Dixon; **56** Gail Johnson/SS; **57** t Pim Leijen/SS, b Nick Baker; **58** t, b David Dixon; **59** Eduard Kyslynskyy/SS; **60** Nadezhda Bolotina/SS; **61** t DavidYoung/SS, bl Chris and Tilde Stuart/FLPA, br Dieter H/SS; **62** Amanda Hsu/SS; **63** t Rebecca Nason, br Gary K Smith/FLPA; **64** Jason Mintzer/SS; **65** t David Dixon, b Rich Cook; **66** t David Dixon, c Julie Dando; **67** t, b David Dixon; **68** Nick Baker; **69** t, b David Dixon; **70** t Nick Baker, b Jeffrey Van Daele/SS; **71** t Nick Baker, b Ms.K/SS; **72** t David Dixon, c Nick Baker, b bojangles/SS; **73** t Nick Baker, b Dieter Hopf/Imagebroker/FLPA; **74** b David Dixon; **75** t Mike J Thomas/FLPA; **76** t David Dixon, b Andrew Parkinson/FLPA; **77** t David Dixon, b David Hosking/FLPA; **78** tr Paul Hobson/FLPA, bl nbiebach/SS, br Debbie Steinhausser/SS; **79** t, b Michael Chinery; **80** tl Jiří Hodecek/SS, c Sergey Plakhotin/SS, b Steve McWilliam/SS; **81** tr Stocksnapper/SS, cl Nick Baker, br Michael Chinery; **82** t Nigel Cattlin/FLPA, b Dr. Morley Read/SS; **83** t QUAN ZHENG/SS, b Richard Becker/FLPA; **84** t, b Nick Baker; **85** t D. Kucharski K. Kucharska/SS, b Richard Becker/FLPA; **86** tr Rosser1954 Roger Griffith/Wiki media, c Martin Fowler/SS, b Michael Chinery; **87** t Erica Olsen/FLPA, b Anatoli Dubkov/SS; **88** tr Elliott Neep/FLPA, bl Michael Callan/FLPA, br Dieter Hopf/Imagebroker/FLPA; **89** tl John Watkins/FLPA, tr Peggy Heard/FLPA, br Michael Lawrence; **90** tl Erica Olsen/FLPA, ct David Dixon, c Richard Davies, b David Dixon; **91** tr IbajaUsap/SS, cl Rebecca Nason, cr ImageBroker/Imagebroker/FLPA; **92** tl John Hawkins/FLPA, c Konrad Wothe/Minden Pictures/FLPA; **93** t George Nystrand/FLPA, bl Betty Rizzotti; **94** tc Steve Byland/SS, cl Dietmar Nill/Minden Pictures/FLPA; **95** tl Paul Sawer/FLPA, cr ImageBroker/Imagebroker/FLPA; **96** t Duncan Usher/Minden Pictures/FLPA, b Florian Andronache/SS; **97** tl Ron Bury, b

Derek Middleton/FLPA; **98** t Arto Hakola/SS, b Rebecca Nason; **99** t CreativeNature.nl/SS, b John Hawkins/FLPA; **100** t Martin H Smith/FLPA, b David Hosking/FLPA; **101** t Nick Baker, b Jackie Walton; **102** S Charlie Brown/FLPA; **103** tr Richard A. Evans/SS, ct Sylvie Lebchek/SS, cr Wild Arctic Pictures/SS, b Wouter Tolenaars/SS; **104** t tarczas/SS, ct Paul Sawer/FLPA, c Nataliia Melnychuk/SS, b Grigorii Pisotsckii/SS; **105** t Florian Andronache, ct, c, b Rebecca Nason; **106** t Nick Baker, b Doug Matthews/SS; **107** t BMJ/SS, c Rebecca Nason, b Chrislofotos/SS; **108** tl Micha Klootwijk/SS, tr Ann W. Kosche/SS, b Graham Calow; **109** t Rebecca Nason, c mycteria/SS, b Vishnevskiy Vasily/SS; **110** t Alena Brozova/SS, bl David Hosking/FLPA, br Roberto Cerruti/SS; **111** t Alexander Chelmodeev/SS, c Paulius Bacinskas/SS, b Rebecca Nason; **112** t John Hawkins/FLPA, b Duncan Usher/Minden Pictures/FLPA; **113** t Â© Biosphoto , J.-L. Klein & M.-/Biosphoto/FLPA, b Roger Hosking/FLPA; **114** t Ingo Arndt/Minden Pictures/FLPA, b Nick Baker; **115** t Feng Yu/SS, b Vishnevskiy Vasily/SS; **116** David Dixon; **117** t Nick Baker, b Jim Lopes; **118** t Nick Baker, c 111106586/SS; **119** t Nick Baker, c David Dixon, b Nick Baker; **120** t Nick Baker, c, bl, br David Dixon; **121** t Patryk Kosmider/SS, c Nick Baker, b Stephen Finn/SS; **122** c Debbie Steinhausser/SS, b marilyn barbone/SS; **123** tl David Dixon, tr Nick Baker, bl Torsten Lorenz/SS, br Alexey Stiop/SS; **124** tl Neil Burton/SS, tr Maxim Kulko/SS, bl Vital Che/SS, b mradlgruber/SS; **125** tl Christopher Elwell/SS, tr, br Nick Baker; **126** tl Erica Olsen/FLPA, c Ian Rentoul/SS, b David Dixon; **127** t David Dixon, b Nick Baker; **128** tl David Dixon, tr Nick Baker, b David Dixon; **129** t Nick Baker, b Roger Tidman/FLPA; **130** tl Volodymyr Burdiak/SS, tr Nick Baker, b Kurkul/SS; **131** t David Dixon, b Richard Costin/FLPA; **132** t xpixel/SS, b Mircea BEZERGHEANU/SS; **133** t Alison Taylor, c Menno Schaefer/SS, b BMJ/SS; **134** tl Nick Baker, c Sebastian Knight/SS, b Gertjan Hooijer/SS; **135** cl, c, cr Nick Baker; **136** tl David Dohnal/SS, c IbajaUsap/SS; **137** Gary K Smith/FLPA; **138** t woodygraphs/SS b Richard Becker/FLPA; **139** tr pzAxe/SS, c Henrik Larsson/SS, b Ed Phillips/SS; **140** t vblinov/SS, b Jeremy Early; **141** t Hintau Aliaksei /SS, b Derek Middleton/FLPA; **142** t, b Nick Baker; **143** c Nigel Cattlin/FLPA, b xpixel/SS; **144** tl Rebecca Nason, c Robin Chittenden/FLPA, b Bogomaz/SS; **145** tl N Mrtgh/SS, tr Surachai/SS, b Serg64/SS; **146** t Julie Dando, b Eric Isselee/SS; **147** t Marek R. Swadzba/SS; c Jane Bowman, b Tony Emmett/SS; **148** bl Wendy Wilde, br Nigel Cattlin/FLPA; **149** bl John Eveson/FLPA, br Chris Manley; **150** cl Nick Baker, cr Nazzu/SS; **151** t B. Borrell Casals/FLPA, b Jeremy Early/FLPA; **152** t Wiki media Auguste Le Roux, b David Fenwick; **152** tl Nick Baker, tr Steve Trewhella/FLPA; **154** t Erica Olsen/FLPA, b D P Wilson/FLPA; **155** Mike Lane/FLPA, **156** Stephen Bonk/SS; **157** tr David Dixon, bl Nick Baker; **159** t mlorenz/SS, b Elena Elisseeva/SS; **160** tl BMJ/SS, ct Nick Baker, cr Menno Schaefe/SS, bl Roberto Cerruti/SS; **161** t David Hosking/FLPA, c Dmitrijs Bindemanis/SS, b Nick Baker; **162** t, b Nick Baker; **163** tr Frederic Desmette/Biosphoto/FLPA, ct hauhu/SS, cr Nick Baker; **164** Nick Baker; **165** t David Dixon, b Nick Baker; **166** t kzww/SS; c Nick Baker, b Tyler Olson/SS; **167** tr Roger Tidman/FLPA, c David Dixon; **168** t Nick Baker, c David Dixon, b Jody./SS; **169** tr David Dixon, ct Alan, cr Gunnar Pippel/SS, bl cristi180884/SS; **170** t David Dixon, cl, cr Nick Baker, b Mary Selk; **171** tl Derek Crawley at Staffordshire Mammal Group, b Marcus Webb/FLPA; **172** t Nick Baker **173** t Sandy Slaymaker, cl Sarah Gregg, cr Hannes E, b Rebecca Nason; **174** t Nick Baker, bl David Dixon, br Nick Baker; **175** Nick Baker, cr Peter38/SS; **176** tl David Dixon, cr Nick Baker, bl Phil McLean/FLPA; **177** tl, tr Nick Baker, c Derek Whiteley, Sorby Mammal Group, b Mike Mottram, **178** t Nick Baker, c Jody./SS, b David Dixon; **179** t Matt Jeppson/SS, c, b Nick Baker; **180** David Dixon; **181** tl Henrik Larsson/SS, tr Hugh Lansdown/FLPA, b Mau Horng/SS; **182** t Nick Baker, b Jane Bowman; **183** t scubaluna/SS, c Richard Andrei R. Sebastian, b Dr Roger S. Key; **184** tl Matt Cole/FLPA, tr Nigel Cattlin/FLPA; **185** t, c, b Michael Chinery; **186** tr Michael Chinery, c © Biosphoto, Sylvain Cordier/Biosphoto/FLPA, b Gary K Smith/FLPA; **187** David Hosking/FLPA; **188** Neil Bowman/FLPA; **189** t Simon Litten/FLPA, br Malcolm Schuyl/FLPA; **190** t Dr. Morley Read/SS, b Gary K Smith/FLPA; **191** t David Dixon, bl Nick Baker; **192** t Lassi Kalleinen & Risto Törnberg, bl Roger Tidman/FLPA, br Dr. Morley Read/SS; **193** tl S.Cooper Digital/SS, tr Jean-Lou Zimmermann/Biosphoto/FLPA, b Lassi Kalleinen & Risto Törnberg; **194** t Lassi Kalleinen & Risto Törnberg, c Rick Wylie, b Roger Tidman/FLPA; **195** cl, c, cr, bl, br Lassi Kalleinen & Risto Törnberg; **196** t Lassi Kalleinen & Risto Törnberg, c Dickie Duckett/FLPA, bl Lassi Kalleinen & Risto Törnberg; **197** tr Monica Johnson; c Roger Tidman/FLPA, br Michael Thornton www.edinburghhawkwatch.org.uk; **198** tl, tr Lassi Kalleinen & Risto Törnberg, c Jason Sturner, b Lassi Kalleinen & Risto Törnberg; **199** David Dixon, cl Nick Baker; **200** t David Hosking/FLPA, b Breffni Martin; **201** Tony Hamblin/FLPA; **202** David Dixon; **203** tr David T. Grewcock/FLPA; **204** Justin Crom; **205** David Trently; **206** t, c, b Nick Baker; **207** t, c, b Nick Baker; **208** Bjorn Heller/SS; **209** cl Rebecca Nason, r David T. Grewcock/FLPA; **210** b Paul Sawer/FLPA; **211** tr Nick Baker; br Rebecca Nason; **212** tl Stanislav Duben/SS, bl Â© Biosphoto , Berndt Fischer/Biosphoto/FLPA; **213** t Nick Baker, br Rebecca Nason; **214** tl Terry Whittaker/FLPA, bl Fabrice Cahez/Biosphoto/FLPA; **215** t Nick Baker, b Michael Callan/FLPA; **216** tl /FLPA, b Michael Callan/FLPA; **217** t, b Nick Baker; **218** János Soproni www.sjfoto.hu; **219** t Roger Wilmshurst/FLPA; b Nick Baker; **220** t TOMO/SS, c Paul Hobson/FLPA, b Nick Baker; **221** David Dohnal; **222** c Erica Olsen/FLPA, b Paul Hobson/FLPA; **223** cl, cr Steve Trewhella/FLPA; **224** c D P Wilson/FLPA, b D P Wilson/FLPA; **225** tr David Fenwick, br Roger Tidman/FLPA; **226** c, b Nick Baker; **227** tr Martin H Smith/FLPA, b Anneka/SS; **228** Richard Becker/FLPA; **229** bl Silvia Reiche/Minden Pictures/FLPA, br Nigel Cattlin/FLPA; **230** Richard Becker/FLPA **231** tl Mike Lane/FLPA, c Evgeni Stefanov/SS, b Marcus Webb/FLPA; **232** mikeledray/SS; **233** cl David Dixon, cr poresh/SS; **234** Nick Spurling/FLPA, **235** Fedorov Oleksiy/SS; **236** Tomas Pavelka/SS; **237** John Stebbins/SS; **238** ImageBroker/Imagebroker/FLPA; **239** tr Natursports/SS, bl Michal Bellan/SS; **240** t PhotoGraphyca/SS, ct, c redefine images, bl © Biosphoto , Fabien Bruggmann/Biosphoto/FLPA, br photowind/SS; **241** tr Barry Blackburn, bl Chris & Tilde Stuart/FLPA; **242** cl Michael Durham/Minden Pictures/FLPA, b Flip De Nooyer/FN/Minden/FLPA; **243** tl Bork/SS, tr David Dixon, br Â© Biosphoto , Fabien Bruggmann/Biosphoto/FLPA; **244** tl, tr David Dixon; **245** tr © Biosphoto , Fabien

Index